HOLY DELIGHT

———————————

HOLY DELIGHT

Typology, Numerology, and Autobiography in Donne's *Devotions Upon Emergent Occasions*

KATE GARTNER FROST

PRINCETON UNIVERSITY PRESS

PRINCETON, NEW JERSEY

Copyright © 1990 by Princeton University Press
Published by Princeton University Press, 41 William Street,
Princeton, New Jersey 08540
In the United Kingdom: Princeton Univesity Press, Oxford

Library of Congress Cataloging-in-Publication Data

Frost, Kate Gartner.
Holy delight : typology, numerology, and autobiography
in Donne's Devotions upon emergent occasions /
Kate Gartner Frost.
1. Donne, John, 1572–1631. Devotions upon emergent
occasions. 2. Devotional literature, English—History and
criticism. 3. Typology (Theology)—History of doctrines.
4. Symbolism of numbers in literature. 5. Autobiography
in literature. I. Title.
PR2247.D483F7   1990   242—dc20   89-70222

ISBN 0-691-06781-3

This book has been composed in Linotron Baskerville

Princeton University Press books are printed on acid-free paper
and meet the guidelines for permanence and durability of the
Committee on Production Guidelines for Book Longevity of
the Council on Library Resources

Printed in the United States of America by Princeton University Press,
Princeton, New Jersey

1   3   5   7   9   10   8   6   4   2

To Robby

Glady wolde he lerne and glady teche

CONTENTS

ILLUSTRATIONS AND CHARTS

ILLUSTRATIONS

CHARTS

PREFACE

In late November 1623, John Donne, dean of St. Paul, fell ill with epidemic typhus or, as it was then called, "spotted fever."[1] The progress of the illness was swift, some fourteen days from first symptom to crisis, and the period of recuperation long, probably exceeding three months. The fever's onset, possibly as early as November 23, corresponded with the beginning of the Advent season (in 1623, the First Sunday of Advent fell on November 30).[2] Donne was out of danger by December 6 and spent the initial month of his recuperation in an invalid chair where he readied for the printer his *Devotions Upon Emergent Occasions and Severall Steps in My Sickness*.[3] In his own words: "Though I have left my bed, I have not left my bed-side; I sit there still, as a Prisoner discharged, sits at the Prison doore, to beg Fees, so sit I here, to gather crummes. I have used this leisure, to put the meditations had in my sicknesse, into some such order, as may minister some holy delight."[4]

Donne's *Devotions* has indeed administered delight over the years, but the nature of that delight has been the subject of some debate. A longish book (630 pages in the 1624 duodecimo edition), it contains twenty-three Devotions outlining the course of the poet's illness and cure preceded by a long poem entitled "*Stationes*" which presents the story of the illness in twenty-two lines of Latin hexameter. Each separate Devotion, bearing for its title a fragment of the "*Stationes*" with an English translation appended, is divided into a Meditation, an Expostulation, and a Prayer. The whole is preceded by an "Epistle Dedicatory" to Prince Charles Stuart. Although its title qualifies the book as a devotional manual, a preoccupation with extremely personal concerns seems to take the work into areas far removed from the traditional patterns of introspection normally associated with that genre. This seeming digressiveness has awakened a like response from critics: The *Devotions* has been accused of dull pedanticism, ob-

[1] My essay, "Donne's *Devotions*: A Case History of Epidemic Typhus," *Journal of the History of Medicine and Allied Sciences* 21 (1976): 421–30, has established the dates and nature of Donne's illness.

[2] Christopher R. Cheney, *Handbook of Dates for Students of English History* (London: Royal Historical Society, 1961), p. 143.

[3] Entered in the Stationer's Register January 9, 1624, by the bookseller Thomas Jones and printed by Augustine Mathewes of Cow Lane, probably in late January.

[4] *Letters to Severall Persons of Honour* (London, 1651), sig. Kkr.

scurity, morbid self-interest, self-indulgent introspection, and de-
based philosophy.[5] Donne himself has been charged with egocentricity and self-display, allegations pertinent not only to the book itself
but to the motives for its publication.[6] The editorial history of the
Devotions mirrors this less-than-enthusiastic reception: five editions
(three in the author's lifetime) in the seventeenth century; none at all
in the eighteenth; two in the nineteenth (stimulated by the Oxford
movement); and three in the twentieth, two of which have appeared
in the last decade. Study of the *Devotions* has suffered not only from
the lack of good editions but also from the scarcity of scholarly sup-
portive works (happily remedied in recent years by the publication of
Bald's *Life* and by the continued updating of the Donne bibliography
and library list) and from the generally unavailable state of Donne's
other prose works (a situation now much alleviated by the publication
of the *Sermons* and, recent and forthcoming, of the other early prose
works). Moreover, with the general turning of critical interest toward
Donne's prose in recent years, serious and enlightening essays have
paved the way for a reevaluation of the *Devotions*. I hope that this
study will contribute to that reevaluation.

Holy Delight is an outgrowth of work undertaken some years ago on
a critical edition of the *Devotions*, completion of which has had to be
postponed. The present work is a response to my reading of the *Devotions* in the light of premodern poetics and of the conventions of
devotional literature. It seeks to identify the work as a link in the
chain of spiritual autobiography, a chain that reaches from the present far back into antiquity but whose continuity has not been recognized by recent critics. In reading Donne's book in the light of this
genre, I hope to draw attention to two problems that engage the
reader of Renaissance literature: the identification or location of the
individual sense of "self" and the feasibility of exploring a work like
the *Devotions* within the limits of the occasion of its creation and the
generic and poetic possibilities open to its author. To arrive at some
understanding of this, Donne's great work of his later years, one
must take into account not the mere confines of a single genre, always

---

[5] Edmond Gosse, *The Life and Letters of John Donne, Dean of St. Paul's* (London, 1899),
2:186; Helen C. White, *English Devotional Literature 1600–1640*, University of Wisconsin Studies in Language and Literature 19 (Madison: University of Wisconsin Press,
1931), p. 248; Evelyn M. Simpson, *A Study of the Prose Works of John Donne*, 2d ed.
(Oxford: Clarendon Press, 1948), p. 243; T. S. Eliot, "Donne's *Devotions*," *Times Literary
Supplement*, March 11, 1926, p. 178; Eliot, p. 178—in that order.

[6] See Joan Webber, *The Eloquent I: Style and Self in Seventeenth-Century Prose* (Madison:
University of Wisconsin Press, 1968), pp. 18–21; Paul Delany, *British Autobiography in
the Seventeenth Century* (New York: Columbia University Press, 1969), pp. 16–18.

a dangerous ploy with Donne, but must examine the work in terms
of its own structure in the entire—in terms of the circumstances and
milieu of its writing, of the creative life of its author before and after
its production, and of the formal and aesthetic expectations that he
sought to satisfy. To that end, I will explore in chapter 1 the place of
the *Devotions* within the tradition of English devotional literature, especially within the traditions of the meditation (both Augustin and
Ignatian) and the *ars moriendi*, both of which have been held up by
critics as models for Donne's work. In chapter 2 I shall make a case
for the *Devotions* as a form of spiritual autobiography, part of an on-
going tradition that manifested itself in the English Renaissance in
forms as varied as the sonnet sequence and the revelatory essay.
Chapter 3 is devoted to the complex use of biblical typology in the
Devotions, one that points back to the tradition of spiritual autobiography within which Donne worked and forward to the historical circumstances of the book's composition. The reliance on underlying
number structures, manifest in so many early autobiographies, is derived from a poetic rooted in pre-Copernican cosmology. Chapter 4
will explore Donne's adherence to that poetic. Chapter 5 will attempt
to reveal the autobiographical and numerologically structured calendars, based on the hexaemeral week and the solstitial day, which underlie the discursive fabric of the *Devotions*. Finally, I have appended
to this study an example of the kind of underlying schema that must
have preceded a work like Donne's. Composed by the fourteenth-
century scribe Opicinus de Canistris, this spatially organized autobiographical chart came to my attention after the completion of this
study, and I have hence been unable to incorporate it in any major
fashion.

A caution to the reader: This is an exercise in literary history and
not the product of any one critical disposition. If there is any bias, it
is against the imposition, without judicious hesitation, of modern sensibility and theories of poesy on a literature which asks first to be understood on its own terms. This book is not an attempt to force the
Devotions into the confines of a narrow genre. Nor is it an attempt to
force Donne into the confines of a restrictive medieval mold. Nonetheless, it does explore very ancient paths—but the Donne scholar
who does so inevitably finds the poet's own footprints there.

Moreover, this is the study of one particular, even "peculiar," work.
The majority of its critical readers have been rather uncomfortable
with its place among Donne's verse, essays, and sermons. My contention is that we find the *Devotions* peculiar on our terms, not on
Donne's, and I hope that this study will warrant another look at the
corpus of his work.

What *Holy Delight* will accomplish, I hope, will be threefold: It will draw attention to Donne's traditional and conservative poetic practice, so that we may begin more carefully to distinguish Donne as innovator from Donne as imitator. Secondly, it will call for a closer look at a subject much occupying recent thought: the tradition of self-scrutiny and its expression in a variety of self-examinative genres, not confined to spiritual autobiography. Finally, *Holy Delight* may promote a more cautious reading of the Donne canon in the light of literary history. I feel strongly that the student who is not well fortified by the work of careful and creative literary historians and who seeks unaided to approach the literature of the English Renaissance via the new, often exciting critical currents that today engage the literary community may find herself unfulfilled, even misled, by her studies. It is for the reader to accept or discard the findings of this study, but to do so fully informed of the terms and conditions of the making of Donne's *Devotions*.

The preparation of this study gave rise to several difficulties which I hope I have resolved to the reader's satisfaction. Biblical quotations are in general taken from the Authorised Version. Where the text or the commentator cited in the text refers specifically to the Vulgate, I have employed the Douay-Rheims translation. In cases of possible ambiguity, a footnote provides the biblical source. For the sake of consistency, spellings of biblical names—for example those of Hezekiah and Isaiah—other than in quotations, are drawn from the Authorized Version. My adventures in the world of hand-press printing have convinced me of the widespread unreliability of early pagination. Therefore, I have generally cited signature rather than page numbers in pre-1700 references. Quotations from the *Devotions* are drawn from the 1624 edition, aware as I am of the inadequacy of recent editions, and are cited by signature numbers. I have put all Latin quotations into English, with the exception of a few short phrases which should not be distracting to the un-Latined reader, and unless they are cited otherwise, I take responsibility for their translation. The originals appear in notes.

Holy Delight owes its first debt to the scholars who in the last few decades have expanded significantly our understanding of Renaissance literature and that of Donne in particular. I am most grateful to the editors—Gardner, Healy, Milgate, Shawcross, Simpson, Sullivan, and Potter—who have given us sound, informed, readable texts, the foremost of scholarly achievements; to the late R. C. Bald for his biography of Donne, a prized tool to the hand of the scholarly critic; to S. K. Heninger, who has increased substantially our awareness of the cosmological framework that Donne both shared and questioned;

to Barbara K. Lewalski, who has made us aware of Donne's commitment to the Heavenly Muse and the ancient technique of literary typology; to Alastair Fowler, A. Kent Hieatt, and Maren-Sofie Røstvig for their work in uncovering the role of number symbolism in Renaissance poetic practice; to the intellectual historians—Gombrich, Panofsky, Klibansky, Allen, Gordon, Yates—who have taught us to read the Renaissance with informed minds; and finally, because the debt is most deeply felt, to D. W. Robertson, who called me as a student to understand the past on its own terms before speeding to judgment. Answering this call has become, as I find wholly to my delight, a lifetime's work.

Parts of this study were presented as papers at meetings of the Arkansas Philological Society, the College Conference of Teachers of English of Texas (CCTE), and the Modern Language Association; chapter 1, in part, appeared in *CCTE Proceedings*. I am indebted to the American Council of Learned Societies for a summer grant that enabled me to get the work under way and to the University Research Institute of the University of Texas at Austin for support that enabled me to push it to its conclusion. My thanks are extended to the Folger Shakespeare Library, to the libraries of Princeton University and the University of Texas at Austin (especially to the Humanities Research Center there, where much of the research was done). My particular gratitude goes to the many scholars and colleagues who read the manuscript in whatever the state of its current malformation: Ernest Kaulbach and James Wimsatt, who gave constant and sound medieval advice; John Hollander and John Fleming, who led me through some tangled byways of iconography; Christopher Dennis, who helped with some much-needed spadework in the Index of Christian Art; Norman Farmer, for his helpful suggestions over a very long time; John Ruszkiewicz, former head of the Writing Program at Texas, who exposed some very freshmanlike bloopers in the manuscript; Wayne Lesser, whose minute critical examination of the text much mollified the pains of revision; and James Duban, my fellow weekend worker, whose time and energy I have tapped unceasingly, whose ungrudging assistance has often enlarged my own flagging energy. A very special place in my gratitude belongs to my good friends and former teachers at Princeton without whose kindness, scholarly advice, and long-distance encouragement in the most trying circumstances this book might not have been completed: W. S. Howell, Earl Miner, and Thomas Roche. I have to thank A. Kent Hieatt for reading the manuscript and helping to tame its sometimes unruly discourse. Professor Maren-Sofie Røstvig has kept in transatlantic correspondence during the most stressful times, always pointing out the neglected path and the incomplete argument; to her especially do I owe my perception of the connection between the *Devotions* and Augustine's *De Trinitate*, the capstone of my final argument.

Finally, I should like to thank some people who helped this book to completion in very special ways: James Kinneavy, Peter Green, and Brad Knopp, for their constant support; Nancy Phillips, bibliographer par excellence, who kept the books coming my way; Rob Johnson and Ernest Kaulbach, for assistance with my sometimes strangled Latin; Sarah Williams, for typing the manuscript; and Ed Kutac and the avian population of Texas, for preserving my sanity during its preparation. With such assistance, this study should be wise and without error; where it is not, I have only myself to thank.

HOLY DELIGHT

Chapter I

THE *DEVOTIONS* AND THE TRADITION OF DEVOTIONAL LITERATURE

We Take into Our Meditation the Slippery
Condition of Man

AT THE TIME of his bout with typhus in 1623, Donne, as dean of St. Paul's and royal chaplain to James I, was well established as a London preacher. His secular career and most of his major poetry lay some years behind him. Immersed in the duties of his ministry and the composition of the more than 150 sermons that form an important part of his literary legacy, he could be counted among the foremost divines of his day. The *Devotions*, composed during that illness and published immediately upon his recovery, displays his finest powers. Providing a remarkable index to the resources of Donne's memory and poetic invention, the individual segments of each Devotion differ radically in content, style, and tone, ranging from the agitated convolutions of the Meditations to the sonorously rolling periods of the Prayers. In the end, Donne turned an exhausting human experience into a complicated artifact.

But to the modern eye, the *Devotions* is a difficult book, one that merges such unlikely companions as odd bits of natural history, personal-life data, quotations from Scripture, and unpleasant medical nostrums with the most personal and inspired of religious outpourings. While it is difficult for me to agree with Gosse that "nothing like them had been noted down before,"[1] or even with R. C. Bald that the work is "unique in the annals of literature,"[2] it is not hard to acknowl-

---

[1] *The Life and Letters of John Donne, Dean of St. Paul's* (London, 1899) 2:186.

[2] *John Donne: A Life* (New York: Oxford University Press, 1970), p. 451. A case may be made for the *Essayes in Divinity* as structural predecessor to the *Devotions*: They too are composed of meditations, preceded by a verse of Scripture (in contrast to the "*Stationes*" fragment, which begins each Devotion), and prayers which differ sharply from each other in tone and style. The *Essayes*, however, show no equivalent to the Expostulations of the *Devotions*. On the other hand, while no devotional work within the English tradition parallels Donne's in the use of experience as a matrix coupled with an extremely formal tripartite structure, there is a rather startling parallel in Sir John Hayward's *Sanctuary of a Troubled Soule* (1604). This work consists of four meditations

edge that the *Devotions* had no contemporary parallel. Yet it appeared at an optimal time.

After the unhappy lacuna proceeding from the sixteenth-century emphasis on religious polemic, the literary stage was prepared by the beginning of the seventeenth century for a renaissance of devotional literature. Thoroughly Protestant forms and conventions had been established,[3] and a generation of great Anglican divines was waiting in the wings—among them, Joseph Hall, Bishop Morton, Lancelot Andrewes, and (not least among his brethren) Donne himself. William Crashaw and the Fletchers, Giles and Phineas, were about to take up their pens, and the Puritan thunder of Bayly and Dent was rumbling in the distance. Best of all, an avid reading public had formed, and weekly fair days at St. Paul's churchyard were thronged with citizenry who manifested strongly independent tastes.

The market was very competitive, and by the end of the first quarter of the seventeenth century, the production of devotional literature was very healthy indeed. In the year 1620, for example, of the 130 books entered in the Stationers' Register, just over half were religious in intent: sermons, scriptural exegeses, polemics, sacred verse, prayers, hagiographies, martyrologies, and—these in large proportion—works of prayer and devotion.[4]

By 1650, the devotional tradition had reached its literary zenith with the simultaneous publication of Richard Baxter's *The Saints Everlasting Rest* and, the masterpiece of the Protestant tradition, Jeremy

---

on the *novissima*, each divided into a discourse on the subject, a consideration, and a prayer. In addition, each of the four sections is followed by a Latin verse tag, just as each of Donne's is preceded by Latin verses. Although there are few thematic parallels between the two, the structural resemblance is very strong.

[3] See Nancy Beaty, *The Crafte of Dying*, Yale Studies in English, 175 (New Haven: Yale University Press, 1970); Frances Comper, *The Book of the Craft of Dying and Other Early English Tracts Concerning Death* (London: Longman's, Green, 1917); F. A. Gasquet, "The Bibliography of Some Devotional Books Printed by the Earliest English Printers," *Transactions of the Bibliographical Society [of London]* 8 (December 1904): 163–89; Sr. Mary Catherine O'Connor, *The Art Dying Well: the Development of the Ars Moriendi*, Columbia University Studies in English and Comparative Literature, 156 (New York: Columbia University Press, 1942); Charles Stranks, *Anglican Devotions: Studies in the Spiritual Life of the Church of England between the Reformation and the Oxford Movement* (Greenwich, Conn.: Seabury Press, 1961); Helen White, *English Devotional Literature 1600–1640*, University of Wisconsin Studies in Language and Literature, 19 (Madison: University of Wisconsin Press, 1931); "Sixteenth-Century English Devotional Literature," in *Joseph Quincey Adams Memorial Studies* (Washington, D.C.: Folger Shakespeare Library, 1948); "Some Continuing Traditions in English Devotional Literature," *PMLA* 57 (1942): 966–80, *The Tudor Books of Private Devotion* (Madison: University of Wisconsin Press, 1951).

[4] White, *English Devotional Literature*, p. 50.

Taylor's *Holy Living*, succeeded by *Holy Dying* the following year—which combined in two volumes the salient features of the prayer book, the meditative tract, the book of directions for the godly life, and the rules for the conduct of dying fostered by the *ars moriendi* tradition.

By virtue of its title, the *Devotions* seems to belong to this tradition, but even after the most superficial reading, its place therein is puzzling, for the book seems to fit, comfortably or uncomfortably, no easily recognized category of contemporary devotional literature, whether one examines prayer books, spiritual conduct books, manuals for the sick or the dying, or even popular meditative forms.

Some of these traditions have been examined for their pertinence to Donne's book. Jonathan Goldberg, for example, has drawn attention to the many commonplaces in the *Devotions* that are drawn from the manuals for the sick, such as M. M.'s *An Ease for a Diseased Man* (1625) and the "Order for the Visitacion of the Sicke" from the Book of Common Prayer.[5] But the *Devotions* is clearly not a manual for the sick: its intensely personal address and what Janel Mueller has called its "anguished intellection" belie the deepest conventions of that soothing genre.[6] The language of the "Order for the Visitacion of the Sicke," however, seems to have informed the *Devotions*, Expostulation 2 especially, a natural enough phenomenon if one realizes that just such a visitation likely occurred (Donne was called upon almost daily by his friend Canon Henry King)[7] and that as a priest, he was familiar with the rite and could easily call it to mind during his own sickness.

But Donne was not merely sick; he was, by contemporary witness, near death,[8] and a recent editor of the *Devotions*, Sister Elizabeth Savage, maintains that the book, in "its content, tone, and basic method" and despite many noticeable differences, reflects its strong dependence on the *ars moriendi* tradition.[9] But those differences, many of which Savage allows (the lack of a central emphasis on the *novissima*,

---

[5] Jonathan Goldberg, "The Understanding of Sickness in Donne's *Devotions*," *Renaissance Quarterly* 24 (1971): 507–17.

[6] "The Exegesis of Experience: Dean Donne's *Devotions Upon Emergent Occasions*," *Journal of English and Germanic Philology* (*JEGP*) 67 (January 1968): 17.

[7] Bald, *John Donne*, p. 455.

[8] The Jacobean letter writer John Chamberlain recorded in his correspondence with Sir Dudley Carleton the steady progress of the spotted fever in 1623–24. He reported Donne's "grave danger," noted his eventual recovery, and commented on the publication of the *Devotions; The Letters of John Chamberlain*, ed. N. E. McClure (Philadelphia: The American Philosophical Society, 1939) 2:531.

[9] *John Donne's "Devotions Upon Emergent Occasions": A Critical Edition with an Introduction and Commentary* (Salzburg: *Institut für englische Sprache und Literatur*, 1975), pp. xxxii–lvi.

the temptations and their remedies, and the conflict of devil and angel for the soul of *Moriens*; the traditional prayers for the dying; the fact that Donne, unlike *Moriens*, was not foredoomed) far outweigh the similarities, indicating that the *Devotions* does not really fulfill the generic purpose of the *ars moriendi*: to teach men to die well. Although the book shares so much thematically and stylistically with the *ars moriendi*—for example, its revulsion at what Louis Martz calls the depravity of "the feeble flesh"[10] and the consequent fear and horror of judgment; its meditative structure, with the implicit expectation that the reader will participate actively as he goes along; the universality of its personal anguish; and finally, according to Savage, its stress "on the acceptance of death, the conquest of those things which could turn the soul from God in its last moments"[11]—still, the *Devotions* is not simply a book on the art of dying. The *ars moriendi* makes formal demands that are not met by Donne's book. Much of the richness is there, but it is a contributory richness. Had Donne not been familiar with the tradition (and as a pastor, he almost certainly knew examples of the genre—probably at least Becon, Crashaw, and his old subject of study Bellarmine),[12] the *Devotions* would be the less. At the same time, however, it is a work the main thrust of which lies elsewhere. It is something more.

The extent of Donne's debt to the meditative tradition has given rise to much controversy. Asserting that "the imprint of Jesuit methods of meditation stayed with Donne throughout . . . his life," Louis Martz has attributed the emotional violence of the "Holy Sonnets" and "The First Anniversary" to Donne's having found a "fundamental affinity and satisfaction in the methods of the Jesuit exercises."[13] Since Professor Martz's arguments are extremely persuasive, it has become rather the fashion in recent years to track down Donne, the closet Jesuit.

Although in her edition of *The Divine Poems* she agrees with some reservation that "both in meditation and in the writing of his sonnets [Donne] converts traditional [Jesuit] material to his own use,"[14] Helen Gardner concludes that "the influence of the formal meditation lies

---

[10] *The Poetry of Meditation: A Study in English Religious Literature of the Seventeenth Century* (New Haven: Yale University Press, 1962), p. 134.

[11] *"Devotions"* 1:xxxii.

[12] Thomas Becon, *The Sicke mannes Salve* (London, 1561); William Crashaw, *A Manuall for true Catholikkes or a Handfull: rather a Heartfull of Holy Meditations and Prayers Gathered out of certaine Ancient Manuscripts written 300. yeares agoe, and more* (London, 1616); Robert Bellarmine, *The Art of Dying Well* (St. Omer, 1622).

[13] Martz, *Poetry of Meditation*, p. 141.

[14] (Oxford: Clarendon Press, 1952), p. xxxiii.

behind the 'Holy Sonnets,' not as a literary source, but as a way of thinking, a method of prayer."[15] Janel Mueller, on the other hand, has identified the prototype of Donne's meditations not as the Ignatian meditation but as the series of sermons on the Penitential Psalms delivered early in the year of Donne's illness,[16] and N.J.C. Andreasen has focused attention not on the Ignatian but the Protestant meditative tradition exemplified by Bishop Hall.[17] Certainly Donne could have been influenced by the Spiritual Exercises, even aside from the meditational literature popular in his day and his own delving into theology and Jesuit lore. Bald, who examined Donne's boyhood connections with the order through his Jesuit uncles, admits a possibility that Donne as a youth visited the English College in Rome, where he may have known some who had undergone the rigors of an Ignatian retreat if he did not do so himself.[18]

Nevertheless, it is a fact that Donne became a bitter and lifelong opponent of the Jesuits, as *Ignatius His Conclave* so amply testifies. Still, Jesuit training dies hard, and one must admit to certain parallels with Jesuit meditation in Donne's work. Unfortunately, most of those who seek to make a case for Donne's use of an Ignatian model have drawn upon his verse, ignoring the *Devotions*, the one work in which he deliberately set out a formal meditative mode.[19] Enough similarities exist between Donne's book and the Spiritual Exercises to make their comparison fruitful: Both must be considered in their entirety; both are thematically and formally concerned with the passage of time and the *imitatio Christi*; and both are derived from a method of meditation which concentrates on the three powers of the soul. Yet I propose that examination of apparent similarities and close consideration of the formal differences between the two works will cast doubt on the extent to which Ignatian meditation influenced Donne's work in general.

Both the *Devotions* and the Spiritual Exercises are valid only as total

---

[15] *Divine Poems*, p. iv.

[16] Mueller, "Exegesis of Experience," 1–19.

[17] Donne's *Devotions* and the Psychology of Assent," *Modern Philology* 62 (1965): 207–16.

[18] Bald, *John Donne*, p. 52. A recent critic, Anthony Low, in *Love's Architecture: Devotional Modes in Seventeenth-Century English Poetry* (New York: New York University Press, 1978), p. 41, finds Donne using Ignatian devotional methods only a year before *Ignatius His Conclave*, a practice involving no paradox but rather a "spoiling [of] the Egyptians."

[19] In a letter to Sir Henry Goodyer (ca. 1608), Donne spoke of his poem "A Litanie" as a "meditation in verse" (*Letters to Severall Persons of Honour* [London, 1651], p. 33). The poem bears little overt relation to the Jesuit form, and Donne's reference is private.

entities; although both have been excerpted frequently, neither can be taken effectively in small doses. According to Jesuit historian Joseph De Guibert, the effectiveness of the Exercises "comes not so much from the value of each one of the exercises that make it up, taken one by one in isolation, but rather from the logical sequence that bends the single exercises into a whole and from the impact of that whole upon the soul of the exercitant."[20] The *Devotions* also constitutes a long work, although fragmentary anthologizing unfortunately has led to its appreciation more for its prose style than its coherence.

Like the Spiritual Exercises, Donne's book is concerned with the passing from crisis to a state of election under conditions of abstinence and isolation within a particular time span. This inherent structure hinders any attempt to isolate fragments from either work. The passage of the soul through time is a significant factor in both books. In the case of the Exercises, the time span is mandatory and determines the work's very structure. The classic Ignatian retreat, given over the course of a month, falls into four thematic weeks; the first deals with man's sinfulness, the second with Christ as captain in the warfare against sin, the third with the Passion as a source of spiritual renewal and resolution, and the fourth with living with Christ in the Resurrection. The *Devotions*, on the other hand, covers a three-week time span at most, charting Donne's illness from its inception through its crisis and a short period thereafter. Although the progression is clear, it is a metaphorical rather than a mandatory one, one which concentrates on states of illness, crisis, and recovery elevated to a spiritual progress, which in no way attempts the rigid classification of the Ignatian model. In addition, although both books are informed by the *imitatio Christi*, the Spiritual Exercises is an overtly Christocentric work, stressing sensual experiencing of Christ, while the *Devotions* is Trinitarian, committed to an intellectuality that obviates emphasis on the senses. Donne's Christ is Son of God and Savior, but he is not the earthly Christ of Ignatius. His Trinitarian address is typified, for example, in the concluding passage of Prayer 9:

> Yet take me again, into your *Consultation, O blessed* and *glorious Trinitie*; & thogh the *Father* know, that I haue defaced his *Image* receiued in my *Creation*; though the *Son* know, I haue neglected mine interest in the *Redemption*, yet, *O blessed spirit*, as thou art to my *Conscience*, so be to them a witnes, that at this *minute*, I accept that which I haue so often, so often, so rebelliously refused, thy blessed inspirations.

[20] *The Jesuits: Their Spiritual Doctrine and Practice* (Chicago: The Institute of Jesuit Sources, 1964), p. 11.

The question of the extent to which the *Devotions* partakes of the more formal content of the Exercises is a matter of debate. Helen Gardner has maintained that by meditation, "Donne meant something much more discursive, a less rigourous exercise than the Ignatian meditation."[21] And the Ignatian model is indeed rigorous. The classic form of Ignatian meditation is found in the exercises of the first week, which employ the method of the three faculties of the soul. This is the quality which has been called most typically Ignatian—a movement from intellect to will, through a processive tripartite structure based upon the application of the senses. The meditations of this first week are generally divided into five parts: preparation, reading, meditation, thanksgiving, and petition. The exercitant first selects a limited topic and makes a short preparatory prayer for the grace to make all facets of his meditation to the honor and glory of God. Next he considers the two preludes, the famous *composito loci* and a request for particular benefits as the fruit of his exercise. Third is proposed a series of points, or aspects, of the topic for meditation and the application of the memory, understanding, and will to each. The exercise closes with a double prayer: the colloquy, in which the exercitant speaks in familiar tones to Christ, the Virgin, or the saints, and a formal prayer, usually the Pater Noster or Anima Christi.

Donne's book, on the other hand, exhibits little appeal to the senses and demonstrates a far less complicated structure. The poet's wit plays a considerable part in limiting any sensuality, a wit epitomized in the first Meditation:

> So that now, we doe not onely die, but die vpon the Rack, die by the torment of sicknesse; nor that onely, but are pre-afflicted, super-afflicted, with these ielousies and suspitions, and apprehensions of *Sicknes*, before we can cal it a sicknes; we are not sure we are ill; one hand askes the other by the pulse, and our eye askes our own vrine, how we do.

The *Devotions*, moreover, offers no act of the presence of God, no attempt to present visualized scenes as matter for meditation, and no attempt to apply the senses to the matter as an aid to understanding. Each of its sections begins with a Meditation on the Book of the Creatures, followed by an Expostulation that draws heavily on Scripture, and ends with a formal Prayer.

Despite these apparent dissimilarities, Thomas F. Van Laan purports to have found direct structural parallels between the Ignatian model and the *Devotions* by an extended comparison of individual De-

---

[21] Review of *The Poetry of Meditation*, by Louis L. Martz, *Review of English Studies* n. ser. 8 (1957): 194–200.

votions with individual Exercises. He finds the two identical—except that Donne has dropped Ignatius's preliminary prayer and the first prelude (the composition of place) and has moved the second prelude bodily to the end of the Exercise, where, as Donne's Prayer, it becomes in effect a postlude. The Pater Noster has also been discarded. This considerable reshuffling, according to Van Laan, has improved the Jesuit exercise by mitigating the abruptness of the Ignatian ending, thus preparing for the exercitant's return to normal routine, and by freeing the meditation so that his mind may "range with maximum possibilities."[22] The missing, and crucial, composition of place can be found in Donne's Meditations and the colloquy in the Expostulations. Van Laan relates Donne's Latin verse tags to the memory, his Meditations to the understanding, and his Expostulations to the will. The function of the Prayers, other than as a general winding down, he ignores.

Much of this lopping of limbs from the Spiritual Exercises to fit Donne's procrustean bed stems from the confusion generated by the *Devotions'* three-part form, which seems to derive directly from the Ignatian appeal to memory, understanding, and will. Yet, tripartite structure was so common in the Renaissance as to obviate comparison to Ignatian or any other set form. The Ignatian Exercises themselves, admits Martz, were a new and exciting development of an older tradition—one stemming from the Victorines and the later *Devotio Moderna* of the fourteenth century, which stressed the three powers of the mind and offered a solid common ground among the many methods developed by the growing congregational movement of the sixteenth century: the Oratorians, the Minims, the Salesians, and the Jesuits. But, he adds, "it is important to remember that [they] do not stand alone in their kind, but represent a summary and synthesis of efforts since the twelfth century to reach a precise and widely accepted method of meditation. The older methods and treatises which underlie the Exercises continue to exert strong influence in their own right."[23]

[22] "John Donne's *Devotions* and the Jesuit Spiritual Exercise," *Studies in Philology* 60 (1963): 191–202.

[23] Martz, *Poetry of Meditation*, p. 25. Professor Martz has taken a longer look at non-Ignatian meditative forms in his study *The Paradise Within* (New Haven: Yale University Press, 1964), particularly at Augustinian methods. Although these maintain the familiar tripartite appeal to memory, understanding, and will, they are far more diffuse in structure than the Exercises. Moreover, the Augustinian progression can be characterized as a "mining" of associations, "a roving search over a certain field of imagery, a sinking inward upon the mind's resources, until all the evocative ramifications of the memory have been explored" (*Poetry of Meditation*, p. 25)—a process very suggestive of the complex interior articulations of Donne's Meditations.

A good look at the similarities—and more important, at the differences—between the Spiritual Exercises and the *Devotions* may incline one to agree with Martz and to conclude moreover that Donne drew on this older tradition, as exemplified, say, by Bonaventura's *Itinerarium*. Although most study of non-Ignatian meditative forms has until recently centered on the latter part of the seventeenth century, it seems to me that much ground remains to be turned in that span of time, which produced in addition to Donne, such luminaries as Lancelot Andrewes and Joseph Hall. The latter, Donne's lifelong friend, has most particularly been overlooked to our detriment, for his *Arte of Divine Meditation* achieved a workable solution to the problem of Protestant meditation: teaching and exemplifying meditation as an art informed by divine purposefulness rather than a studied ascent by the will toward divine illumination. Indeed, Barbara K. Lewalski not long ago emphasized the near-equation of the sermon and meditation, suggesting the "strong-possibility" of connections between Hall's method and Donne's poetry.[24]

I suggest that there is much to be gained from the study of Hall's "extemporall" or "occasionall" meditation which as Lewalski points out, draws on the Book of the Creatures in combination with chance occurrences—frequently events like Donne's sickness—and centers often on moral topics or scriptural texts.[25] These meditations took the form of short prose essays informally mixed with scriptural passages and ejaculatory prayers. Their topics are sometimes incongruous, as with Meditation 92, "Upon the Sight of a Harlot Carted," or 23, "Upon the Barking of a Dog," but they are also sometimes strongly reminiscent of concerns which pervade the *Devotions*, as in Meditation 37, "Upon a Coal Covered with Ashes"; 56, "Upon the Sound of a Cracked Bell"; 78, "Upon the Tolling of a Passing-bell"; 99, "Upon the Beginning of a Sicknes"; 129, "Upon a Medicinal Potion." Indeed, certain of them bear some similarity in language and address to the *Devotions*. In particular, the very first of the series, "Upon the Sight of the Heavens moving," resembles strongly both Donne's second Meditation ("The *Heauens* are not the lesse constant, because they moue continually one and the same way") and his fourth ("It is too little to call *Man* a *little World*"):

I can see nothing stand still but the earth; all other things are in motion. Even the water which makes up one globe with the earth is ever stirring

<hr />

[24] *Protestant Poetics and the Seventeenth-Century Religious Lyric* (Princeton: Princeton University Press, 1979), pp. 152–53. She also draws attention to the work of Richard Sibbes, Lewis Bayly, Richard Rogers, and Isaac Ambrose.

[25] Ibid., pp. 151–52.

in ebbs and flowings; the clouds over my head, the heavens above the clouds, these, as they are most conspicuous, so are they the greatest patterns of perpetual action. What should we rather imitate than this glorious frame? O God, when we pray that Thy will may be done in earth as it is in heaven, though we mean chiefly the inhabitants of that place, yet we do not exclude the very place of those blessed inhabitants from being an example of our obedience. The motion of this Thy heaven is perpetual, so let me ever be acting somewhat of Thy will. The motion of Thine heaven is regular, never swerving from the due points; so let me ever walk steadily in the ways of Thy will, without all diversions or variations from the line of Thy Law. In the motion of Thine heaven, though some stars have their own peculiar and contrary courses, yet all yield themselves to the sway of the main circumvolution of that First Mover. So, though I have a will of mine own, yet let me give myself over to be ruled and ordered by Thy spirit in all my ways.

Man is a little world: my soul is heaven, my body is earth. If this earth be dull and fixed, yet O God, let my heaven like unto Thine move perpetually, regularly, and in a constant subjection to Thine Holy Ghost.[26]

The recent editor of Hall's *Occasional Meditations* places its composition during the author's rectorship at Waltham Holy Cross,[27] which ended some ten years before Donne's composition of the *Devotions*. Thus the echoes may be attributed to Donne's familiarity with Hall's book or simply with the shared concerns and understanding of long friendship. Certainly Donne draws attention to his own book as participating in the genre by its very title, which, incidentally, gave the phrase "emergent occasion" to the language. At least one reader saw the *Devotions* as part of the tradition: In 1642, the fifteen-year-old Robert Boyle, some years away from his scientific career, composed "Upon the Accidents of an Ague," which is in language and form a direct imitation of Donne's book.[28] But neither Hall nor Boyle can lay claim to Donne's insistent voice—what Janel Mueller has called an "acute state of consciousness."[29] And there seems to be no parallel to Donne's formal setting out of hexameter fragments, Meditations, Expositions, Prayers, at least in contemporary devotional literature.

That the *Devotions* fits only uncomfortably into the ranks of conventional devotional literature should not surprise the student of seven-

---

[26] *Occasional Meditations* (1633), in Frank Livingstone Huntley, *Bishop Joseph Hall and Protestant Meditation in Seventeenth-Century England: A Study with the texts of "The Art of Divine Meditation" (1606) and "Occasional Meditations" (1633)* (Binghamton, N.Y.: Center for Medieval and Early Renaissance Studies, 1981), pp. 123–24.

[27] Ibid., p. 35.

[28] *Occasional Reflections upon Several Subjects* (London, 1665).

[29] Mueller, "Exegesis of Experience," 17.

teenth-century literature. Donne habitually exceeded the confines of any single genre. But even if the book conformed more closely in form or content to any of the devotional forms examined here, it would still prove the exception by virtue of Donne's "morbid delight in analysing his own conflicting emotions."[30] And perhaps the resurgence of its popularity in recent times can be attributed to just such a delight, to a compelling interest in the psychology of the individual, particularly of the individual in a state of stress. Helen White addressed this interest, however prurient, when she identified Donne's book as

> So personal that even the reader who takes no interest in devotion will find the *Devotions Upon Emergent Occasions* of engrossing interest for their highly personal revelations of the author's very recent experience. . . . Donne's restless eyes are forever straying to that object of perennial curiosity, himself. Even in his moments of deepest and sincerest religious feeling—and that passionate heart of his was capable of great depth of feeling in this as in any other realm to which he gave it—even in these moments of what we may call religious passion, Donne could not cease to observe himself. . . . It is as a book of religious psychology, a book of deep and intimate self-revelation, that we treasure Donne's *Devotions*.[31]

She adds that in the end, Donne's book is "much more significant from the literary than the devotional point of view."[32]

I hope to show that for Donne, the literary and the devotional points of view are without borders, that we may legitimately, with Evelyn Simpson, "suspect the writer of artifice."[33] But we must first approach the critical dilemma of self-interest versus devotional intent. Some years ago, N.J.C. Andreasen posed four questions about the *Devotions*, the answering of which is integral, I think, to a clear understanding of the work. First, she asked, what are the principles of organization used in the book, and how do these relate to other contemporary works? Next, "if Donne's work was meant to be used generally as a spiritual guide, how can we account for its peculiarly private and individual point of view, for its apparent self-consciousness and egocentricity?" And if the *Devotions* was not intended for general use, why was the book even published? Finally, and most important: In what sense is Donne's *Devotions* "devotional"?[34] I propose

---

[30] Evelyn M. Simpson, *A Study of the Prose Works of John Donne*, 2d ed. (Oxford: Clarendon Press, 1948).

[31] White, *English Devotional Literature*, p. 253.

[32] Ibid.

[33] Simpson, *A Study of the Prose Works*, p. 251.

[34] Andreasen, "Donne's *Devotions*," 207.

that these questions can be answered, or at the very least discussed with less perplexity, if the *Devotions* is viewed as responding largely to the generic concerns of early spiritual autobiography, a literature both private and public, drawing on a rich formal tradition, only apparently self-conscious—at least in the modern sense of "self"—intended for publication, and viewed by author and reader as both an act of devotion and a teaching exemplum. It is a literature imbued with a sense of occasion, committed to intense self-scrutiny, and one that in the deepest sense belongs within the larger tradition of devotional literature. Viewed in the light of this genre, Donne's book no longer need be defended against the charges of peculiarity and morbidity which have diminished both its reputation and its availability. The *Devotions* is a masterpiece in the tradition of self-scrutiny and deserves to be read within the context of that tradition.

Chapter II

THE *DEVOTIONS* AND SPIRITUAL
AUTOBIOGRAPHY

What is Your Life?

SOME THREE WEEKS before his death, wasted by stomach cancer, Donne mounted the pulpit of St. Paul's for his last sermon. There, a barely erect *memento mori*, he told his audience:

> Wee have a winding sheete in our Mothers wombe, which growes with us from our conception, and wee come into the world, wound up in that *winding sheet*, for wee come to *seeke a grave*; And as prisoners discharg'd of actions may lye for fees; so when the *wombe* hath discharg'd us, yet we are bound to it by *cordes* of flesh, by such a *string*, as that wee cannot goe thence, nor stay there. We celebrate our owne funeralls with cryes, even at our birth; as though our *threescore and ten years of life* were spent in our mothers labour, and our circle made up in the first point thereof. We begge one Baptism with another, a sacrament of tears; And we come into a world that lasts many ages, but wee last not.[1]

A short time later Donne took to his deathbed, some eleven years short of the biblically allotted span—yet so certain of his election that he allowed himself to be painted there, warmed by charcoal fires, lying naked in the shroud in which he was soon to be buried. Even in the face of approaching death, the Donne persona drew on artifice: He stood at the last before his congregation as a living emblem of man's final state, and his self-presentation on his deathbed was as an exemplar.

The language of the *Devotions*, which displays strong parallels to "Death's Duell," also features a forcefully presented, even a dramatic, persona, one which perhaps pertains more to autobiography than to devotion, for while in devotional literature the eye supposedly is on God, in autobiography it is turned inward on the self. In response to this seeming anomaly, Margaret Bottrall has charged that "self-dis-

---

[1] Donne, *Sermons*, ed. G. F. Potter and Evelyn Simpson (Berkeley: University of California Press, 1953–1962) 10:233.

play was as powerful a motive with Donne as self-scrutiny."[2] The consensus has generally been that Donne's book primarily displays a "consuming interest in the validity of his own experience,"[3] with the inference of vanity let lie. That Donne published the book and exercised some care in the matter, adds weight to the evidence. In fact, Donne has never been completely free from the charge of paramount self-interest. However, that paramount self-interest is the duty of every Christian has largely been forgotten by our modern world, which reads the *Devotions* for literary, psychological, even sociological rather than pious edification. But the implications of self-display and self-interest were different to the seventeenth-century reader, who looked to the *Devotions* for moral instruction and "holy delight" rather than for Donne's private self autobiographically embodied. The twentieth-century reader, distracted by the book's intensely personal expression and its use of autobiographical material, is more likely to direct his gaze to author than to Author. His seventeenth-century counterpart, on the other hand, acquainted with a tradition of spiritual autobiography that boasted such giants as Augustine, Abelard, and Dante, was as able to distance himself from Donne's authorial voice as one is still, in most cases, from the voice of the Psalmist.

The modern reader approaches the subject of autobiography equipped with suppositions that do not always serve her well in the seventeenth century. The concept of self has changed a great deal since the philosophical upheavals of that time, and with the stimuli of Rousseau and Freud, autobiography has evolved into a highly sophisticated and largely secular genre. Attempts to come to terms with the genre as such have been, for the most part, rather recent, and by virtue of their limitations, the range of definitions shows the problem of perceiving a continuity in the tradition. Only modern autobiography, for example, tends to fall within the limits recently proposed by James M. Osborn:

> A "sustained" formal autobiography may be considered to have the following minimum characteristics: (1) it should be the history of a life, told by the person himself, usually in the first person; (2) it should be written in conscious literary form of some kind, an orderly plan of narration, usually with a beginning, a middle, and (God permitting) an end; (3) it should be a sustained attempt to delineate a whole life up to the date of termination, albeit with selection of details.[4]

[2] Margaret Bottrall, *Every Man a Phoenix: Studies in Seventeenth-Century Autobiography* (London: John Murray, 1958), p. 23.

[3] Bottrall, *Every Man a Phoenix*, p. 25.

[4] James M. Osborn, *The Beginnings of Autobiography in England* (Los Angeles: William Andrews Clark Memorial Library, 1959), pp. 3–4.

The presence of real autobiographical data in the *Devotions* is a given, although the nature of that data and the principle of its selection is at first glance rather puzzling. We are made aware of the day-by-day progress of Donne's illness, with all its sweats, chills, fears, and tremblings. He alludes to the solitude of his contagious sickroom and to the visits of his faithful servants, his family, his confessor, and his physicians, one of the latter sent by the king himself.[5] He comments on the years before his ordination when he was "sick . . . of a vertiginous giddines, and irresolution,"[6] and on the part played by James I in his eventual decision to enter the ministry. We learn something of his upbringing, his travels, his transgressions and personal vanities. This kind of information led the poet's nineteenth-century biographer, Sir Edmund Gosse, to value the work chiefly for its autobiographical content: "We can imagine him lying there all alone, propped up in state in his great dark chamber; scribbling these funereal conceits on a tablet that rests against the fold of the coverlet, while 'that striking clock which I ordinarily wear' ticks on the table at his side."[7] Gosse's description puts one in mind more of the Land of Counterpane than the fevered actuality of the sickroom,[8] and it is only a small step from this to the mere culling of the *Devotions* for autobiographical chaff.

Despite Gosse's romantic interest, however, the searcher for life data will find within the *Devotions* sparse information, which is selected and arranged to articulate the structure and thematic content of the work rather than to shed any immediate light on the poet's life. As a matter of fact, certain important events which occurred during the illness are strangely lacking in Donne's account. Fearing his imminent death, he hastened the marriage of his eldest and dearest daughter, Constance, to the actor Edward Allyn during the crucial days of his illness, an event important both for its drama and for the light it sheds on Donne's special affection for the girl.[9] Moreover, during the first and worst days of the fever, his longtime friend Henry King, canon of Chichester and a residentiary of St. Paul's, clearly expecting the Dean's death, offered Donne an additional

---

[5] Devotion 7: *The King sends his owne Phisician*, sig. H1r.

[6] Expostulation VIII, sig. K1r.

[7] Edmond Gosse, *The Life and Letters of John Donne, Dean of St. Paul's* (London, 1899) 2:183.

[8] For an extended description of Donne's treatment, see my essay, "Prescription and Devotion: The Reverend Doctor Donne and the Learned Doctor Mayerne—Two Seventeenth-Century Records of Epidemic Typhus Fever," *Medical History* 22 (1978): 408–16.

[9] R. C. Bald, *John Donne: A Life* (New York: Oxford University Press, 1970), pp. 448–50.

prebendary income, lest his children be left in need.[10] Yet neither
Constance nor King finds mention in the *Devotions*. Rather, three central episodes concern the funeral of an anonymous London neighbor—small pickings for the seeker of biographical information. Even
if we interpreted the apparently random life events recorded in the
Devotions as mere ornament or illustration, we would enter not the
realm of autobiography but that of anecdote.

   In the opening pages of *British Seventeenth-Century Autobiography*,
Paul Delany defines the critic's first task as "to decide which works,
among a great mass of more or less personal or self-revelatory writings, should be singled out for inclusion in a history of autobiography. He must commit himself to some kind of formal definition of
the genre, even though it is bound to give rise to anomalies in practice."[11] He then claims for the genre "literary works (1) *primarily* written to give a coherent account of the author's life, or of an extensive
period or series of events in his life, and (2) composed after a period
of reflection and forming a unified narrative."[12] If one abides by Delany's definition, the *Devotions* does not appear to qualify, for its presentation of autobiographical material is seemingly fragmentary and
without coherence, and it apparently forms no unified narrative.
Even if one adopts the more general criteria of Roy Pascal—who
maintains in *Design and Truth in Autobiography* that autobiography is
"a shaping of the past which imposed a pattern on a life, constructs
out of it a coherent story, of relationship between self and the outside
world"[13] the *Devotions* again fails to qualify, for other than in its formal structure of "*Stationes*"/Meditation/Expostulation/Prayer, it seems
to display no pattern, gives merely a fragmentary account of a two-
week illness, and converts the relationship between the self and the
outside world ultimately to a metaphor of the relationship between
the soul and God.

   Actually, very few Renaissance autobiographies—and there are
quite a number—seem to meet the criteria of Osborn, Delany, or Pascal, and consequently there has been of late some scrambling to identify the first "modern" autobiography. Donne's book appeared at a
time when literary awareness of the secular self was just beginning.
In the seventeenth century, the distinction between the medieval tradition of self-scrutiny and that of the *res gestae* or social anecdote was
blurred at best. For example, one is tempted to classify as *res gestae*
the autobiography of Thomas Whythorne (1576), which has been

[10] Ibid., p. 455.
[11] (London: Routledge and Kegan Paul, 1969), p. 1.
[12] Delany, *Autobiography*, p. 2.
[13] (London: Routledge and Kegan Paul, 1960), p. 9.

called "the first sustained autobiography, in the modern sense, in English literature,"[14] until one examines its structure, an alternation of prose and verse which points back to a long-established tradition of self-scrutiny. The line between truth and fiction, anecdote and exemplum, wavers frequently here. Churchyard's and Tusser's brief verse lives and Greene's stunning *Groatsworth of Wit* fall into the latter category, despite their heavy reliance on anecdote. One who seeks the sustained "factual" account of a life finds little reward.

Small wonder that Donald Stauffer has complained that "early autobiography does not attain the literary standard of the biography."[15] This he attributes to the lack of both classical and native models, which tends to diminish the importance of literary form in the genre. Nevertheless, examination of models suggests a plethora, not a lack— but with this difference: Structurally and thematically, their concerns necessitate the subordination of personal anecdote to thematic matter; hence fiction often intrudes upon fact. Jonathan Goldberg, in his consideration of fictive forms in Cellini's autobiography, describes this intrusion of fiction into autobiography as a "mode of self-understanding [in which] the true and the metaphorical are identical."[16] Cellini's autobiography draws both on the spiritual autobiography and the picaresque romance, straddling the "borderline between romance and realism."[17] Yet, Goldberg maintains, "had Cellini crossed those boundaries and made an attempt to tell the truth as a modern man might perceive it, he would have violated the equation of the true and the metaphorical that stood at the center of his mode of perceiving. A realistic autobiography, a novelistic autobiography, would have resulted; a great irony is, that from Cellini's perspective, such a 'truthful' work would not have told the truth at all."[18]

Under the impetus of the new humanism, the English Renaissance saw a turning from the tradition of self-scrutiny, with its mimetic conventions, to the secular autobiography, at first much in the manner of Marcus Aurelius or, more to the active taste, the *Commentaries* of Caesar. The seventeenth century found gentlemen, often soldiers or administrators, rejecting the conventions of Lydgate's *Testament* and More's *Dialogue of Comfort* for those of the memoir or straightforward

[14] Rudolf Gottfried, "Autobiography and Art: An Elizabethan Borderland," in *Literary Criticism and Historical Understanding*, ed. Philip Damon (New York: Columbia University Press, 1967), p. 111.

[15] *English Biography before 1700* (Cambridge: Harvard University Press, 1930), p. 216.

[16] "Cellini's *Vita* and the Conventions of Early Autobiography," *Modern Language Notes* 89 (1974): 82.

[17] Ibid., p. 83.

[18] Ibid., p. 81.

life in the manner of Cardano or Blaise de Monluc, while its first thirty years witnessed such men of prominence as Sir Thomas Bodley, Sir James Melville, Robert Carey, and Thomas Dempster writing short but largely factual memoirs. The life accounts of Sir Kenelm Digby and Lord Herbert of Cherbury bear strong and spicy witness to the new tradition. Although most of this type bear some perfunctory instruction to relatives or to posterity, any pretensions to fictive exempla are soon overcome by narrative. They offer straightforward models for a growing tradition—one on which Donne might have drawn had he so desired.

But the exemplary tradition had not been eclipsed. It was, in fact, given new impetus by the Reformation, for men like Thomas Browne felt the need to define for themselves their stance on doctrine and devotion. Both *Religio Medici* and Bunyan's *Grace Abounding*, while they differ radically in tone, are prime examples of a revivified confessional tradition. Margaret Bottrall has differentiated what she calls the "interior memoir" from the anecdotal autobiography by drawing attention to the "static" representation of the personality which it presents. The author of such a memoir, she says, "has affinities with the philosopher, the poet, and the penitent. His interest is focused upon his inner life, and outward happenings may be regulated to the background."[19] Such accounts often become so engrossed with the inner life that the outer world becomes blurred, and the author's movement and growth in "real" time are subordinated to his spiritual progress. Often too, as in the case of Augustine's pear tree and Abelard's fortunate loss, events in historical time become emblems of spiritual change. Like many of his predecessors in the literature of self-scrutiny, John Bunyan uses the occasion of an illness to juxtapose two temporal planes, the actual and the spiritual:

> At the apprehension of these things, my sickness was doubled upon me, for now I was sick in my inward man, my Soul was clog'd with guilt, now also was my former experience of Gods goodness to me quite taken out of my mind, and hid as if it had never been, nor seen: Now was my Soul greatly pinched between these two considerations. *Live I must not, Die I dare not.*[20]

Modern autobiographers focus attention on their inner lives in their attempt to discover a unique self, while early autobiographers may come to self-awareness through the submission to a generic

---

[19] Bottrall, *Every Man a Phoenix*, p. 3.

[20] *Grace Abounding to the Chief of Sinners*, ed. Roger Sharrock (London: Oxford University Press, 1966), p. 82.

mode.[21] Within these limits, experience merely provides grounds for interior reflection; to dwell on personal history as an end in itself is both vain and beside the point, for the events of historical time gain importance only in the light of eternity. Says Augustine, preeminent among these autobiographers: "Thy years stand all at once, because they stand: nor are those that go thrust out by those that come, for they pass not away; but these years of thine shall all be ours, when all time shall cease to be."[22] If one agrees with Wayne Shumaker that "all autobiographies hold *what was* up to view in light reflected from *what is*,"[23] this convention becomes more understandable: In the timeless presence of God, the past is significant only as evidence of the workings of Providence. And the recounting of that past becomes in itself an act of devotion.

Nevertheless, from Augustine onward, the spiritual autobiography characteristically features narration in real time, although one often emblematic of the inner workings of the spirit. A certain awareness seems to prevail that confession and narrative must achieve a balance if the work is to be both interesting and edifying, for almost without exception, spiritual autobiographies, although they are written as if no one in the world were to read them, were intended for publication. Augustine, for example, follows Paul ("We speak before God in Christ: but we do all things, dearly beloved, for edifying" 2 Cor. 12.19) when he says: "Why then do I lay in order before thee so many narrations? Not to this end I do it, that thou mayest come to know them upon my relation; but thereby I stir up mine own and my reader's devotion towards thee, that we may say all together: Great is the Lord, and greatly to be praised."[24] Augustine sent his *Confessions* abroad to his friends; Abelard's *Historia Calamitatum* prefaced a rule for the nuns of the Paraclete; Petrarch's *Ascent of Mt. Ventoux* was addressed and conveyed to his confessor. These were literary pieces intended for audiences in touch with their intent and their conventions. But for modern audiences, so out of touch with both, the early tradition remains perplexing. Thus, much of the critical thought about spiritual autobiography to date has revolved around the literature of the eighteenth century and the Protestant confessions that led to it. The implications of a more ancient tradition with conventions and expectations of its own have not, to my knowledge, been explored to

[21] Goldberg, "Cellini's *Vita*," p. 71.

[22] *St. Augustine's "Confessions,"* trans. William Watts (Cambridge: Harvard University Press, 1968) 2:237.

[23] Wayne Shumaker, *English Autobiography: Its Emergence, Materials, and Form* (Berkeley: University of California Press, 1954), p. 114.

[24] *Confessions* 2:209.

any extent.[25] Moreover, that Donne's *Devotions* may have an identifiable place within an earlier tradition has not been proposed, although G. A. Starr, in his *Defoe and Spiritual Autobiography*, has cited the work as "a splendid example of autobiographical material essential yet subordinate to a work's main scheme; personal experience . . . assimilated into what is, in effect, an extended homily on the human condition."[26] But Starr sees the autobiographical elements in the *Devotions*, "although transmuted into something universal and impersonal," more as embellishment than as basic to the work's identity.[27] His essentially fragmented perception of the *Devotions* is derived rather from the modern manner of reading than from any disunity in the work itself. Viewed in the light of premodern poetics, the autobiographical elements in Donne's book are not subordinate to the work's main scheme, rather, they are the work's main scheme.

None of the definitions examined up to this point has come to terms with a form of autobiography where the life being examined becomes an artifact itself, a "made" thing and hence fictive. As a result of this lacuna, the history of the genre seems an oddly disrupted one: Autobiography seems to have flourished during classical times, then to have vanished during the Middle Ages, only to reappear during the Renaissance with the recovery of classical emphasis on the *res gestae* and a new commitment to the individual and secular man. In the thousand years of flourishing culture between the death of the pagan world and its attempted resuscitation, the genre either died out or, I would suggest, existed in a form that is not fully comprehended by modern definitions.

This fundamental gap in our understanding of the continuity of the autobiographical tradition has encouraged the study of the genre in early times as a mere milestone on the highway "to the period of its greatest flowering, which [was] subsequent to the Renaissance,"[28] so that "the earlier era is of paramount interest from an aetiological

---

[25] For attempts to identify and define the tradition, see Andrew Fichter, *Poets Historical: Dynastic Epic in the Renaissance* (New Haven: Yale University Press, 1982); Mary M. McLaughlin, "Abelard as an Autobiographer," *Speculum* 42 (1967): 463–88; T. C. Price Zimmerman, "Confession and Autobiography in the Early Renaissance," in *Renaissance Studies in Honor of Hans Baron*, ed. Anthony Molho and John A. Tedeschi (Dekalb, Ill.: Dekalb University Press, 1971); Paul Zumthor, "Autobiography in the Middle Ages?" *Genre* 6 (1973): 29–48.

[26] (Princeton: Princeton University Press, 1965), p. 5. Joan Webber, *The Eloquent I: Style and Self in Seventeenth-Century Prose* (Madison: University of Wisconsin Press, 1968), p. 6, goes one step further when she describes the *Devotions* as being "a kind of spiritual autobiography."

[27] Starr, *Defoe*, p. 34.

[28] Zimmerman, "Confession and Autobiography," 122.

standpoint, since during its primary stages autobiography betrays more clearly the evidence of its origins."[29] The problem with this statement is one shared by many studies of early literature: the assumption that modern literary forms, modern modes of experience, are the final culmination of a long formative period of growth from fairly primitive beginnings. Thus Wayne Shumaker can note with a frown that autobiography before the eighteenth century seems unable to confront experience directly; it presents metaphor, not "reality."[30] T. C. Price Zimmerman, one of the few scholars presently directing his attention to medieval autobiography, can theorize that Petrarch's having written no life history in "modern" form attests to the rudimentary nature of the fusion between Christian and classical traditions.[31] Rudolf Gottfried can maintain that autobiography in the modern sense "hardly exists for Elizabethan literature, and the single bona fide example of it which has survived [Thomas Whythorne's alternating prose and verse life, which the author himself compared to the *Vita Nuova*] is not . . . very fully developed."[32] Finally, in his study of seventeenth-century British autobiography, Paul Delany can claim that no tradition of secular autobiography in England existed, that no clearly defined spiritual autobiography appeared until Richard Norwood's *Journal* of 1639–1640, that autobiographers lacked interest in formal and stylistic excellence, that no generally accepted norms of good autobiographical writing existed, and that sophisticated and carefully structured autobiography is exceptional in the seventeenth century.[33]

[29] Ibid.

[30] Shumaker, *English Autobiography*, p. 10.

[31] Zimmerman, "Confession and Autobiography," 128.

[32] Gottfried, "Autobiography and Art," 110. Gottfried echoes Osborn, who holds that Whythorne was influenced by no earlier autobiographical tradition. Nevertheless, Whythorne's 1576 autobiography, in its use of Menippean satire form alone, shares in a tradition at least as old as late-antique autobiography, one employed by Lucian, Aelius Aristides, Commodianus, and, in the Christian tradition, the Pastor of Hermas (ca. 145), Boethius, Acilius of Spain (ca. 360), and, of course, Dante. See Georg Misch, *A History of Autobiography in Antiquity*. 2 vols., trans. E. W. Dickes (Cambridge: Harvard University Press, 1951).

[33] Delany, *Autobiography*, p. 173. That Delany writes from a modern perspective is evident in his language: In the absence of any tradition, he says, "each author was free to write the kind of autobiography that seemed best to him," "secular writers . . . were not bound by the constraints of sectarian doctrine," and "the loosening of rigid conventions of prose style" had a positive effect on the development of the modern genre. Viewed from a seventeenth-century perspective, Delany's freedom from conventions might rather be termed an indication of generic decay. What he sees is not so much the growth of a new tradition as a change in world view. Indeed, he comes very close at times to such an awareness, as when he states: "It would seem that few men were

It is clear that a great many questions are still to be answered regarding the roots of seventeenth-century autobiography. Although
the tradition descending from the Old Testament through the Pauline Epistles to the *Confessions* has been recognized, it has generally
been associated with devotional literature or with "works so subjective
as to be rhapsodies or intimate essays rather than true autobiographies."[34] Perhaps there *is* no tradition that continued down to the autobiographers of the Renaissance. And perhaps Donne will again be
proved to wear one of his many masks, this time that of Augustine.
But if this is not the case, some hard questions should be asked about
the literature of the period. If Donne is acting not as a man of "exceptional sensibility who extended the boundaries of personality
while the mass of [his] contemporaries stuck to age-old habits,"[35] but
as a deliberate exploiter of such habits, as I think this study will demonstrate, then we must look more closely at Milton, Browne, and Burton; at Whythorne and Greene; at the Pauline typologists Francis
Bamfield and Sir William Waller.[36] Did these latter two "distort the

---

willing to concede to the individual sensibility an autonomous field of action, outside
of religion or the external observances of the state. In a pre-romantic age, the profane
creed of self-realization as the highest good did not hold sway, and man's relation to
his God was held to be more vital than any concern with personal, secular development" (p. 172).

[34] Delany, *Autobiography*, p. 2. Nevertheless, he does recognize a "long tradition of
devotional literature—descending from the Old Testament, and becoming directly im-
itable with the Pauline epistles and Augustine's *Confessions*—[which] made self-analysis
respectable" (p. 107), but he neither relates it to autobiographical intent nor sees any
significant influence upon British authors of the period. "Not," he maintains, "until
Richard Norwood wrote his Journal in 1639–40 do we find a clearly defined spiritual
autobiography, though diaries and religious meditations were commonly written, by
men whose piety took an introspective turn, from the last decades of the sixteenth
century onward" (p. 171).

[35] Ibid., p. 14.

[36] One might begin by taking a closer look at the fifteenth-century lives of Margery
Kempe and John Lydgate, as well as Hoccleve's *Mal Regle* (1406). More's *Dialogue of
Comfort against Tribulation* (1535) shares formal concerns with the Boethian and Augustinian traditions. The verse lives of Churchyard, Tusser, and Gascoigne (the latter
perhaps modeled on Lydgate's) and the prose confessions of Greene also deserve
closer examination of their structural and formal conventions. Finally, for the sixteenth century anyway, the verse/prose autobiography of Thomas Whythorne, which
Osborn terms "unique in early literature" (p. 24), is suspiciously similar to Gascoigne's
Master F.J.; both use a series of poems around which a picaresque prose narrative is
developed. Seventeenth-century autobiographies which may participate in the tradition are many. I list briefly here Kenelm Digby's *Loose Fantasies* (1609), with its resemblance to *The Golden Ass* and to Sidney's *Arcadia*; the life of Herbert of Cherbury, which
participates in the tradition shared by Cellini; the overtly Augustinian life of Sir Tobie
Matthews; the lives of William Chappell and Matthew Robinson, boldly patterned after
Virgil and Suetonius; and, finally, the biblical life of the horse doctor's son, Lodowick

true pattern of their lives by trying to fit every detail into the Pauline archetype," forcing spiritual autobiography "into an unduly rigid convention"?[37] Or did they find the "true pattern" of their lives by participating in a literary tradition through which the written life was made eternally meaningful, a tradition which blurred, even negated, the lines between secular and spiritual life history? Moreover, are the Puritans, as Joan Webber has maintained, as the only practitioners of autobiography "in its literal, chronological sense," by implication the only "really self-conscious men" of the period?[38] Or does the Anglican, who, she says, gives the audience "a sense of confusion about whether what it sees is real or artificial," expect his audience to be not at all confused? Does he further expect it to be cognizant that his "turning life into art" is a form of autobiography as literal, sometimes as chronological, as that of the Puritans, but one operating within a framework to which the modern world responds, if at all, with confusion?[39]

To identify such a framework requires a reexamination of our definitions of autobiography and of the nature of self-consciousness which informed the genre during the Middle Ages and the Renaissance. I quote two more critical definitions. The first, that of Zimmerman, works perhaps because of its looseness; it could, with little effort, be stretched to cover a remarkable range of literature:

> Ideally practiced, autobiography involves the formulation of a coherent interpretation of the self from a particular viewpoint in time. What distinguishes it from memoirs, diaries, writing is the author's viewing of his past life in an effort to construe it as a whole. Through the process of reflection there emerges an interpretation of past experience which attempts to clarify the development of the self.[40]

Zimmerman places emphasis on the act of construing, a grammatical term—seeing one's life as syntax, as a statement deserving of expla-

---

Muggleton, divided into chapter and verse, and those of Sir William Waller and Francis Bamfield, which were closely modeled on St. Paul. The last of these mirrors the early tradition in its very title: *A Name, an After-one; or a Name, a New-One, In the Later-day Glory. Or, An Historical Declaration of the Life of Shem Acher* [Francis Bamfield], *Especially as to some more eminent Passages of his Day, relating to his more thorow lawful Call to the Office and Work of the Ministry, for about Twenty Years last past. Wherein Paul is propounded for an Example, and the Case, so far as it doth run Parallel, is set down before it; tho the Prehiminence is given unto Paul* (1681). Waller's life, entitled *Recollections*, is to be found in *The Poetry of Anna Matilda* (1788).

[37] Delany, *Autobiography*, p. 30.

[38] Webber, *The Eloquent I*, p. 28.

[39] Ibid., p. 56.

[40] Zimmerman, "Confession and Autobiography," 33.

nation—a term attributable perhaps to his commitment to medieval studies. His thinking is echoed in a startling fashion by Donne himself, who, in a letter accompanying a presentation copy of the *Devotions*, described his own life in grammatical terms:

> To make myself believe that our life is something, I use in my thoughts to compare it to something; if it be like anything that is something. It is like a sentence, so much as may be uttered in a breathing; and such a difference as is in styles is in our lives, contracted and dilated. And, as in some styles there are open parentheses, sentences within sentences, so there are lives within our lives. I am in such a parenthesis now (in a convalescence) when I thought myself very near my period.[41]

This is no piece of easy wit. As I shall demonstrate in the following chapters, Donne saw his life, and the written expression of it, in terms of models and structures that allowed the blending of chronology, experience, anecdote, and insight into the fullness of extended metaphor, even readable symbol, and that entailed an essentially mimetic act of self-creation. James Olney, in his exhaustive and penetrating study, *Metaphors of the Self: The Meaning of Autobiography*, has made such literary self-fashioning a central concern in his attempt to define the genre:

> I do not mean, for autobiography, that it is a definition of the writer's self in the past, at the time of action, but in the present, at the time of writing. . . . In the great autobiographers, whether it be autobiography as such or poetry, consciousness of this continuing creation of the self accompanies the creation, and, in the moment after, becomes it. . . . If these men succeeded in creating symbolic images in their autobiographies, then one cannot doubt that it is because they lived symbolic lives and that they continue to live them in their autobiographies.[42]

This definition is one to which the work of Augustine, Dante, Donne, and others of the early tradition can be said to conform, for they employed both typology and formal structure to convey a portrait of the self in continuing creation—that is, in the timeless presence of a loving, creating God. That they, and Donne, saw their lives as symbolic will, I think, become evident in the course of this study.

Unfortunately, like many present writers on the subject of autobiography, Olney does not substantively address the premodern forms. But he could be confronting the intensity of the *Devotions* (he is in

---

[41] Gosse, *The Life and Letters* 2:208.
[42] (Princeton: Princeton University Press, 1972), p. 44.

actuality speaking of Hopkins) when he describes the self-awareness
embodied in the act of creating an autobiography:

> There are unquestionably times when the self is more highly "pitched"
> or intensely concentrated, more fully realized or richly "selved" or self-
> possessed; in some moments, why or how one does not know, we succeed
> in incorporating more of the energy of the body of the unconscious into
> the narrow wedge of consciousness, and the self is defined in those mo-
> ments of great capability as the relation between consciousness and the
> unconscious, or as the process of bringing unconscious contents into the
> area of consciousness and under the control of awareness and the will.
> These highest peaks of self, when the largest areas of the vague uncon-
> scious are brought to an intensity of consciousness, when the whole po-
> tential of humanity seems realized in the individual, cannot be analyzed
> or explained but only experienced and, if the artist's faith is justified,
> perhaps reexperienced in metaphors and symbols: in autobiography and
> poetry.[43]

Donne would, I think, have identified these as moments of grace.
They came, surely, as the gift of God, but they were occasions prepared for by prayer, discipline, and constant self-scrutiny.

Donne's own preparation, like that of his kinsman Thomas More,
was concentrated in prayer and meditation; where More devoted the
whole of his Friday hours to the chapel at New Building, Donne rose
alone each morning before dawn and gave himself to contemplation
for hours at a time (a practice to which he alludes in the sixteenth
Expostulation, when he comments on his habit of meditating on illustrations of the Gospels). Stephen Greenblatt has recently pointed to
the role which such sessions played in fashioning the interior awareness that was to strengthen More at the scaffold,[44] and much of the
intensity that informs the *Devotions*, particularly that found in the
Meditations and Expostulations, results, I would maintain, from just
such a habit of prayer, where Donne confronted himself alone in the
presence of God. Indeed, at such times the individual sense of self,
to repeat Olney, is "more highly 'pitched,' " more "richly 'selved,' "
more deeply self-aware, even "transcendent and more than individual."[45]

But I must part company with Olney on the point of the limitations
of this self-awareness. "Self as concept," he maintains, "is defined, if

---

[43] Olney, *Metaphors of the Self*, p. 25.

[44] *Renaissance Self-Fashioning, from More to Shakespeare* (Chicago: University of Chicago Press, 1980). See especially his chapter "The Implications of the More-Tyndale
Controversy."

[45] Olney, *Metaphors of the Self*, p. 30.

such be a definition, in self as experience, but only there. What a writer about the self and its life, or an autobiographer, cannot give us, nor is there any reason to desire it, is a view of himself from without."[46] Early spiritual autobiography adheres to a literary and philosophical tradition that subordinates individual experience to an external reality, one which enables the autobiographer to view himself from without and to communicate that view to his reader. It focuses, through the examination of an individual soul, upon the place of that soul in the schema of Eternity and upon the ways in which God can work in any soul to produce Christian conviction, for its author hopes that sins similar to his own will be acknowledged by the reader, who will be vicariously purified by the author's sufferings. It is a tradition that demands the subordination of personal experience to thematic matter, where the subject's movement and growth in real time play a secondary role to his spiritual progress. The autobiographies it produced are "true" life histories, but their truth is that of poetry: The whole is informed by the articulation of its components, and the persona upon which the account centers is only one of these—one often perceived and delineated in terms of the larger pattern of the Creation. Unfortunately, the modern reader looks for a different autobiographical persona, for post-Renaissance awareness has restructured the genre, so that, in the words of Alfred Whitehead, "the individual subject of experience [has] been substituted for the total drama of reality."[47]

That early autobiographers saw themselves as participating in such a tradition is evidenced by their acceptance of an ancient iconography that follows the pattern of conversion established in the New Testament by Paul (Acts 11.1–22), itself reflecting the Old Testament literary motif of King Hezekiah: a casting down, a period of blindness and abstinence, cure and raising by a specially appointed messenger of God, and immediate preaching of the good news by the recovered sinner. This pattern in the conversion of Paul, a *locus classicus* for the extremists and visionaries of the English commonwealth, was adopted early on by autobiographers. In his great study of early autobiography, Misch has pointed to an efflorescence of typological confessions as early as the first century of the Christian era. That of Dio-Chrysostom is, he maintains, "the first time that we meet with . . . a man's elaboration of his experience on a literary model not only in style but in content, perhaps really understanding it in that conven-

---

[46] Ibid., p. 35.

[47] *Science and the Modern World* (New York: Macmillan Co., 1928), p. 201.

tional way,"[48] and another from the same period, *The Shepherd* of Hermas (ca. 145), is "the first [example] in Christian literature of a characteristic type of presentation of religious experiences, in which the individual and the typical proceed together without distinction."[49] The tradition was thus established quite early, and it featured prominently the motif of a casting down by sickness; consequent healing, frequently accompanied by a dream or vision (sometimes cast as a visit to another, an "under," world); and repentance and conversion to a holier life.

The individual work was often cast in hexameters or in forms of Menippean satire, the latter perhaps borrowed from pagan autobiographies like that of Lucian (ca. 120–180). Early on, too, came the convention of epistolary autobiography, as in Jerome's confession to Eustochia (384), which fills some forty printed pages:

> While the old serpent was thus making me his plaything, about the middle of Lent a deep-seated fever fell upon my weakened body. . . . Meantime preparations for my funeral went on; my weakened body grew gradually colder. . . . Suddenly I was caught up in the spirit and dragged before the judgment seat of the Judge; and here the light was so bright, and those who stood around were so radiant, that I cast myself upon the ground and did not dare to look up. Asked who and what I was, I replied: "I am a Christian." But he who presided said: "Thou liest, thou art a follower of Cicero and not of Christ. For 'where thy treasure is, there will thy heart be also.'" Instantly I became dumb, and amid the strokes of the lash—for he had ordered me to be scourged—I was tortured more severely still by the fire of conscience, considering with myself that verse, "In Sheol who shall give thee thanks?" . . . Accordingly, I made oath, saying: "Lord, if ever again I possess worldly books or if ever again I read such, I have denied Thee." Dismissed, then, on taking this oath, I returned to the upper world.[50]

Jerome here recollects both the hymn of Hezekiah (Isaiah 38.18) in the Vulgate, "For hell shall not confess to thee, neither shall death praise thee; nor shall they that go down into the pit look for thy truth," and Psalm 6.5–6, "Return, O Lord, rescue my soul, save me for thy mercy's sake, because there is none in death who remembers thee: who is there that praises thee in the abode of the dead?" The story of Hezekiah, which seems to me a primary source of the iconography employed by early autobiographers, appears four times in the

---

[48] Misch, *A History of Autobiography* 2:489.
[49] Ibid., 513.
[50] Quoted in Misch, *A History of Autobiography* 2:578.

Vulgate Old Testament: 2 Kings 32.24–33, 4 Kings 20.1–20, Isaiah 38.1–22, and Ecclesiasticus 24.20–28. In brief: Son of the backsliding Ahaz, Hezekiah restored the altar of the temple desecrated by his father and was rewarded for his piety by a victory over Sennacherib. In his pride, however, he neglected to render proper thanks to God and was stricken with a fever, its outward manifestation an "impostume" on the chest or side. When, turning his face towards the temple wall, he protected his general faithfulness and righteousness, God sent Isaiah to promise a cure after three days (wrought by means of a plaster of figs laid upon the ulcer), victory over the Assyrians and the protection of Jerusalem, and the addition to Hezekiah's life of fifteen years, the sign of which was the return of the sun ten degrees on the "Dial" of Ahaz—the latter probably a staircase ascending to the temple, its steps (made from broken parts of the altar Ahaz had desecrated) used to tell time by the progression of the sun along their course. The king recovered in the promised time and celebrated his cure by composing an intricate hymn of thanksgiving (given in its entirety in Isaiah 38.10–20 and containing the verse quoted by Jerome). The figure of Hezekiah and the pattern of his illness and repentance inform the tradition of spiritual autobiography consistently through the Middle Ages and eventually appear in Donne's own attempt in the genre, the *Devotions Upon Emergent Occasions*.

A good number of medieval autobiographical and confessional works can also be connected with the Hezekiah/Paul iconographical pattern exemplified in Jerome, among them the *Confessio* formerly attributed to Prosper of Aquitania (ca. 410), that of Paulinus of Pella (ca. 459), those ascribed to St. Patrick (ca. 460), the early-sixth-century "Confessio" of Ennodius, the *Histoire de sa vie* of Guibert de Nogent (ca. 1115), and the "notes de caractère à la fois mystique et autobiographique" of Opicinus de Canistris (1296–ca. 1350).[51] The eleventh-century life of Jean de Fecamp, with its alternating verse and prose, also bears witness to the tradition.[52] Its great manifestation, however, was Augustine's *Confessions*. Suffering from what he calls "my disease of incontinency,"[53] and deeply moved by the examples of Simplicianus and Ponticianus, Augustine, in Book 8 of the *Confessions* is overcome with remorse at his own inability to turn from the love of the flesh to the love of God. Accompanied by his friend Alypius, he withdraws into the garden of his dwelling at Milan, into a kind of intense retreat that results in his total conversion to celibacy and the

---

[51] Pierre Courcelle, *Les Confessions de S. Augustin dans la tradition littéraire: Antécédents et Postérité* (Paris: Études Augustiniennes, 1963), pp. 206–13, 329.

[52] Ibid., p. 263.

[53] Confessions, 1:441.

life of the spirit. He views the struggles in the garden in terms of impending death and in a moment of existential terror, describes his exhausted soul: "All its arguments were already spent and confuted, there remained a silent trembling; and it feared, like the death, to be restrained from the sore of custom, which made it pine away even to the very death."[54]

His body no longer obeys his will: He tears his hair, beats his forehead, wrings his hands, even staggers and stumbles in a physical parody of his interior indecision. Significantly, even in the midst of the vocabulary of physical decay and death, there is a strong admixture of the language of birth: "And thou, O Lord, pressedst upon me in my inward parts, by a most severe mercy redoubling my lashes of fear and shame, lest I should give way again, and lest that small and tender tie, which now only was left, should not break off but recover strength again, and hamper me again the faster."[55] As he sits in the garden with Alypius, who witnesses his torment in respectful silence, Augustine experiences a kind of dream vision in which Lady Continency invites him to join her train of joyful youths and maidens: "[C]heerful was she, but not dissolutely pleasant, honestly coaxing me to come to her, and doubt nothing; yea, stretching forth those devout hands of hers, so full of the multitudes of good examples, both to receive and to embrace me."[56] This vision agitates him extremely, and he flees even the patient silence of Alypius to seek the solitude of the inner garden. There he literally flings himself down under the fig tree and at last gives vent to tears of sorrow and compunction.

Only then, when he is physically prostrate and calling on God in the words of Psalm 6—which contains the verses remembered by Hezekiah and Jerome, "And thou, O Lord, how long, how long, Lord wilt thou be angry, for ever? Remember not our former iniquities" (3.76)—comes the visionary response: "Tolle lege." He does take, and he reads Paul (Rom. 13.13–14): "Let us walk honestly, as in the day; not in rioting and drunkenness, not in chambering and wantonness, not in strife and envying. But put ye on the Lord Jesus Christ and make not the provision for the flesh, to fulfill the lusts thereof." Augustine now rises both literally and figuratively, his moral blindness cured by this messenger of God, "by a light as it were of confidence now darted into my heart, all the darkness of doubting vanished away."[57] His final act in the garden repeats the pattern of Paul, who straightaway preached Christ in the synagogues, for "with a well-qui-

[54] Ibid., 443.
[55] Ibid., 457.
[56] Ibid., 459.
[57] Ibid., 465.

eted countenance" he announces the good news to Alypius. Alypius, himself converted almost by the force of Augustine's struggle, joins his friend in announcing the good news to Monica, and the pattern is completed when Augustine publishes the *Confessions* as the testimony to his conversion and his *vita nuova*.

The pattern of Hezekiah and Paul, and of Augustine, is echoed strongly in two medieval autobiographical works which bear interesting relations to the *Devotions*, Dante's *Vita Nuova* and the *Life of the Servant*, composed by his near contemporary, the Dominican mystic Henry Suso. The latter work might be more properly called a teaching exemplum; that is, an exemplary self-revelation of past sinfulness and conversion, sometimes, as employed by Suso and by Peter Abelard, coupled with a set of epistles and a rule for nuns. Abelard's *Historia Calamitatum* (ca. 1130), which prefaced a rule for the nuns of the Paraclete, has been identified as a "tightly structured literary work, . . . [and] a record of conversion in the Augustinian manner reinforced with Boethian themes."[58] Suso's *Life* (ca. 1362) resembles the *Historia* in form and content; assembled and published with some eleven letters by his spiritual daughter, Elsbeth Stagel, it formed the first of a four-part *Exemplar*, the whole intended for the edification and instruction of women religious.[59] Interestingly, the question of this work's autobiographical veracity was unasked until the nineteenth century, when the exemplary nature of its content, replete with visions and the most arduous penances, began to arouse doubt in Suso scholars. "Is this extraordinary ascetic," asks his most recent editor, "whom we consider with alternating feelings of admiration and pity, a historical character or merely a kind of prototype, the product of a pious imagination which looked as Suso more through the prism of its fantasy than in the light of historical reality?"[60] He opts for the latter, ascribing the composition of the *Life* to a hagiographer-compiler, presumably an impressionable female. Yet Suso's book bears all the marks of a conventional early spiritual autobiography. Like the *Historia Calamitatum*, it is a highly structured autobiographical confession, prefacing a rule for nuns; like the *Confessions*, like the *Vita Nuova*, like the *Ascent of Mt. Ventoux*, it embodies an ico-

---

[58] D. W. Robertson, *Abelard and Heloise* (New York: Dial Press, 1972), p. 110.

[59] Elsbeth Stagel collected twenty-seven of Suso's letters (*das grosse Briefbuch*), which she recast into eleven, published as *das Briefbuchlein*, which formed the fourth part of *The Exemplar*. Thus *The Exemplar* consists of *The Book of Life, The Book of Eternal Wisdom, The Book of Truth*, and *The Little Book of Letters*.

[60] *The Exemplar: Life and Writings of Blessed Henry Suso, O.P.*, ed. Nicholas Heller, trans. Sister M. Ann Edward, O.P. (Dubuque: Priory Press, 1962) 1:xvi.

nography ancient even in the thirteenth century.[61] Like all of these, it is frankly literary, and its authorial voice is best understood in literary terms; that is, in terms of its author's and its audience's conception of autobiographical, revelatory literature—in terms of imitation, of structure, or a persona at once fictive and real.

Of particular interest to readers of the *Devotions* is the twenty-third chapter of Suso's *Life*, which begins with a series of worldly injuries and then concentrates on an illness—a burning fever caused by an abscess not unlike Hezekiah's posthume—that supposedly has brought Suso near to death. In his illness, the holy man meditates on Christ's suffering and is rewarded by angelic messengers who comfort him and request that he join with them in a song of praise. When he demurs, fearing death, they quote Psalm 30.25: "Take courage and be stouthearted. Cheer up, act like a man. Death is still a hundred leagues from your door. You have many earthly days ahead of you in which you will praise God and console your weary fellow men with the carols of eternity."[62] Thereupon the abscess bursts, and Suso is cured.

Although Suso's *Life* follows the *Vita Nuova* by some fifty years, and although many of the parallels between the two can be explained by their drawing upon the same general tradition, certain similarities, to each other and to the *Devotions*, are almost uncanny. Like Suso, in the twenty-third chapter of the *Vita Nuova* Dante is prostrated with fever; in a delirium, he confronts in a dream-vision first the passing of Beatrice ("Vero e che morta giace la nostra donna") and then his own imminent ("Tu pur morrai") and actual ("Tu se morte") death. There is a vision of angels, and, after his cure, the recounting of the experience in song ("Donna pietosa e di novella etate").[63] What these

---

[61] John Fleming, *The "Roman de la Rose": A Study in Allegory and Iconography* (Princeton: Princeton University Press, 1969), p. 21.

[62] Suso, *The Exemplar* 1:64.

[63] *La Vita Nouva of Dante Alighieri*, trans. Mark Musa (New Brunswick, N. J.: Rutgers University Press, 1957), pp. 43–51. An interesting variation of this tradition may be found in Petrarch's *Ascent of Mt. Ventoux*, which takes the act of rising from metaphor to reality. With his brother Gherardo (later a contemplative Carthusian) ascending the mountain by a shorter, if more arduous, route, Petrarch attempts the easier winding path to the summit, although it is one that more often than not leads him away from his goal and into difficulties. Upon reaching the top, his mind already drawing comparisons between his ascent and the art of contemplation, he reads from his pocket copy of the *Confessions* (much as Augustine had read Paul in the garden at Milan): "Men go abroad to wonder at the heights of mountains . . . and yet pass themselves by." Like Augustine, Petrarch is moved with compunction. He compares his reading to the conversion of Augustine: "I thought in silence of the vanity of men's purposes. . . . This thought possessed me for a time: if we were willing to endure so much labor and sweat to raise our bodies a little closer to Heaven, what cross, what prison, what

works share is a threefold movement of prostration, fevered wake-fulness, and healing dream-vision. The *Devotions* demonstrates a like movement. Donne's prostration after all is evident; it is the historical occasion of the *Devotions*. But in Expostulation 12, it is a station on the way to the completion of Paul's instruction, "Put ye on the Lord Jesus Christ":

> When thine *Angels* fell from heauen, thou tookst into thy care, the rep-aration of that place, & didst it, by assuming, by drawing vs thither; when we fel from thee here, in this world, thou tookst into thy care the reparation of this place too, and didst it by assuming vs another way, by descending down to assume our nature, in thy *Son*. So that though our last act be ascending to glory, (we shall ascend to the place of *Angels*) yet our first act is to goe the way of thy *Sonne, descending*, and the way of thy blessed *spirit* too, who *descended in the Doue*.

Like Dante, Donne is beset in his prostration by a cruel insomnia: "I sleep not night or day." Meditation 15, which follows this introductory tag, takes the reader through an extended and rather conventional discourse on sleep as the figure of fearful death, and the Expostula-tion concludes with Donne himself presented as an icon of sleepless-ness:

> And therefore giue me leaue, O my blessed *God*, to inuert the words of thy *Sonnes Spouse*: she said, *I sleepe, but my heart waketh*; I say, *I wake, but my heart sleepeth*; My body is in a sicke wearinesse, but my soule in a peacefull rest with thee; and as our *eies*, in our health, see not the *Aire*, that is next them, nor the *fire*, nor the *spheares*, nor stop vpon any thing, till they come to *starres*, so my *eies*, that are open, see nothing of this world, but passe through all that, and fix themselves vpon thy *peace*, and *ioy*, and *glory* aboue.

I do not find it perplexing that immediately after this Devotion there should follow a kind of dream-vision. Devotions 16, 17, and 18 depict Donne in a delirium passing through the fevered crisis of his illness and witnessing as in a dream the drama of his own death and burial played out by the funeral bells rung for fellow victims: "Here the *Bells* can scarse solemnise the funerall of any person, but that I knew him, or knew that hee was my *Neighbour*: we dwelt in houses

---

rack should terrify the soul in its approach to God, treading down upthrusting pride and all man's moral lot? How few are they who are not tempted from this path by fear of hardship or by desire or ease? How happy is such a man, if there be any such." Petrarch immediately writes an account of his "conversion"; the *Ascent of Mt. Ventoux* is actually a letter to his friend and former confessor, the Augustinian canon Father Dionigi da Borgo San Sepolcro.

neere to one another before, but now hee is gone into that house, into which I must follow him."[64] The message of these three Devotions, made explicit in their hexameter headings, is that contained in chapter 23 of the *Vita Nuova:* Beatrice is dead ("From the bels of the church adioyning, I am daily remembered of my buriall in the funeralls of others"); you will die ("Now, this Bell tolling softly for another, saies to me, Thou must die"); you are dead ("The bell rings out, and tells me in him, that I am dead"). The remaining five Devotions quickly move to the conclusion of Donne's illness, both physical and spiritual: Signs of digestion are perceived in the urine; the patient is purged, rises from bed, embarks on convalescence, and fortifies himself against relapse. And as the "Epistle Dedicatory" manifests, Donne must then publish the account of his healing, fully aware that he does so within an ancient tradition: "*It might bee enough, that* God *hath seene my* Deuotions: *But* Examples *of* Good Kings *are* Commandements; *And* Ezechiah *writt the* Meditations *of his* Sicknesse, *after his* Sicknesse." Like Paul, Augustine, Dante, and Suso before him, he makes public his restoration and conversion.

I return at this point to our definers of autobiography, in particular to reconsider the statement of Zimmerman that "ideally practiced, autobiography involves the formulation of a coherent interpretation of the self from a particular viewpoint in time" and Olney's, that "what a writer about the self and its life, or an autobiographer, cannot give us, nor is there any reason to desire it, is a view of himself from without." Neither, of course, holds up in the face of early spiritual autobiography, but I have chosen to reexamine them because they so clearly demonstrate the tendency to examine the literature of all ages in the light of modern sensibilities.

The true object of spiritual autobiography is not merely self-scrutiny, nor even edification, but rather Wisdom herself, who partakes of the Godhead. This predicated a more general sense of self than that presented in the modern autobiography, one tied to what Donne calls on his title page the "Humane Condition." Jonathan Goldberg, commenting on the discovery by Augustine "[of] the suprapersonal and generic identity of a saint," maintains that "the location of the individual dilemma in a universal content allows for a definition of self centered in essential matters of self-concern. Paradoxically, this focus produces an impersonal sense of self."[65] For the Christian, the painful process of self-scrutiny led to a perception of himself as the image of fallen Adam and of redeeming Christ, an identification best

[64] Meditation 13, sigs. S3v, S4r.
[65] Goldberg, "Cellini's *Vita*," 74.

perceived in times of adversity. The spiritual autobiography is concerned with the movement between these two poles; that is, conversion—sudden or progressive—as a point in the soul's turning from love of creatures to contemplation of divine wisdom, with the crux of conversion often occupying a central position, both thematically and structurally. At its heart is the movement from prostration, often the literal prostration of illness, to an ascendancy of divine love, where the death to carnal affection is followed by a putting-on of Christ. The movement of the whole reflects the downward path from God to man and the upward and the returning path of love from man to God—a Jacob's ladder complete with rocky pillow. The lesson of the *Devotions* is that the true means of ascending the ladder is first downward, and Donne, meditating on his own prostrate condition, describes the tensions between the two points: "As yet God suspends mee betweene *Heaven* and *Earth*, as a *Meteor*; and I am not in Heauen, because an earthly bodie clogges me, and I am not in the Earth, because a heauenly *Soule* sustaines mee."[66] In this light the *Devotions* may be seen as an exercise in autodidacticism rather than mere self-display. Not so much egocentric as "theocentric,"[67] Donne's self-exploration becomes in itself an act of devotion that leads toward wisdom and the discovery of the image of God in himself. From the intense preoccupation with the created world in the Meditations, he works his way through the self-questioning of the Expostulations, to the identification of himself with Christ in the Prayers. The ending of Prayer 3, for example, is so syntactically involved that the equation of the speaker with Christ is assured: "Doe this, *O Lord*, for his sake, who did, and suffered so much, that thou mightest, as well in thy Iustice, as in thy Mercy, doe it for me, thy *Sonne*, our *Sauiour, Christ Iesus*."

If the *Devotions* is an exercise in autodidacticism, Donne's life provides the text. But this autobiographical material is of greater scope than mere data of the sickroom or of conversion. N.J.C. Andreasen has come nearest to seeing the nature of the autobiographical impulse in the work:

> Literally, he writes as John Donne, as an individual man who has been dangerously, almost fatally, ill and who has been cured by his physician. In a larger sense, however, the "I" is really "we," the individual man is Everyman, the "Sickness unto death" is sin, the physician is Christ, and the curative is divine grace. Donne in describing his own experience, is actually doing much more; he is meditating "upon our Humane condi-

---

[66] Expostulation 3, sig. D4v.
[67] "Donne's *Devotions* and the Psychology of Ascent," *Modern Philology* 62 (1965): 209.

tion" (which he in his sickness, frailty, and weakness typifies) and revealing how human weakness may be transformed through the power of divine love; he, at the end of the *Devotions*, is a witness to the love.[68]

Although, like the incident of Augustine's pear tree, Donne's illness is very real, it is given a broader range of application by its metaphorical function: Donne reveals a deliberate distancing between himself as author and as object by showing himself in his sickness and frailty as a type of human weakness healed and called to rise again through the power of divine grace. One recalls Paul: "To the weak became I as weak, that I might by all means save some" (1 Cor. 9.22).

This perception Donne makes clear in the "Epistle Dedicatory" to the *Devotions*, where he identifies himself literally with the progenitor of the tradition, the poet-king Hezekiah. A figure in Christian typology of the entombment and resurrection of Christ, Hezekiah takes his place in the *Devotions* among a gallery of nearly forty figures, among them Paul and Augustine. By reading the words and experiences of Hezekiah, Paul, and even Augustine as his own, and by participating in the iconography of their tradition, Donne could discover his own identity in the eyes of God, for in the realm of grace all Christian experience is essentially common. As Augustine is Paul, so Donne can be both Augustine and Paul. All Christians, remade in the image of Christ, speak as one. Thus, by subordinating the individual personality to the more general Christian identity, Donne manifests both his Christianity and his artistry. The author of spiritual autobiography is not only a self-conscious self, "aware of himself making himself," but also a literary construct meant to be a figure of humanity; for Donne, the spiritual autobiography truly becomes an interior memoir that is "self-reflecting, man-reflecting, and God-reflecting simultaneously."[69]

To ask whether the author of that memoir functions primarily as historical entity or as prototype is off the mark, for he bears the entire pattern. He is both old Adam, fallen, and new Adam, bearing the image of Christ within him. The spiritual autobiography follows the scheme of the redemption within the individual soul as set out by Paul: "I am crucified with Christ: nevertheless I live; yet not I, but Christ liveth in me: and the life which I now live in the flesh I live by the faith of the Son of God, who loved me, and gave himself for me" (Gal. 2.20). Donne's *Devotions* enables the author and his audience to

---

[68] Ibid.
[69] Goldberg, "Not Unto Death: The *Devotions* of John Donne" (Ph.D. diss., Columbia University, 1971), 133.

experience the throwing down and rising up through Christ that make for humility and that, reliving the pattern of the Incarnation and the Resurrection, enable the Christian to rise above his individuality to a true imitation of Christ. Its composition was, in the most profound sense, itself an act of devotion.

Chapter III

PERSONAL AND POLITICAL TYPOLOGY
IN THE *DEVOTIONS*

A Type and Earnest of thy Gracious Purpose

ESSENTIAL to the "construing" of the self in the tradition of spiritual autobiography—a literary urge to self-statement that prompted Dante to paint an essentially scribal persona in the *Vita Nuova*—is the reflecting of the author's identity in the mirror of literary type. The choice of Hezekiah for such a function goes far toward explaining the problem of publication which has for so long clouded the reputation of the *Devotions*. "*It might bee enough,*" Donne says in his "Epistle Dedicatory," "*that* God *hath seene my* Deuotions." And there are those who would agree with all but his use of "*might.*" It is to be remembered that T. S. Eliot once accused Donne of publishing his book "for the purpose either of self-indulgent introspection or to astonish his fashionable audience, or for both purposes at once."[1] Self-indulgence and sycophancy, nonetheless, do not fit the pattern of Donne's attitude toward the publication of the *Devotions* or for that matter, toward the publication of his work in general. It is a pattern manifest as early as 1607 or 1608 and once which continued under a clear rationale nearly to his death. Throughout his career, he demonstrated a knowledgeable respect for the power of print, paying close attention to those efforts he deemed publishable and withholding others as either unwise or unworthy.[2]

Of the round dozen publications to his credit by the time of the *Devotions*, his earliest effort, the *Juvenilia*, fell in the latter category, and was published posthumously in 1633, although "An Essay of Valour" and one of the "Characters" had found their way into the 1622 edition of Sir Thomas Overburie's *The Wife*.[3] Donne was aware that these "swagerers," as he called them, were immature both in content

---

[1] "Donne's *Devotions*," *Times Literary Supplement*, 11 March 1926, p. 178.

[2] Edwin H. Miller, *The Professional Writer in Elizabethan England: A Study of Nondramatic Literature* (Cambridge: Harvard University Press, 1959), p. 7, cites Donne for "contempt of the printing press." The facts demonstrate the contrary.

[3] Geoffrey Keynes, *A Bibliography of Dr. John Donne, Dean of Saint Paul's* (Oxford: Clarendon Press, 1973), p. 34.

and style, for in 1600 he wrote his friend Sir Henry Wotton that "they are not hatcht: they are rather alarums to truth to arme her then enemies."[4]

His second effort, *Biathanatos*, written probably in 1607 or 1608, was also, because of its delicate and controversial content, deemed unpublishable by its author and withheld from the press, although Donne allowed it the customary circulation among his friends. Moreover, he seems to have been unwilling to destroy the work, aware of both its merit and the scope it gave for possible misinterpretation. In 1619 Donne, now dean of St. Paul's, was apparently even more conscious of the sensitive nature of the work, for he sought to rid himself of the responsibility for the manuscript, entrusting it on going to Germany to his close friend Sir Robert Carr with instructions: "Reserve it for me, if I live, and if I die, I only forbid it the Presse, and the Fire: publish it not, but yet burn it not; and between those, do what you will with it."[5] *Biathanatos* was at last published in 1646/1647.

Donne's third prose effort, *Pseudo-Martyr*, was his first to be published. Although the story that the work was commissioned by James Stuart is probably apocryphal, the book does fall among Donne's efforts to gain royal favor with his pen. *Pseudo-Martyr* was entered in the Stationers' Register by the printer Walter Burre in 1609. Evidently Donne was satisfied with the man's work, for his choice fell on Burre for the printing of *Conclavi Ignati* early in 1611. This first Latin edition, although published anonymously, shows meticulous preparation for the printer. The English version, published in 1611 by Richard More, is less perfect both in text and accomplishment; again, the work is anonymous—Donne's name was not attached until the edition of 1614.

Donne's attitude toward the publication of his poetry seems to have paralleled that toward his prose. A small number of his poems can be found in four anthologies: Ferrabosco's *Ayres* (1609), Coryat's *Crudities* (1611), *The Odcombian Banquet* (1611), and Corkine's *Second Booke of Ayres* (1612). These show little or no sign of the author's hand in their printing. On the other hand, Donne did see some of his occasional verse through the press. His elegy on Prince Henry, which appeared in Joshua Sylvester's *Lachrymae Lachrymarum* (1613), was carefully prepared for publication. The 1611 and 1612 editions of the *Anniversaries* also show signs of careful supervision, although Donne seems not to have dealt directly with the printer.[6]

---

[4] Evelyn Simpson, *A Study of the Prose Works of John Donne*, 2d. ed. (Oxford: Clarendon Press, 1948), p. 316.

[5] *Letters to Severall Persons of Honour* (London, 1651), pp. 21–22.

[6] Anticipating his journey to France with the Drurys—which was actually delayed

His last effort at poetic publication was an abortive one. At the end of 1614, when he appears to have been preparing a collection of his poems, he wrote to Sir Henry Goodyer: "I am brought to a necessity of printing my poems, and addressing them to my Lord Chamberlain . . . not so much for publique view but at mine own cost, a few Copies . . . for I must do this, as a valediction to the world before I take orders."[7] Gosse suggests that Donne's abandonment of the project may have signaled not only the end of his quest for secular preferment but also an unwillingness to risk the loss of favor with Archbishop Abot.[8] The edition was to have been dedicated to "my Lord Chamberlain" Robert Carr, earl of Somerset, who met with strong disapproval in the eyes of the archbishop—not without reason as time was to prove. The project, for whatever cause, did not see fruition, and the first edition of the collected poems was not published until 1633. This edition, though posthumous, shows an attention to detail very like the author's.

With the taking of orders, Donne's stated rationale for publication changed. Where previously his efforts had been bent primarily on obtaining preferment, now he was also dealing with the matter of edification. From 1615 until his death in 1631, Donne allowed the publication of only six sermons and the *Devotions*. At least one of these sermons, that on Judges 10.15, was published on royal instruction, for it set forth James I's directions for preachers, which directions had created a great deal of controversy among the Puritan clergy.[9] More interesting, in the dedicatory epistle to *Encaenia*,

---

beyond the date of publication—he gave over supervision of *An Anatomy of the World* to his friend Joseph Hall, whose "To the praise of the Dead and the Anatomy" is prefixed to the "Funerall Elegy." Hall gave the work to the printer Samuel Macham, a boyhood friend with whom he had been associated in the publication of two of his works in 1611. The next year, Donne sent copy for *The Second Anniversarie* from France, and Hall again saw it through Macham's press.

[7] Edmond Gosse, *The Life and Letters of John Donne, Dean of St. Paul's* (London, 1899), 2:68.

[8] Ibid., 69–70.

[9] One questions whether, left to his own devices, Donne would have published the sermon. One contemporary observer accords it a less-than-welcome reception: "On the 15th of this present the Dean of Paules preached at the Crosse to certifie the Kings goode intention in the late orders concerning preachers and preaching, and of his constancie in the true reformed religion, which the people (as shold seeme) began to suspect; his text was the 20th verse of the 5th chapter of the booke of Judges, somewhat a straunge text for such a business, and how he made yt hold together I know not, but he gave no great satisfaction, or as some say spake as yf himself were not so well satisfied" (Chamberlain, 2:518). Nevertheless, the sermon ran through two editions. It is reprinted in *The Sermons of John Donne*, ed. George R. Potter and Evelyn M. Simpson (Berkeley: University of California Press, 1962) 4:178–209. The matter of

preached in 1623 at the dedication of the new Lincoln's Inn Chapel, Donne set forth expressly a rationale for publication:

> It pleased you [the Masters of the Bench of Lincoln's Inn] to exercise your interest in me, and to expresse your favour to mee, in inviting mee to preach this Sermon: and it hath pleased you to doe both over againe, in inviting me to publish it. To this latter service I was the more inclinable, because, though in it I had no occasion to handle any matter of Controversie between us, and those of the *Romane Perswasion*, yet the whole body and frame of the *Sermon*, is opposed against one pestilent calumny of theirs, that wee have cast off all distinction of places, and of dayes, and all outward meanes of assisting the devotion of the Congregation. For this use, I am not sorry that it is made publique, for I shall never bee sorry to appeare plainly, and openly, and directly, without disguise or modification, in the vindicating of our *Church* from the imputations and calumnies of that Adversary. If it had no publique use, yet I should satisfie my selfe in this, that it is done in obedience to that, which you may call your Request, but I shall call your Commandement upon
>
> *Your very humble Servant in Christ Jesus,*
> Iohn Donne[10]

He implies that publication of a sermon is justified only if it contains something beyond mere homiletic instruction; that is, it should have either special reference to contemporary problems or value in the enduring battle with Rome. The 6 sermons published during his lifetime seem to have met this criteria. Seven more appeared shortly after his death, including the magnificent *Death's Duell*, and Walton maintains that at the time of his death, Donne had ready for the printer nearly 120 sermons copied in his own hand. The three folio volumes collected by John Donne the younger between 1640 and 1660 contain 154 sermons, delivered from notes and written out later by their author with a view toward publication.

In the light of this stated rationale, the question becomes more pertinent: If the *Devotions* is to be defined not as a deliberately crafted

---

Donne's personal disinterestedness, as opposed to his natural desire for preferment in what was a highly politicized church, is presently under debate. Two recent studies which deal with the subject are John Carey, *John Donne: Life, Mind, and Art* (New York: Oxford University Press, 1981) and Arthur Marotti, *John Donne, Coterie Poet* (Madison: University of Wisconsin Press, 1986), although the latter confines itself to Donne's secular career. Recently, Dennis Flynn has cast some doubt on Donne's opposition to the church of Rome: "Donne, the Survivor," in *The Eagle and the Dove: Reassessing John Donne*, ed. Claude J. Summers and Ted-Larry Petworth (Columbia: University of Missouri Press, 1986).

[10] *Sermons*, 4:362–63.

spiritual autobiography but as an idosyncratic prose-poem, private in scope and intention—as indeed it has so been defined by many critics—then why is the book among the few works that Donne allowed to be published during his lifetime? An examination of the data of its publication does, to some extent, reveal his purpose in sending it to press. Donne was ill from November 24–25 through at least December 6; by early January, the work was in the hands of Thomas Jones, his bookseller, and was entered in the Stationers' Register by Augustine Mathewes, who had printed the second edition of the *Anniversaries*. In the interim, Donne had revised his meditations, imparted to them their twenty-three-part structure, composed the "*Stationes*," and prepared a fair copy (albeit one deficient in correct marginal citations) for the printer. By February 1, copies were available in some stage of completion, for on that date Donne sent one to Sir Robert Carr with the remark: "They arise to so many sheetes (perchance 20.) as that without staying for that furniture of an Epistle, That [as] my Friends importun'd me to Print them, I importune my Friends to receive them Printed."[11] (It is possible that the work was just then coming off the press, for, minus the "Epistle Dedicatory," the *Devotions* comes to some twenty-seven sheets.) In the letter to Carr, Donne wonders whether "there be any uncomeliness or unseasonableness" in dedicating the work to Prince Charles.

A letter of that same date to Princess Elizabeth, the exiled queen of Bohemia, speaks of the *Devotions* as completed. But has the *Devotions* aught to do either with contemporary problems or the enduring battle with Rome? The letters of compliment accompanying presentation copies to Princess Elizabeth, the duke of Buckingham, and an unidentified court lord (perhaps the earl of Dorset)[12] throw revealing light on Donne's intentions in publishing his book. His purpose, he wrote the princess, then in exile in Holland, was exemplary: "In the hearing of me deliver my messages to God, I can hope for the continuance of your Majesty's patience."[13] To Buckingham he expressed the wish that the "*Devotions*" and "*Mortifications*" might help him prepare for death: "And as the reading of the actions of great men may affect you for great actions, so for this our necessary defect of dying . . . you may receive some remembrances for the *Meditations and Devotions* of your Grace's devoted Servant."[14] The letter to the unknown lord, which I have already quoted in part, plays upon elements of structure and discourse in the book:

[11] *Letters*, p. 249.
[12] Gosse, *The Life and Letters* 2:208.
[13] Ibid., 205.
[14] Ibid., 207–8.

To make myself believe that our life is something, I use my thoughts to compare it to something; if it be like anything that is something. It is like a sentence, so much as may be uttered in a breathing; and such a difference as is in styles is in our lives, contracted parentheses, sentences within sentences, so there are lives within our lives. I am in such a parenthesis now (in a convalescence) when I thought myself very near my period. God brought me into a low valley, and from thence showed me high Jerusalem upon so high a hill as that He thought it fit to bid me stay and gather more breath. This I do by meditating, by expostulating, by praying; for, since I am barred of my ordinary diet, which is reading, I make these my exercises, which is another part of physic. And these meditations, and expostulations, and prayers I am bold to send to your Lordship; that, as this which I live now is a kind of second life, I may deliver myself over to your Lordship in this life with the same affection and devotion as made me yours in all my former life; and as long as any image of this world sticks in my soul, shall ever remain in your Lordship's.[15]

The dedication to Prince Charles is the most revealing of all. There Donne pictures himself as one not only recovered from an illness but reborn: "I *Haue had three* Births; *One*, Naturall, *when I came into the* World; *One* Supernatural, *when I entred into the* Ministerie; *and now, a* preter-naturall Birth, *in returning to* Life, *from this* Sicknes." The book is *"This* Image *of my* Humiliation." He might, he says, have kept his devotions private (as had Lancelot Andrewes), *"But* Examples *of* Good Kings *are* Commandements; *And* Ezechiah *writt the* Meditations *of his* Sicknesse, *after his* Sicknesse." It is my contention that the evidence of these statements, considered carefully in the light of the internal evidence of the *Devotions* and in the light of contemporary poetic practice, will reveal that Donne's publication of this work was well within the boundaries imposed by his rationale for publication of his sermons; that is, the *Devotions* refers both to contemporary problems and to the conflict with Rome. Moreover, as we shall see, it embodies this reference in a structure that refers directly to Donne himself—to the structure of his life, his role within the church, his place within God's universe.

For Donne, Hezekiah's was a situation uncannily like his own: Both fell ill at the winter solstice,[16] and both seemed under the sentence of

---

[15] Ibid., 208.

[16] Nicolaus de Lyra, *Postilla Super Totam Bibliam* (Strasburg, 1492; facsm. ed. Minerva GmbH., Frankfurt/Main.: Unveränderter Nachdruk, 1971), I, sig. UU*vv*, col. 2, in his commentary on 4 Kings, voices the common opinion: "Notadum que iste due figure facte sunt secundum unus viam quam posui—qui dies elongata sub ezechia fuerat in

imminent death at a crucial time of life—Hezekiah in the middle of his years,[17] and Donne in his fifty-first year when he was entering astrological "old age." Both, unable to approach their God in his sanctuary, called to him from the sickbed, and both were treated by a poultice put to the breast.[18] Donne is certain to have been reminded of these similarities by the liturgy for December 12 and 13, which called for the reading at Morning and Evening Prayer of Isaiah 37 through 40, the story of Hezekiah—his victory, illness, cure, and hymn of thanksgiving—culminating in the great Advent prophecy of chapter 40: "Every valley shall be exalted, and every mountain and hill shall be made low: and the crooked shall be made straight and the rough places plain." It seems very likely that Donne was aware of and probably followed the liturgy from his sickbed. Devotions 16 through 18 reveal that he could hear not only the daily ringing to prayer of the bells of St. Gregory but also the playing of the organ: "Where I lie, I could heare the *Psalme*, and did ioine with the *Congregation* in it."[19] The third Expostulation indicates his distress at his physical inability to join with the congregation in prayer: "It is not a *Recusancie*, for I would come, but it is an *Excommunication*, I must not."

Hezekiah had recited as thanksgiving for his cure not a traditional psalm but a hymn of his own making, one which had become a prototype within the English church of the private act of thanksgiving for relief from illness. A metrical paraphrase had appeared as early as the 1545 primer of Henry VIII, and in the very year of Donne's illness, George Wither published such a paraphrase in *The Hymnes and Songs of the Church*. His introductory comments to "Hezekiah's Thanksgiving" are enlightening:

> Hezekiah, having beene sicke and recovered, made this *Song of Thanksgiving*: And setteth forth the mercie of God by considering these particulars: The time of his age; the feares of his soule; the rooting out of his

---

solstitio hyemali, et sic brevior die prolongata est." (Please note that those two figures were constructed according to the way I proposed—the day was prolonged under Hezekiah in the winter solstice, and so the shorter one was prolonged by a day.)

[17] According to Cornelius a Lapide, *Commentaria in Isaiam Prophetam, Commentaria in Scripturum Sacrum* (Paris: 1866), p. 477; Hezekiah was thirty-nine: "quae aetas est quasi dimidia vitae humanae," referring specifically to the seventy-year limit of Psalm 89 ("si autem in potentatibus, octoginata").

[18] The Vulgate 4 Kings 20 tells us that Hezekiah was cured by a paste made of figs. Donne's physicians applied to his breast an electuary of egg—a glutinous sweet paste which contained countervenoms, heart stimulants, and febrifuges. See my essay "Prescription and Devotion: The Reverend Doctor Donne and the Learned Doctor Mayerne—Two Seventeenth-Century Records of Epidemic Typhus Fever," *Medical History* 22 (1978): 412.

[19] Expostulation 16, sig. S9v.

posteritie; the violence of his disease; and the forgiveness of his sinnes, added to the restoring of his health. Then (seeming to have entred into a serious consideration of all this) hee confesseth who most are bound to praise God; and voweth this Deliverance to everlasting memorie. This *Song* may bee used after deliverance from temporall sicknesse: But in the principall sense it is a speciall thanksgiving, for that cure which *Iesus Christ* Wrought upon the *humane Nature*, being in danger of everlasting perdition. For, *Hezekiah*, which signifieth, *helped of the Lord*, typified Man-kind, labouring under the sicknesse of sinne and death. *Isaiah*, who brought the medicine that cured him (and is interpreted) *The salvation of the Lord*, figured our blessed *Redeemer*, by whom the *humane Nature* is restored; and whose sending into the world, was mystically shewed by the Miracle of the *Sunnes* retrogradation. To praise God for that mys-terie therefore (the circumstances being well considered) this *Hymne* seemeth very proper; and, doubtlesse, for this cause it was partly pre-served for these our times; and ought often and heartily to bee sung to that purpose.[20]

Hezekiah's hymn "seemeth very proper," and, following his example, Donne did not exercise his devotions privately but strove to make them overheard. In contrast to those Anglicans who were inhibited by what has been called "genteel inhibitions against self-revelation"[21] and consequently left their devotions to be published posthumously if at all, Donne saw his *Devotions* as a work of edification for his au-dience, so that his meditations on his own condition reveal something about the nature of God's salvific action both to himself and to his reader. To the latter, the *Devotions* reveal the "Humane Condition," a sense of common identity and purpose with one's neighbor which is the foundation of charitable love; to Donne, the *Devotions* vow "this Deliverance to everlasting memorie." For the poet, the composition of his book became an act of devotion; for his reader, the taking of edification from the book becomes in itself a spiritual act.[22]

Donne's close friend Bishop Joseph Hall displayed a like frame of mind for the publication of his own autobiography:

Not out of a vain affectation of my own Glory, which I know how little it can avail me, when I am gone hence; but out of a sincere desire to give glory to my God, (whose wonderful Providence I have noted in all my

[20] (London: 1881), p. 70. John Hall, *The Court of Virtue* (1565), manages to expand Hezekiah's delicately concise hexameters to seventy-two lines of riming doggerel.

[21] Paul Delany, *British Seventeenth-Century Autobiography* (London: Routledge and Ke-gan Paul, 1969), p. 28.

[22] Gerald H. Cox, "Donne's *Devotions*: A Meditative Sequence on Repentance," *Har-vard Theological Review* 66 (July 1973): 38.

wayes) have I recorded some remarkable passages of my fore-past life: what I have done is worthy of nothing, but silence and forgetfulness; but what God hath done for me, is worthy of everlasting and thankfull Memory.[23]

Hall writes on the unhappy occasion of his being forced from his bishopric into private life by the exigencies of civil war. Donne's role, however, by virtue of his exceedingly public position as dean of St. Paul's, royal chaplain, and foremost preacher in London, had become that of a spokesman to and for the Christian community. The dedication of his book to Prince Charles and the language of the "Epistle Dedicatory" indicate that he saw his situation as spiritually profitable to the English church and to its monarch, present and future.

His calling up the image of Hezekiah had ample precedent, for during the Tudor monarchy, it had been used frequently to encourage the monarch in piety and to remind her or him of sacred dynastic obligations. Particularly, the image was used to remind the ruler of the obligations of Protestant succession. Early on, Henry Bullinger, "Minister of the Church of Zurich," who had dedicated his multivolume *Decades* of sermons to Edward VI, had compared the boy-king to a number of biblical sons: "Salomon, the son of David, the wisest and most commended king of all the world, did so long enjoy prosperity and praise at the mouth of the Lord, as he did not neglect with reverence to obey his word."[24] "Abia, the son of Roboam, overcame the host of Israel . . . because he believed the word of the Lord."[25] "Joas, a child yet but seven years old, being by the labour, faith, and diligence of the faithful priest Joiada restored to and settled in the place of his father, who was slain before him, reigned, after the wicked Athalia was put to death, most happily and in a prosperous state. . . ."[26] Among these exemplary types of fathers and sons, Hezekiah functions both as son and as father to a son:

> The good and godly king Ezechias succeeded his ungodly father in the seat and kingdom. Of him we have this testimony in the scripture: "He did that which was right in the sight of the Lord, according to all that his father David did. He put away the high places, and brake the images, and cut down the groves, and allto[gether] brake the brasen serpent which Moses had made: for unto those days the children of Israel burnt

[23] Cited in Delany, *Autobiography*, pp. 47–48.
[24] *The Decades of Henry Bullinger. Minister of the Church of Zurich* (Cambridge, 1849–1852) 8:6.
[25] Ibid., p. 7.
[26] Ibid., p. 8.

sacrifice to it. He trusted in the Lord God of Israel. For he clave to the
Lord, and departed not from him, but kept his commandments, which
the Lord commanded Moses" [2 Kings 18]. And now, let us hear what
followed upon this obedience and faith of his. The scripture goeth forward, and saith: "And the Lord was with him, so that he prospered in
all things that he took in hand." While he did reign, the most ancient
and puissant monarchy of the Assyrians was broken and diminished: for
when Senacherib, king of Assyria, besieged the city of Jerusalem, the
angel of the Lord in one night slew in the Assyrian camp one hundred
fourscore and five thousand soldiers. And the king of Babylon also did
very honourably by his ambassadors send prince-like gifts unto Ezechias,
desiring earnestly his amity and friendship: for the glory of that most
godly king was blown abroad, and known in all the world. Again, when
his son Manasses, a very wicked man, did not tread the path and express
the deeds of his most holy father, but, being made king in the twelfth
year of his age, did of purpose cross the word of God, and brought in
again all the superstition which his father had abolished, he was taken
captive and carried away to Babylon.[27]

Considering the Romish location of Babylon in his own day, this was
a sorry fate for the staunchly Protestant Edward. The pattern is clear:
Like Hezekiah, Edward can be the instrument of God's justice in destroying papist idolatry; he can also strive to be unlike the unfaithful
son Manasseh, who delivered his people into the Babylonian captivity, an event which seemed imminent until 1588 at the very least, and
one just as easily envisioned in the political climate of 1623–1624,
when Spain seemed again to threaten English Protestant autonomy
and Charles could easily be cast in the role of Manasseh in his quest
for the hand of the Infanta.

The example of Hezekiah held up to Edward omits the story of his
miraculous cure. Not so for Elizabeth. The Accession Day prayers
added to the liturgy in 1576 (when the Queen had successfully passed
the age of forty-two, an important climacteric) presented for Morning Prayer a first lesson consisting of a reading of "The history of
King Hezekia, taken out of the fourth book of Kings, the 18. 19, and
20. Chapters." This reading contains the account of Hezekiah's victory over Sennacherib and his consequent illness and healing, although it omits the hymn of thanksgiving found in the Isaiah account. The remainder of the service is consistent in its underwriting
of monarchial power: The second reading (Vulgate 4 Kings 22.23
and 2 Chronicles 34) tells of Josiah, who strengthened the priesthood
of Israel; the second lesson (Romans 13.3: "For rulers are not a terror

[27] Ibid., pp. 9–10.

to good works, but to the evil. Wilt thou then not be afraid of the power? do that which is good, and thou shalt have praise of the same"); the epistle (1 Peter 2.11–18, at 13: "Submit yourselves to every ordinance of man for the Lord's sake: whether it be to the king, as supreme; Or unto governors, as unto them that are sent by him for the punishment of evildoers, and for the praise of them that do sell"); and the gospel (Matthew 22.16–23, at 21: "They say unto him, Caesar's. Then saith he unto them, Render therefore unto Caesar the things which are Caesar's; and unto God the things that are God's")—all these reinforce the image and lawful rule of the monarch.[28]

They underscore as well the season, for the sun had entered Sagittarius, an event noted in the Prayerbook, the last and darkest sign of autumn which would end in "the yeares deep midnight" of the winter solstice and Capricorn. The liturgy abounds with apocalyptic overtones, a reminder of the eschatological mystique of the Protestant Tudor monarchy: the second reading—"And that, knowing the time, that now it is high time to awake out of sleep: for now is our salvation nearer than when we believed. The night is far spent, the day is at hand: let us therefore cast off the works of darkness, and let us put on the armour of light" (Romans 13.11–13); the epistle—"Dearly beloved, I beseech you as strangers and pilgrims, abstain from fleshly lusts, which war against the soul; Having your conversation honest among the Gentiles: that, whereas they speak against you as evildoers, they may be your good works, which they shall behold, glorify God in the day of visitation" (1 Peter 11–12); and the psalm—"Then we made our complaint unto our God, and cried unto the Lord in our trouble: and he heard the voice of our prayer out of his holy temple, and delivered us out of our distress. He gathered us home again out of the lands; from the East, and from the West, from the North, and from the South. He delivered our souls from death, our eyes from tears, and our feet from falling: he hath set us at liberty, he hath light[ed] our candle; the Lord our God hath made our darkness to be light (Psalms 18.5; 107.12; 107.3; 116.8, 4, 1, 18, 27). The seamless fabric of the liturgy delicately reiterates the matter of Hezekiah, with its motifs of complaint and crying to the Lord, of the winter solstice, of the godly king, of the Second Coming.

The figure of Hezekiah seems to have been a standard one for English churchmen to apply to their monarch. At the end of her days, the comparison with Elizabeth must have seemed apt: She had fought the good fight and championed mightily the English church. That

[28] *Liturgical Services. Liturgies and Occasional Forms of Prayer Set Forth in the Reign of Queen Elizabeth* (Cambridge, 1847), pp. 550–52.

the comparison was made openly is evidenced by a funeral eulogy preached and later published by William Leigh, wherein Elizabeth is extolled as another Hezekiah in "her pietie, to reforme the Church."[29] Leigh touches on many elements of the Hezekiah motif, including the returning of the sun on the Dial of Ahaz, Hezekiah's association with the virtues of justice and temperance, his role as son and father ("*Ezekia* succeeded *Ahaz*, a good sonne to a bad father, So did *Queene Elizabeth Mary*, a Religious Prince, a superstitious sister"),[30] his purgation of the sanctuary (Elizabeth does so by calling back the Marian exiles and purging "that pregnant Idoll the Masse"),[31] his association with the counting of life years, and even his association with the flight of contemplation ("I may say, then, as of all these, so of good *Ezechias, Nihil habuit vulgare*, he had no base minde, hee contended for no trifles, but for the honour of his God, and good of his Church, his generous spirit carried him above the pitch of vulgar conceit, which hovereth belowe, and aymeth at mediocrities, and therefore Hesiodus speaking of such high hearts, calleth them not without cause *Kera epamenoi*. Whose minds soare. on high, without commerce of earth, or earthly things").[32] The seventeenth-century churchman could draw on a tradition hoary with antiquity, one which obviously held much meaning for the English monarchy.

If Edward and Elizabeth Tudor merited this kind of typological attention, how much more James Stuart! Elizabeth's was, even in her declining years, an exceedingly difficult act to follow, and James rose as best he could to the occasion by touting his inconsiderable talents as poet and theologian. Of the many works ascribed to him, few are fully by his own hand, but the weight of his name insured their publication well into the period of the Civil War, when the need for a royal David—or better, an English Solomon—was all too evident to the faltering Royalist cause. Early in his reign he had taken pains to establish continuity with the literary tradition which depicted the English monarch as eschatological ruler. Elizabeth's claim to this distinction had been reiterated continually by such luminaries as Bishop Jewel and John Foxe. The latter, who dated the struggle with Antichrist from the fourteenth century, read history as a continuing action fought between the English monarchy and the papal Whore of Babylon. As the centuries passed and Apocalypse neared, the conflict was to climax in the struggle of the Elizabethan church against Rome.

[29] William Leigh, *Queene Elizabeth, Paraleld In Her Princely Virtues, with David, Joshua, and Hezekia . . . In three Sermons, as they were preached three severall Queenes dayes* (London, 1612), sig. A1r.

[30] Ibid., sig. K5v.

[31] Ibid., sig. K6v.

[32] Ibid., sig. I5r.

Thus, by the accession of James, popular writing had devolved into near legend, and the monarch was well aware of the mythic expectations of his people in his taking up the cause.[33] James's answer was to identify himself strongly with Revelation, thereby, as James Bobrick has pointed out, doing nothing to prevent his further identification with the powerful emperor of Sibylline eschatology who, appearing toward the close of the world's sixth age, was to initiate the final struggle against the hosts of Satan.[34] To this end, in *A Premonition to all most Mightie Monarchs, Kings, Free Princes, and States of Christendome* (1609), James attacked the papacy's temporal claims by means of a systematic exegesis of Revelation, identifying the Roman church, of course, with the Scarlet Woman and the Pope with Antichrist. It was a situation ripe for typological exploitation.

Hezekiah, as we have seen, was a figure associated strongly with the concept of a reforming monarch. It is this association that attracted Joshua Sylvester who, in the fourth book of the fourth day of the second of his *Divine Weekes*, marginally identifies the biblical king as "the true pattern of an excellent Prince." His Englishing of Du Bartas's Hezekiah account points a loyal finger in the Stuart direction:

> So, all the Vertues of the most and best
> Of Patriarchs, meet in this Prince's brest:
> Pure in Religion, Wise in Counselling,
> Stout in Exploiting, Just in Governing;
> Un-puft in Sunshine, un-appal'd in Storms
> (Not, as not feeling, but not fearing Harms)
> And therefore bravely hee repels the rage
> Of proudest Tyrants (living in his Age)
> And (ay un-daunted) in his God's behalf
> Hazzards at once his Scepter and himself.
>
>   For, though (for Neighbours) round about him reigne
> Idolaters (that would him gladly gain)
> Though Godlings, here of wood, and there of stone,
> A Brazen here and there a Golden one,
> With Lamps and Tapers, even as bright as Day,
> On every side would draw his mind astray:
>
> (449–64)

> Hee first of all sets up th' Almightie's Throne
> And under that, then, hee erects his own.

---

[33] William Haller, *The Elect Nation: The Meaning and Relevance of Foxe's "Book of Martyrs"* (New York: Harper and Row, 1963), p. 224.

[34] "The Structure of Giles Fletcher's *Christs Victorie, and Triumph*," Texas Studies in Literature and Language, 21, 1979, 522–52.

Th' establishing of God's pure *Law* again,
Is as the Preface of his happy Reigne.

(477–80)

This zealous Hate of all Abhomination,
This royall Work of thorough-*Reformation*,
This worthy Action wants not recompence:
God, who his grace by measure doth dispense,
Who honours them that truly honour him,
to EZECHIAH not so much doth seem
His sure Defence, as his Confederate.[35]

(504–10)

Likewise Donne, in a sermon on Isaiah 32.8, delivered to King Charles at Whitehall some four years after his illness: The commentators dispute, he says,

> whether this prophecy of *Esay*, in this Chapter, beginning thus, (*Behold, a King shall reigne in righteousnesse, and Princes shall rule in judgement*) be to be understood of an *Hezekias*, or a *Iosias*, or any other good King, which was to succeed, and to induce vertuous times in the temporall State, and government, Or whether this were a prophecy of Christs time, and of the exaltation of all vertues in the Christian Religion, . . . it may very well subsist so, That in a faire proportion, all these blessings shall be in the reignes of those *Hezekiasses*, and those *Iosiasses*, those Kings which God affords to his people; But the multiplication, the exaltation of all those blessings, and vertues, is with relation to the comming of Christ, and the establishing of his Kingdome.[36]

In the same sermon, Donne identifies Hezekiah as "a Type of Christ, but yet but a Type of Christ,"[37] while "the King is Christ,"[38] moreover, he is "our King, our God, our Christ, our Jesus."[39] By extension, the entire government takes on a divine cast: "Thy King, thy Christ, is a liberall God; His Officers, his Ministers, by his instructions, declare plentifull redemption."[40] And for Donne himself, in Expostulation 7 of the *Devotions*—which embodies a paean of praise to James—the King is Araumah, David, Jehosophat, Hezekiah, a "man of God, and God of men." He is both correlative with his Old Testament proto-

---

[35] *The Complete Works of Joshua Sylvester*, ed. Alexander B. Grosart (Edinburgh, 1880; reprint, New York: AMS Press, 1967), 2:255.
[36] *Sermons*, 8:238–39.
[37] Ibid., 245.
[38] Ibid., 249.
[39] Ibid., 251.
[40] Ibid., 252.

types and a recapitulation of Christ, since in his public role as Christian monarch he bears within him the image of Christ and outwardly acts as his viceregent.[41]

All of this is in accord with a political and historical typology which manifests Donne's belief in the special providential eye turned toward the place of England and her monarchs in Christian history. In this view, as one historian has recently maintained, "God's provident hand touches the world and history and time, and at each touch, divine echoes are set up which reverberate and reinforce one another across the barriers of historical times. . . . This divine resonance is actually the result of the impact of Eternity upon historical time, of the meeting of the Infinite and the finite at a given moment in the historical evolution of God's salvific will."[42] It is a vision not so much linear and sequential as it is vertical; the figure or event of the Old Testament is fulfilled in the New Testament, which it adumbrates, and these are figures of events to happen in the end of time.[43]

Thus, every occurrence in history is part of the larger plan of God's providence, with the Incarnation as its central focus. The events and characters of Scripture are perennial: Old Adam is fulfilled in Christ who will be fully revealed in glory at the end of time. It took only a small step to construe political structures and events in the light of Old Testament typology. Stephen Zwicker maintains that the resulting "political typology" is based on a "theology of federal grace,"[44] which developed in Reformation theology by means of a reevaluation of the relationship between the faithful of the Old Testament and the elect of the New. From this theology developed the theory of the new covenant, one which, invoked by the English church, could exalt the monarch to near divinity, and invoked by dissenters could bring him to the block.[45] The change in focus resulted, as Barbara Lewalski has demonstrated, in the identification by Christians not so much with

[41] Ernst H. Kantorowicz, *The King's Two Bodies* (Princeton: Princeton University Press, 1957), p. 45. See also Barbara K. Lewalski, *Donne's "Anniversaries" and the Poetry of Praise: The Creation of a Symbolic Mode* (Princeton: Princeton University Press, 1973), pp. 15ff.

[42] Joseph A. Galden, S.J., *Typology and Seventeenth-Century Literature* (The Hague: Mouton, 1975), pp. 47–48.

[43] Ibid.

[44] Steven N. Zwicker, "Politics and Panegyric: The Figural Mode from Marvell to Pope," in *Literary Uses of Typology*, ed. Earl Miner (Princeton: Princeton University Press, 1977), p. 116.

[45] Francis Oakely, "Jacobean Political Theology: The Absolute and Ordinary Powers of the King," *Journal of the History of Ideas* 29 (1968): 323–46; William Haller, *The Rise of Puritanism* (New York: Columbia University Press, 1938); *Foxe's "Book of Martyrs" and the Elect Nation.*

the sacramental and institutional church as with the continuing effect
of providential history upon his mystical body and upon the individual within that body. English Protestants thus were likely to identify
their national experiences, spiritual and political, with those of the
Old Testament faithful, when "a strong millenarian impulse led them
to view their own contemporary history as the last age spoken of in
the millennial prophecies."[46]

Donne was very much a man of his time, and the *Devotions* provides
an example of his loyal adherence both to the British monarchy and
to a belief in its central place in salvation history, a belief he had demonstrated as early as the Prince Henry elegy of 1613.[47] He wrote at a
crucial time in the history of that monarchy: James I was clearly in
mental and physical decline—he would die in little more than a
year—and his son Charles was embarked on a foolhardy course of
alliance by marriage and then war with Spain.[48] The winter of 1623–
1624—feared by some as the time of the Second Coming[49]—marked
a period of extreme national anxiety. The prince, spurred by Buckingham, seemed bent on forcing this policy on James, who remained
in morbid alcoholic seclusion. A letter from the Venetian ambassador
describes the unhappy state of affairs:

> The King seems practically lost; he comes to various decisions and in-
> clines to his usual negotiations; he does not care to fall in with the wishes
> of his son-in-law and the favourite. He now protests, now weeps, but

[46] Barbara K. Lewalski, *Protestant Poetics and the Seventeenth-Century Religious Lyric*
(Princeton: Princeton University Press, 1979), 130. She also describes "correlative"
types, who rather than fulfilling millenarian expectations, recapitulate the Old Testament in that they too await the coming of the millennium (pp. 123–39).

[47] See Lewalski, *Donne's "Anniversaries,"* pp. 18ff. Donne's view of Henry was clearly
eschatological:

> Was it not well believ'd, that hee would make
> This general peace th'eternall overtake?
> And that his times might have stretcht out so far
> As to touch those of which they emblems are?
>
>   (35–38)

[48] Donne, like most Englishmen, did not give the Spanish match anything like whole-
hearted support. See R. C. Bald, *John Donne: A Life* (New York: Oxford University
Press, 1970), pp. 446-47.

[49] Thomas Swan, *Speculum Mundi* (1637), sig. C4v: "for the year 1623, thus was the
fancie, IUDICare VIVos & Mort Vos, *To judge the quick and the dead*: Now here (as
before) they were led by numerall letters, having so many as would make 1623, in
which year they dreamed of the world's ending." A sidenote in Swan's text refers the
reader to the *Institutiones dialecticae* (post Dom. 2. adven.) of Conrad Dieterich. The
prediction attached itself to the Second Sunday of Advent, December 7, 1623, when
Donne was coming out of his febrile crisis.

finally gives in. . . . [He] descends deeper and deeper into folly every day, sometimes swearing and calling upon God, heaven and the angels, at other times weeping, then laughing, and finally pretending illness in order to play upon the pity of those who urge him to generous actions and to show them that sickness renders him incapable of deciding anything, demanding only repose, and, indeed, the tomb.[50]

The illness was real, if perhaps exaggerated. James suffered from painful and increasingly debilitating arthritis, exacerbated by his alcoholism. More to the point, however, in the last year of his life, increasingly severe senile depression caused him virtually to withdraw from his regal duties, which were thrown upon Charles and the increasingly powerful Buckingham. In the light of this situation, the "Epistle Dedicatory" of the *Devotions* smacks less of sycophancy than of advice:

> *This* Child *of mine, this* Booke, *comes into the world*, from *mee, and* with *mee. And therefore, I presume (as I did the* Father *to the* Father) *to present the* Sonne *to the* Sonne; *This* Image *of my* Humiliation, *to the liuely* Image *of his* Maiesty, *your* Highnesse. . . . *Besides, as I haue liu'd to see,* (not as a Witnesse *onely, but as a* Partaker) *the happinesses of a part of your* Royal Fathers *time, so shall I liue,* (in my way) *to see the happinesses of the times of your* Highnesse *too, if this* Child *of mine, inanimated by your gracious Acceptation, may so long preserue aliue the* Memory *of*

Your Highnesse
Humblest and
Deuotedst
IOHN DONNE.

The *Devotions* remind the Prince of his coming twofold responsibility: As a monarch, he must fulfill the type of the good King Hezekiah, and as head of the Church, he must promulgate the Word through the support of its preaching priesthood, of whom Donne is a living example. The message of Bullinger to Edward VI is repeated: Like the father/son Hezekiah, Charles can be a destroyer of idolatry and the enemies of Israel, but he can also fall like Manasseh, the undutiful son who delivered his people into the Babylonian captivity. (Donne did not live to witness Charles's ultimate humiliation.) On the other hand, Charles could imitate his father in building a strong church and fortifying it with learned preachers. James himself was aware of this necessary and to him eschatological role when he inter-

---

[50] D. Harris Willson, *King James VI and I* (London: Jonathan Cape, 1956), pp. 441-42.

preted the two witnesses of Revelation 11.3, "And I will give power unto my two witnesses, and they shall prophesy a thousand two hundred and threescore days, clothed in sackcloth," usually held to be the risen Eliah and Elijah: "In the one taking it to be the Word of *God* it self, in the other, the Word of *God* too, but in the mouths of his Preachers."[51] He adds: "And yet (praised by God) we begin now with our eyes, (as our Predecessors have done in some ages before) to see these *Witnesses* rise againe, and shine in their former glory: God as it were, *setting them up again on their feet*, and *raising them to the Heavens* in a triumphall cloud of glory, like *Eliah* in his fiery Chariot."[52] Donne will be such a witness; it remains for Charles to put him to use, as had his father when, in Donne's words, "he, first of any man conceiu'd a hope, that I might be of some vse in thy *Church*, and descended to an intimation, to a perswasion, almost to a solicitation, that I would embrace that calling."[53]

Donne's embracing the ministry had committed him to the public role that determined, in large part, the monarchial orientation of the *Devotions*. But the impact of eternity upon historical time, that "divine resonance," extends beyond the state and its representatives to the individual Christian, for the workings of God upon one sinner are as important as his workings upon history at large. And, as the letter to the earl of Dorset amply demonstrates, the experience which generated the *Devotions* was intensely personal: "God brought me into a low valley, and from thence showed me high Jerusalem upon so high a hill as that He thought it fit to bid me stay and gather more breath."[54] Donne's emphasis on the figure of Hezekiah reveals not only his identification of that ancient king with James and Charles Stuart but equally its private application to himself as suffering victim and Christian poet. It was not difficult for him to see the pattern of Hezekiah's illness as his own: a casting down to near death, a healing by emissary, and a rising. Hezekiah was traditionally representative of the Christian in affliction, and Isaiah's injunction to the king, "Set

---

[51] *King James His Divine Prophecie, of the Warres and Distractors of the present and future Times, in Relation to the two Witnesses their coming downe from Heaven, fighting, and how slaine by Antichrist, and being again risen in imitation of Christ, and cloathed in sackcloth, they work miracles and wonders, such as we have seen some already* (London, 1645), p. 5. In 1609, James had, through exegesis of Revelation, demonstrated that the Pope is indeed "the peste of all Religion," the Antichrist, leaving the way clear for his own identification with the predestinate ruler of the sixth age in *A Premonition to all most Mightie Monarchs, Kings, Free Princes, and States of Christendome*, which followed his *Apologie for the Oath of Allegiance* (1607).

[52] *King James His Divine Prophecie*, p. 6.

[53] Expostulation 8, sigs. I12v–K1r.

[54] Gosse, *Life and Letters*, 2:208.

thine house in order; for thou shalt die, and not live" (2 Kings 20.1), quoted by Donne in Expostulation 17 and applied to his own case, was a common starting point in the *ars moriendi* tradition. The prayer of Hezekiah (Isaiah 38.3; 2 Kings 20.3) was advocated for the sick,[55] and his hymn for the safely recovered.[56]

That Donne saw himself as one of "Mankind, labouring under the sicknesse of sinne and death" is obvious, for the *Devotions* echoes and reechoes the conventions of the literature of ministering to the sick. The "Order for the Visitacion of the Sicke" from the Prayerbook has the priest exhort the sick person to "know . . . that almighty God is the Lorde over lyfe, and death, and over all thynges to them perteyning. . . . Wherfore, whatsoever your sickness is, knowe you certaynly, that it is God's visitacion."[57] Donne, in his pastoral life committed to visitation of the sick, could see his own illness as God's visitation, and hence in the fourth Expostulation he says: "I knowe, that euen my weakenesse is a reason, a motiue, to induce thy mercie, and my sicknes an occasion of thy sending health"; in Expostulation 14: "This is the day of thy *visitation*, thy coming to me; and would I looke to be welcome to thee, and not entertaine thee in thy coming to me?"; in the second Prayer: "*A sound heart is the life of the flesh*; & a heart visited by thee, and directed to thee, by that visitation is a sound hart. *There is no soundnesse in my flesh, becaues of thine anger.* Interpret thine owne worke, and call this sicknes, correction, and not anger, & there is soundnes in my flesh."

The body of literature concerned with devotions during illness— books like *The Sicke Mans Salve* (1561) or Becon's *The Physyke of the Soule* (1549)—displays motifs shared by the spiritual autobiography, such as the paradox of falling as rising, suffering as medicament, and Christ as physician; Donne does not neglect these. Indeed, the first Expostulation promotes the commonplace of sin as sickness: "I fall sick of *Sin*, and am bedded and bedrid, buried and putrified in the practise of *Sin*, and all this while haue no presage, no pulse, no sense of my *sicknesse*; O heighth, O depth of misery, where the first *Symptome* of the sicknes is *Hell*, & where I neuer see the feuer of lust, of enuy, of ambition, by any other light, then the darkness and horror

[55] Sylvester, *The Complete Works*, 1:257; a marginal note reads: "A Prayer for a sick Person, *mutatis mutandis*," referring to the Hezekiah prayer.

[56] Wither, *Hymnes and Songs of the Church*, p. 70.

[57] *The First and Second Prayer Books of Edward VI*, ed. Ernest Rhys (London: J. M. Dent, 1938), pp. 260–61. See also Lancelot Andrewes, *Manual of Directions for the Sick*, trans. Richard Drake, in *Two Answers to Cardinal Perron and other Miscellaneous Works* (Oxford, 1854), p. 181; Jonathan Goldberg, "The Understanding of Sickness in Donne's *Devotions*," *Renaissance Quarterly* 24 (1979): 507–17.

of *Hell* it selfe." Although his doctors are the effective dispensers of his cure, they receive no real attention—they are allowed neither names nor speech—for they give place to Christ: "I send for the *Phisician*, but I will heare him enter with those wordes of *Peter, Iesus Christ maketh thee whole*; I long for his presence, but I look, *that the power of the Lord, should bee present to heale mee*."[58] The Christ-physician, whom Augustine called "medice meus intime,"[59] prescribes, like Donne's own doctors, cordials for fortifying the heart:

> And as thou hast not deliuered vs, thine *adopted sonnes*, from these infectious tentations, no neither hast thou deliuered vs ouer to them, nor withheld thy *Cordialls* from vs. I was baptized in thy *Cordiall water*, against *Originall sinne*, and I haue drunke of thy *Cordiall Blood*, for my recouerie, from actuall, and habituall sinne in the other *Sacrament*. Thou, *O Lord*, who hast imprinted all medicinall vertues, which are in all creatures, and hast made euen the flesh of *Vipers*, to assist in *Cordialls*, art able to make this present sicknesse, euerlasting health, this weaknes, euerlasting strength, and this very deiection, and faintnesse of heart, a powerfull *Cordiall*.[60]

The passage from Hebrews, so popular in prayer books and devotional manuals for the sick (a passage Donne must have been familiar with in the course of his pastoral duties), demonstrates the questioning of identity proper for the sick and dying, one central to the language of the *Devotions*: "For whom the Lord loveth he chasteneth, and scourgeth every son whom he receiveth. If ye endure chastening, God dealeth with you as with sons; for what son is he whom the father chasteneth not? But if ye be without chastisement, whereof all are partakers, then are ye bastards, and not sons" (Hebrews 12.6–8). Donne's Expostulation 2 presents something very close to verses 9 and 10 of that chapter ("Furthermore we have had fathers of our flesh which corrected us, and we gave them reverence: shall we not much rather be in subjection unto the Father of spirits, and live? For they verily for a few days chastened us after their own pleasure; but he for our profit, that we might be partakers of his holiness") when he says: "It is thou; Thou *my God*, who hast led mee so continually

---

[58] Expostulation 4, sigs. E5v–E6r. Among Donne's physicians were Theodore Turquet de Mayerne, eminent light of the Royal College of Physicians and the king's own doctor, and Simon Foxe, son of the author of the *Book of Martyrs* and Donne's lifelong friend.

[59] George Gusdorf, *La Découverte de Soi* (Paris: Presses universitaires de France, 1948), p. 19. See also Rudolf Arbesmann, "The Concept of *Christus Medicus* in St. Augustine," *Traditio* 10 (1954): 1–28.

[60] Prayer 11, sigs. N8v–N10r.

with thy hand, from the hand of my Nurce, as that I know, thou wilt not correct mee, but with thine own hand. My parents would not giue mee ouer to a *Seruants* correction, nor my *God*, to *Satans*."

Through chastisement, the Christian is led to recognize his true identity: He is child of God, fallen with Adam but risen in Christ. In acknowledging this relationship—"I cannot say with thy seruant *Ieremy, Lord, I am a child, and cannot speake*; but, *O Lord*, I am a sucking childe, and cannot eat, a creeping childe, and cannot goe; how shall I come to thee?"[61]—Donne also acknowledges a personal and generic Christian sense of selfhood. He is concerned not so much with the display of personal angst as with the movement, through the discovery of his participation in sinful humanity redeemed by Christ, from particular identity to a new and general identity of Christian, where individual differences are subordinate. This is the true context of Donne's famous definition of the human condition, so often taken out of context: "Any Mans *death* diminishes *me*, because I am in-uolued in *Mankinde*."[62] All men are sick of sin; for all, healing is possible. Donne speaks as one of them whose fallen condition and potential for redemption have been revealed by the adversity of his illness. That the pattern and occasion of that illness so closely echoed that of Hezekiah was singularly fortuitous, for like the Old Testament king, Donne was a poet capable of giving public voice to his thanksgiving. Hence Hezekiah figures in the *Devotions* as a type of the Christian monarch and of the individual Christian soul as well.

In recent years, the subject of Renaissance typology, and in particular the employment of typology by Donne and the Protestant poets of seventeenth-century England, has been the focus of enormous critical energy.[63] Barbara K. Lewalski has demonstrated that the

[61] Expostulation 3, sig. C12v.

[62] Meditation 17, sig. T4v.

[63] See Eric Auerbach, "Figura," in *Scenes from the Drama of European Literature* (New York: Meridian Books, 1959), and *Mimesis*, trans. Willard Trask (Garden City, N.Y.: Doubleday, 1959); Sacvan Bercovitch, "Annotated Bibliography [of Typology]," in *Typology and Early American Literature* (Amherst: University of Massachusetts Press, 1972), and "Typology in Puritan New England: The Williams-Cotton Controversy Reassessed," *American Quarterly* 19 (1967): 167–91; Victor Harris, "Allegory to Analogy in the Interpretation of Scriptures," *Philological Quarterly* 45 (1966): 1–23; Richard D. Jordan, *The Temple of Eternity: Thomas Traherne's Philosophy of Time* (Port Washington: Kennikat Press, 1972); Paul J. Korshin, *From Concord to Dissent: Major Themes in English Poetic Theory, 1640–1700* (Menstone: Scolar Press, 1973); Barbara K. Lewalski, *Milton's Brief Epic: The Genre, Meaning, and Art of Paradise Regained* (Providence: Brown University Press, 1966); William Madsen, "Earth the Shadow of Heaven: Typological Symbolism in *Paradise Lost*," *PMLA* 75 (1960): 519–26, and *From Shadowy Types to Truth: Studies in Milton's Symbolism* (New Haven: Yale University Press, 1968); Joseph Mazzeo, "Cromwell as Davidic King," in *Renaissance and Seventeenth-Century Studies* (New York:

transfer of emphasis from Christ as antitype, recapitulated in the sacramental and ecclesiastical Church, to the active mystical body of the Church itself and particularly to the individual Christian, opened new possibilities for the divine poet, who was enabled to bring to his work an energy rising from intensified self-scrutiny.

But as in all things, Donne fits no simple mold. His use of typology as a literary device is as complex and multivalent as his use of language, address, persona, tropes, figures, and all the other tools of his poetic practice. His early sermons, for example, employ the ancient fourfold method of exegesis and, while he can conform to the formula which sees Christ as strict antitype completing all that was foreshadowed by Scripture, he can also find in the Christian—the individual, his collective audience, the body of the church, himself—a recapitulation of the words and events of the Old Testament through participation in Christ.[64]

It has not escaped critical notice that Donne's *Devotions* is deeply involved in such typology. Whether one perceives Donne's illness as a type of his sickness of sin and regeneration through grace,[65] or as an extended explication of God's word through an anatomy of the world which is his body,[66] it is clear that the concerns of the *Devotions*

Columbia University Press, 1964); J. S. Preus, *From Shadow to Promise: Old Testament Interpretation from Augustine to the Young Luther* (Cambridge: Harvard University Press, 1969); Steven N. Zwicker, *Dryden's Political Poetry: The Typology of King and Nation* (Providence: Brown University Press, 1972).

[64] In his sermon on Psalm 38.3 (*Sermons* 2:75–76), Donne makes this recapitulation explicit: "Which words we shall first consider, as they are our present object, as they are historically, and literally to be understood of *David*; And secondly, in their *retrospect*, as they look back upon the first *Adam*, and so concern *Mankind collectively*, and so *you*, and *I*, and all have our portion in these calamities; And thirdly, we shall consider them in their *prospect*, in their future relation to the *second Adam*, in *Christ Jesus*, in whom also all mankinde was collected, and the calamities of all men had their *Ocean* and their confluence, and the cause of them, the anger of God was more declared, and the cause of that anger, that is sin, did more abound, for the sins of all the world were *his* by imputation; for this Psalm, some of our Expositors take to be a *historicall*, and *personall* Psalm, determin'd in *David*; some, a *Catholique*, and *universall* Psalm, extended to the whole condition of *man*; and some a *Propheticall*, and *Evangelicall* Psalm, directed upon *Christ*. None of them inconveniently; for we receive help and health, from every one of these acceptations; first, *Adam* was the *Patient*, and so, his promise, the promise that he received of a *Messiah*, is our *physick*; And then *David* was the *Patient*, and there, his *Example* is our *physick*; And lastly, *Christ Jesus* was the *Patient*, and so, his *blood* is our physick. In *Adam* we shall finde the *Scriptum est*, the medicine is in our books, an assurance of a Messiah there is; In *David* we shall find the *Probatum est*, that this medicine wrought upon *David*; and in *Christ* we finde the receit it self; Thus you may take this physick, thus you may apply it to your selves."

[65] Lewalski, *Donne's "Anniversaries,"* p. 159.

[66] See Leonard Barkan, *Nature's Work of Art* (New Haven: Yale University Press, 1975), pp. 51–60, for an extended discussion of the *Devotions* as microcosm.

range far beyond the narrow scope of personal malaise and do so through a questioning and "trying on" of Scripture. Moreover, the "Epistle Dedicatory" and the evidence of individual Devotions indicate that Donne was using the model of Scripture in an exciting and supremely artful fashion, for his emphasis on the figure of Hezekiah reveals not only his identification of that ancient king with James Stuart but also with himself in his role as divine poet.

James had focused attention on the role of "divine poesie" with his translation of Du Bartas's *L'Uranie*.[67] The latter had sought a Christian alternative to the Pleiade, and his effort was strengthened by renewed interest in the book of Psalms occasioned by Protestant biblical commentary.[68] The duty of the Christian poet had, of course, been defined early on by the church fathers, and good Protestants looked back to them as, for example, did Henry Peacham: "Nazianzen, S. Augustine, Bernard, Prudentius, with many others, beside the allowance they haue giuen of Poetrie, they teach vs the true use and end therefore, which is to compose the Songs of Sion, and addresse the fruite of our inuention to his glorie, who is the author of so goodly a gift, which we abuse to our loues, light fancies, and basest affections."[69] Thus Urania, the muse of astronomy, became as well "heavens high holy Muse"[70] and a figure of the Holy Spirit, for as George Wither informs us: "Verse is the forme of speech which the holy Ghost hath often chosen to expresse his mysteries in, when they were first penned in the Hebrew tongue."[71]

For the divine poet of the Renaissance, so often in England literally a divine who sought to imitate both the life and the ministry of Christ, the process of creating poetry became one of self-conversion as well as the preaching of the Word to others. Poetry, reflecting as it did the actual music of the spheres, acted as a "tuner" of the disordered sphere of the soul. Wither says, paraphasing Chrysostom: "We should orderly compose our selues, and make so tuneable our disagreeing affections, that our words and workes might be conformable."[72] Divine numbers were essential to the process:

[67] "The Vranie, translated," *The Essayes of a Prentise* (Edinburg, 1584), sigs. C2r–G1r.

[68] Jean Plattard, *La Renaissance des Lettres en France* (Paris: Libraries Armand Colin, 1952), p. 156.

[69] *The Compleat Gentleman* (1622), p. 118.

[70] "Upon the translation of the Psalmes by Sir Philip Sydney, and the Countesse of Pembroke his Sister." The Psalms are "songs . . . which heavens high holy Muse / Whisper'd to *David*, *David* to the Jewes: / And *Davids* Successors, in holy zeale, / In formes of joy and art do re-reveale" (ll. 31–34).

[71] Wither, *Hymnes and Songs*, p. 64.

[72] Ibid.

You must truely endeuour to sing them, not with your voyce, or a little heartie deuotion for the time: but learne to sing them vnto the *Psaltery*. ... For, the *Psaltery* was an Instrument to be played on with the hand: which consisting of ten strings was aunciently vsed by those who sung these *Psalmes* in the Temple. And it was appoynted for that purpose, mystically to teach vs, that hee whose tongue shall truely prayse God, with the Songs of Faith in the Gospell must also haue hands, making the *Musicke* of good workes vpon the ten strings of the Law.[73]

Urania wore a seven-starred crown—originally denoting the planets but now signifying as well the gifts of the Holy Spirit. She guided the divine singer in the turning of his own soul away from carnal to divine love, so that he "tuned" himself and his audience in an ascending scale from the carnal to the eternal, a movement made explicit by Du Bartas in *L'Uranie*:

> Et le sage écrivain n'éloigne dans ses vers
> Le sçavoir du plaisir, le jeu de la doctrine.
>   Tels serés–vous sans doute en chantant choses telles:
> Car enseignant autrui, vos mesmes aprendrés
> La regle de bien vivre, et, bien-heureus, rendrés
> Autant que leurs sujets, vos chansons immortelles.[74]

Holy Scripture, specifically the lyric genres contained within the book of Psalms, became a favorite source of both outward and inward form for the divine poet. He was not limited to Psalms alone, and various lyrics within the Old Testament, such as the songs of Moses and Miriam, the lamentations of Jeremiah, and of course the hymn of Hezekiah, became matter for imitation and paraphrase. Donne

---

[73] Ibid.

[74] Guillaume Du Bartas, *Works*, ed. U. T. Holmes et al. (Chapel Hill: University of North Carolina Press, 1938), p. 183. The lines are translated by James I, in *The Essayes of a Prentice* (Edinburgh, 1581), sig. F3r:

> In singing kepe this order showen you heir,
> Then ye your self, in teaching men shall leir
> The rule of liuing well, and happely shall
> Your songs make, as your thems immortall all.

Joshua Sylvester (*The Complete Works* 2:6) gives the lines in a rather more clear, if similarly talented fashion:

> Such shall you be, if such a taske you take:
> For, teaching others you your selves shall learn-all
> Rules of good life; and happy so shall make,
> As is your subject, your own Songs eternall.

had already done so with Moses and Jeremiah,[75] and in the *Devotions* he allows both internal content and external form to echo the narrative of Isaiah 38. Indeed, the parallels are tantalizing. I proceed now through the Isaiah chapter, demonstrating from the scriptural text itself and from generally accepted commentary on the text, the similarities between the two and the suitability of the Hezekiah story to Donne's literary purposes.

. . .

Isaiah 38.1: "In those days was Hezekiah sick unto death. And Isaiah the Prophet the son of Amoz came unto him, and said unto him, Thus saith the Lord, Set thine house in order: for thou shalt die, and not live."

There is some disagreement over the cause of the king's illness: One school has it that Hezekiah neglected to show proper thanks to God for his overwhelming victory against Sennacherib,[76] while the other, cited and approved by Cornelius a Lapide, who is a fairly good source of contemporary received opinion and one frequently consulted by Donne,[77] holds that God intended the illness as a purgation from sin, designed to increase his own glory and Hezekiah's love. According to Lapide: "Add that God wished to purge the devout king and to test him and perfect him with this affliction so that he would attach himself more ardently to God and call upon Him, as he did; and so that God would make plain His glory and the glory of Isaiah and Hezekiah, as we shall see that He did in the course of the text."[78] The importance of purgation in the *Devotions* cannot be underestimated: two full Devotions, 20 and 22, are preoccupied with the med-

---

[75] See Lewalski, *Protestant Poetics*, pp. 253–82.

[76] The *Glossa Ordinaria*, for example, cites Jerome: "Quia de victoria dignas Deo grates no retulit, sed in superbia evanuit, sicut Regum et Paralipomenorum liber aperit; unde: Quem Deus diligit, corripit, ne elevetur in superbiam post incredibiles triumphos" (*Pat. Lat.* 113, col. 1279). "Because he did not return due thanks to God for his victory but sunk himself in pride as is obvious from the Books of Kings and Paralipomenon; hence, whom God loves, he afflicts, lest he be elevated into pride after unbelievable victories."

[77] *Sermons*, Appendix 8:393–96, describes the strong dependence on Lapide demonstrated by the Christmas sermon of 1627; *Sermons*, "Donne's Sources (cont.)" 10:370–74, continues to outline "Donne's considerable indebtedness to Lapide."

[78] Lapide, *Commentaria in Isaiam*, p. 471. "Adde Deum voluisse pium regem purgare, probare et perficere hac afflictione, ut ardentius se Deo conjungeret, eumque invocaret, uti fecit; itaque novis miraculis Deus tam suam quam Isaiae et Ezechiae gloriam illustraret, uti eum fecisse videbimus in decursu textus."

ical purgations given Donne in his illness and with their spiritual implications.

38.2: "Then Hezekiah turned his face toward the wall, and prayed unto the Lord."

Says Lapide: "Because he could not go to the temple, he turned his face to the wall of the temple next to which Solomon had built the palace."[79] Jerome was of the opinion that not only proximity to the temple wall, but the king's humility had caused him to turn, so that his prayer might not smack of ostentation.[80] Lapide adds: "It is so arranged in [human] nature that, if someone should hear our prayers to God, we become embarrassed with inborn shame; and the shame distracts the mind of the one praying, pushes him away, and interrupts and weakens the prayer's force and fervor."[81] In the third Expostulation, soon after taking to his bed, Donne bemoans his inability to join with the congregation:

> But when I am cast into this bedd, my slacke sinewes are yron fetters, and those thin sheets, yron dores vpon me; And, *Lord, I haue loued the habitation of thy house, and the place where thine honour dwelleth*: I lye here, and say, *Blessed are they, that dwell in hy house*; but I cannot say, *I will come into thy house*: I may say, *In thy feare will I worship towards thy holy Temple*, but I cannot say in thy holy *Temple*: and, *Lord, the zeale of thy House, eats me vp*, as fast as my feuer; It is not a Recusancie, for I would come, but it is an *Excommunication*, I must not.

38.3: "And said, Remember now, O Lord, I beseech thee, how I have walked before thee in truth and with a perfect heart, and have done that which is good in thy sight. And Hezekiah wept sore."

Hezekiah is possessed of a good conscience through his destruction of idolatry and restoration of the worship of the one God in the temple.[82] Jerome relates conscience to health: "It is a happy conscience,

---

[79] Ibid., p. 472. "Quia ad templum ire non poterat, convertit faciem ad parietem templi, juxta quod Salomon palatium extruxerat."

[80] *Commentariorum in Essaiam*, Liber 11, *Corpus Christianorum, Series Latina* (Turnholt, 1958), 73, 443.

[81] Lapide, *Commentaria in Isaiam*, p. 472. "Natura enim ita comparatum est, ut si quis preces nostras ad Deum audiat, ingenito pudore verecundemur; et pudor hic mentem orantis distrahat, deprimat, ejusque vim et fervorem incidat et hebetet."

[82] Lapide (p. 472) comes down here very firmly: "The mind well aware of itself gives great confidence to prayer and impetration, . . . destroying idols, opening the doors of the temples, destroying the brass serpent [of Moses]. For in this worship of the one God he has been distinguished and perfected. In some other things he was imperfect, and he failed." ("Magnam fiduciam orandi et impetrandi dat animus sibi bene conscious . . . idola destruens, templi valvas aperiens, serpentem aeneum comminuens,

he says, which recalls good works in time of affliction."[83] In the fourth Prayer, Donne combines these elements of health, weeping, and state of conscience:

Heale this *earth*, O my *God*, my repentant tears, and heale these *waters*, these teares from all bitternes, from all diffidence, from all deiection, by establishing my irremouable assurance in thee. *Thy Sonn went about healing all manner of sickenesses.* (No disease incurable, none difficult; he healed them *in passing*) *Vertue went out of him, and he healed all,* all the multitude (no person incurable) he healed them *euery whit,* (as himselfe speaks) he left no relikes of the disease; and will this vniuersall *Phisician* pass by this *Hospitall,* and not visit mee? not heale me? not heale me wholy? *Lord,* I looke not that thou shouldest say by thy Messenger to mee, as to *Ezechias, Behold, I will heale thee, and on the third day thou shalt goe vp to the house of the Lord.*

38.4–8: "Then came the word of the Lord to Isaiah, saying, Go, and say to Hezekiah, Thus saith the Lord, the God of David thy father, I have heard thy prayer. I have seen thy tears: behold, I will add unto thy days fifteen years. And I will deliver thee and this city out of the hand of the king of Assyria: and I will defend this city. And this shall be a sign unto thee from the Lord, that the Lord will do this thing that he hath spoken; Behold I will bring again the shadow of the degrees, which is gone down in the sundial of Ahaz, ten degrees backward. So the sun returned ten degrees, by which degrees it was gone down."

In the twenty-second Devotion, Donne explicitly compares Hezekiah's fifteen-year extension to his own deliverance from death.[84] The lore and controversy surrounding the miracle of the sun is intriguing. Primarily, argument centered around the applicability of Hezekiah's extension of life not only to the king himself but to Israel, for it was held that the fifteen-year period referred as well to the postponement of the coming Babylonian captivity until the reign of Manasseh, the son begot by Hezekiah after his cure. Such an application both to king and state would thus prefigure Christ and his Church.[85]

---

etc. In hoc enim unius Dei cultu insignis et perfectus fuit; in aliis tamen nonnullis deliquit.")

[83] *Commentariorum in Essaiam,* p. 443: "Felix, ait, conscientia quae afflictionis tempore bonorum operum recordatur."

[84] Prayer 22, sig. Cc8r.

[85] According to the *Glossa Ordinaria, Pat. Lat.,* 113, col. 1279: "Of the present and future time, so that, as the sun returns to its beginning, the life of Hezekiah returns to years that have passed. And for us living in the seventh and eighth [ages] after the resurrection of Christ the times of life are measured out." ("Praesentis scilicet temporis et futuri, ut quomodo sol revertitur ad exordium sui ita Ezechiae vita ad evolutos re-

The point at issue, which shall be discussed more fully in chapter 5, was the problem of the shadow on the dial and of the dial itself: Was the miracle particular or universal? That is, did the shadow on the dial merely retrograde, or did the heavens themselves change their wonted course? If the latter, was the action of the sun related to the season of the year—most commentators are in agreement that the miracle took place at the winter solstice—or was the movement an act of divine intervention that foreshadowed the heavens of the Epiphany and the eclipse of the Passion? Was the Dial of Ahaz actually a sundial, or was it a series of fifteen steps leading from the royal palace to the sanctuary, constructed from the fragments of the temple altar which had been broken by Hezekiah's apostate father? Great effort was expended to demonstrate that the amplified day of Hezekiah did not, in effect, eclipse the longest day of Joshua 10.14.

Hence the winter solstice with its shortest day which, even thus extended, could not equal that of Joshua, thus leaving Scripture uncontradicted. And finally, even more effort was spent on estimating the hours of Hezekiah's day and the ten degrees on the dial, and in establishing their significance in terms of God's numerically structured universe. Among the results of this kind of thinking was an application of the ten degrees of the dial to the descent of Christ at his incarnation to earth and his ascent to heaven, through all the choirs of angels and the spheres of the universe—a total of twenty-three "layers" of the cosmos—or to the progression of time through the patriarchal and prophetic ages to the moment of the Incarnation.[86]

Lapide, committed to the fourfold sense of Scripture, thus interprets the Hezekiah miracle:

> Morally, this sign indicated how much God esteems his own, how much he should be loved and worshipped as a result. Tropologically, it insinuated to those converting themselves to God that they are restored to their original merits and perfection as they joined Hezekiah in penance. Anagogically, in light of eternity, it signified that fifteen years of life

deat annos. Nobis quoque in hebdoade et ogdoade viventibus post resurrectionem Christi vitae spatia protelentur.")

[86] In his return from the harrowing of hell, Christ passed through twenty-three "layers" of the universe to reach Paradise. The actual numbering of these layers differed; in some cases, the spheres of the cosmos were reckoned at fifteen (including hell, earth, water, air, and fire) and to these were added eight as the number of the Resurrection, while in other accountings fourteen spheres were added to the nine choirs of angels; all accountings, however, arrived at twenty-three as a number of the universe or, more particularly, of ascent to paradise. Hence the number's popularity in treatises on the art of contemplation and in poetic accounts of divine ascendancies, such as Dante's in the *Paradiso* and Milton's in *Paradise Lost*.

were to be given us, that is, fifteen years of eternity. The number fifteen factors into seven and eight; the seventh day being the Sabbath, the eighth, the day of the Lord. Both are symbols of the resurrection and of eternal peace. . . . Allegorically, it represented Christ about to descend in ten strata, most especially within the choirs of Angels and of men in His passions, and again His process of ascent to the Father.[87]

The echoes in the *Devotions* are many and complex, and I shall give separate special attention in chapter 5 to Donne's references to time and season. Nevertheless, several are worth examining here: Where Hezekiah, for example, was given the shadow as a sign of his healing, for Donne the indication is a cloudy urine, by which sign his physicians offer hope of recovery.[88] Moreover, like Hezekiah's, Donne's illness means both purgation and conversion, and in the latter case both indicate a turning toward the temple and an interior turning to God. Donne's conversion, typically, is expressed in geometric terms:

> As hee that would describe a *circle* in paper, if hee haue brought that *circle* within one *inch* of finishing, yet if he remoue his *compasse*, he cannot make it vp a perfit *circle*, except he fall to worke againe, to finde out the same *center*; so, though setting that *foot* of my *compasse* vpon *thee*, I haue gone so farre, as to the *consideration* of my selfe, yet if I depart from *thee*, my *center*, all is vnperfit. This proceeding to *action* therefore, is a returning to thee, and a *working* vpon *my selfe* by thy *Physicke*, by thy *purgatiue physicke*, a free and entire euacuation of my *soule* by *confession*.[89]

In the fourteenth Expostulation, Donne compares his sickness to the week of Creation, ending in "my *Seuenth day*, my *Euerlasting Saboth* in *thy rest, thy glory, thy ioy, thy sight, thy selfe*." But most exciting is the great aria of ascent and descent that is the twelfth Expostulation—and the numerical center—of the *Devotions*, which concludes:

> When thine *Angels* fell from heauen, thou tookst into thy care, the reparation of that place, & didst it, by assuming, by drawing vs thither; when we fel from thee here, in this world, thou tookst into thy care the

[87] Lapide, *Commentaria in Isaiam*, p. 476: "Moraliter, hoc signum indicabat quanti Deus aestimet suos, quam potens, quam pius, quam consequenter amandus et colendus sit. Tropologice, innuebat convertentibus se ad Deum cum Ezechia per poenitentiam, pristina merita et perfectionem restitui. Anagogice, in aeternitate reddendos nobis esse annos vitae quindecim, id est aeternos: quindecim enim conflantur ex septem et octo: septima dies est sabbatum, octava est Dominica: quarum utraque est symbolum resurrectionis et quietis aeternae. . . . Allegorice, representabat Christum descensurum decem lineis, id est summe infra omnes Angelorum et hominum choros in passione; inde rursum ascensurum ad Patrem."

[88] Meditation 19, sigs. X7r–X12v.

[89] Expostulation 20, sigs. Z11r–Z12r.

reparation of this place too, and didst it by assuming vs another way, by descending down to assume our nature, in thy *Son*. So that though our last act be an ascending to glory, (we shall ascend to the place of *Angels*) yet our first act is to goe the way of thy *Sonn, descending,* and the way of thy blessed *spirit* too, who *descended in the Doue*. Therefore hast thou bin pleased to afford vs this remedy in *Nature*, by this application of a *Doue,* to our lower parts, to make these *vapors* in the *bodies,* to descend, and to make that a *type* to vs, that by the visitation of thy *Spirit,* the *vapors* of sin shall descend, & we tread them vnder our feet. At the baptisme of thy *Son,* the *Doue* descended, & at the exalting of thine *Apostles* to preach, the same spirit descended. Let vs draw down the *vapors* of our own *pride,* our own *wits,* our own *wils,* our own *inuentions,* to the *simplicitie* of thy *Sacraments,* & the obedience of thy word, and these *Doues,* thus applied, shall make vs liue.

38.9 "The writing of Hezekiah king of Judah, when he had been sick, and was recovered of his sickness."

The thanksgiving hymn of Hezekiah in metrical paraphrase was, by Donne's time, a common poetic exercise.[90] Donne presents his own rather idiosyncratic version in the "*Stationes.*" Indeed, the *Devotions* itself forms the "hymn" of thanksgiving offered at the end of Donne's illness. Some opinion held that the Hezekiah hymn actually was composed by Isaiah at the behest of the king.[91] It is an easy, albeit chancy leap to envision Donne composing his *Devotions,* "*This* Image *of my* Humiliation, [to present] *to the liuely* Image *of his* Maiesty, *your* Highnesse." In this case, one might ask just who is "helped of the Lord" and who is "salvation of the Lord"?

38.10: "I said in the cutting off of my days, I shall go to the gates of the grave: I am deprived of the residue of my years."

The commentaries make a point of Hezekiah's age at the time of his cure, citing Psalm 90.10: "The days of our years are threescore

---

[90] See Terence C. Cave, *Devotional Poetry in France c. 1570–1613* (Cambridge: Cambridge University Press, 1969), pp. 94 ff; Lewalski, *Protestant Poetics,* pp. 31 ff.

[91] Lapide, *Commentaria in Isaiam,* p. 477: "This is a eucharistic song which pious Hezekiah composed by himself, or rather with the help of Isaiah, in thanksgiving to God for his restored health. He commanded that it be written or engraved in brass and publicly pronounced as a perpetual song of praise and a memorial to divine clemency. . . . The style and brilliance of the song seem to argue that Isaiah was its author. What the king had stated in simple parts of a prayer, Isaiah converted into a decorous song." ("Hoc est carmen eucharisticum, quod pius Ezechias per se, vel potius per Isaiam composuit, in gratiarum actionem Deo pro sanitate restituta, quodque scribi, vel in aes incidi, publiceque proponi jussit, in perpetuum divinae clementiae praeconium et monumentum. . . . Stylus et nitor carminis videtur arguere Isaiam ejus esse auctorem, qui quod rex plana et soluta oratione dixerat, in elegans carmen convertit.")

years and ten; and if by reason of strength they be fourscore years, yet is their strength labour and sorrow; for it is soon cut off, and we fly away." Hezekiah's age of thirty-nine was more than half the seventy-year limit, and almost exactly half the eighty-year one, the prime-of-life years "which is the age of quiet and cessation—full, mature, vigorous, and flourishing. On that account that age is one half of human life, which is circumscribed by eighty years. And so for this reason our conversion should be reckoned in a half."[92] One notes that the Septuagint translates what in the Vulgate reads, "in dimidio" ("Ego dixi in dimidio dierum meorum vadam ad portas inferi, quaesivi residuum annorum meorum") as "in excelso," a point the commentators make much of,[93] and, when one remembers the arch of Dante's *Convivio*, with its apex falling at the thirty-fifth year of life, that point makes spatial sense in terms of the *Devotions*, the center of which falls, at Expostulation 12, the thirty-fifth prose segment. When one remembers as well that Donne was writing at the age of fifty-one, when astrologically he had reached the Tropic of Capricorn, the so-called Gates of Death, this verse takes on new relevance. Both the eighth and the fifteenth Meditations draw attention to man's span of

---

[92] Ibid.: "the age of rest and withdrawal, a full and mature and vigorous and productive time. For that reason it is one half of human life, described at eighty years. For this reason it says 'in the half.' " ("aetas quietis et cessationis, hoc est plena, matura, vigens et florens, ideoque eadem est dimidium vitae humanae, quae 80 annis circumscribitur; atque hac de causa censet Nostrum vertere in dimido.")

[93] Jerome, for example, and Gregory as well (23 *Moralium, cap.* xxiv), held that God sent the virtuous long life and that life was shortened by sin. Sinners and the disloyal, says Jerome in his commentary on this verse, die in one half of their days. The Psalmist says of them: "Bloody and deceitful men do not live out half their days." ("Peccatores vero et impii in dimidio dierum suorum moriuntur, de quibus, et psalmista loquitur: Viri sanguinum et colosi non dimidiabunt dies suos.") *Commentariorum in Essaiam*, p. 446. Lapide elaborates, pp. 477–78: "The Septuagint translates 'on high': for . . . the daleth, reading 'the attached' resch and for . . . bidmi, that is, in the middle, they have read . . . beromi, that is, 'on high.' The sense comes to the same thing: for in half a lifetime is the flourishing of an age of life; and then there is as it were the whole, where one takes his status. And so remains a number of years after which one diminishes and decays. This is the opinion of Leo Castrius. But Cyril explains the τò as 'on high': 'Carried to the threshold of power, glory and happiness, Look, I fall.' Theodoret says this: qd. 'When I have been entombed and I have raised myself proudly on high, then I am made into earth by God and struck with a deadly disease.' " ("Septuaginta vertunt, *in excelso*; nam pro . . . *daleth* accipientes affine . . . *resch*, pro . . . *bidmi*, id est *in medio*, legerunt . . . *beromi*, id est *in excelso*. Eodem redit sensus: nam in dimidia aetate est id est vigor aetatis; tumque est quasi in summo, in quo statum sumit, permanetque aliquot annos, post quos sensim decrescit et deficit. Ita Leo Castrius. Sed Cyrillus τò *in excelso* sic exponit, *q. d.* Evectus ad fastigium regni, gloriae et felicitatis, ecce cado. Theodoretus vero sic, *q. d.* Cum intumui et in altum superbe me extuli, tunc a Deo humiliatus sum, et percussus morbo lethali.")

life as limited to threescore and ten years, and Expostulation 21 cites Donne's age at the time of composition.

38.11–14: "I said, I shall not see the Lord, even the Lord, in the land of the living: I shall behold man no more with the inhabitants of the world. Mine age is departed, and is removed from me as a shepherd's tent: I have cut off like a weaver my life: he will cut me off with pining sickness: from day even to night wilt thou make an end of me. Like a crane or a swallow, so did I chatter: I did mourn as a dove: mine eyes fail with looking upward: O Lord, I am oppressed; undertake for me."

Again there are verbal echoes within the text of the *Devotions*, particularly those of the twelfth Prayer:

> O Eternall and most gracious *God*, who though thou haue suffred vs to destroy our selues, & hast not giuen vs the power of reparation in our selues, hast yet afforded vs such meanes of reparation, as may easily, and familiarly be compassed by vs, prosper I humbly beseech thee this means of bodily assistance in this thy ordinary *creature*, and prosper thy meanes of spirituall assistance in thy holy *ordinances*. And as thou hast caried this thy *creature* the *Doue*, through all thy wayes, through *Nature*, and made it naturally proper to conduce medicinally to our *bodily health*, Through the *law*, and made it a *sacrifice* for *sinne* there, and through the *Gospel*, and made it, & thy spirit in it, a witnes of thy *sonnes baptisme* there, so carry it, and the qualities of it home to my *soule*, and imprint there that *simplicity*, that *mildnesse*, that *harmelesnesse*, which thou hast imprinted by *Nature* in this *Creature*. That so all *vapours* of all disobedience to thee, being subdued vnder my feete, I may in the power, and triumphe of thy *sonne*, treade victoriously vpon my *graue*, and trample vpon the *Lyon*, and *Dragon*, that lye vnder it, to deuoure me. Thou O *Lord* by the *Prophet* callest the *Doue*, the *Doue of the Valleys*, but promisest that *the Doue of the Valleyes shall bee vpon the Mountaine*: As thou hast layed mee low, in this *Valley* of sickenesse, so low, as that I am made fit for that question, asked in the field of bones, *Sonne of Man, can these bones liue*, so, in thy good time, carry me vp to these *Mountaynes*, of which, euen in this *Valley*, thou affordest mee a prospect, the Mountain where thou dwellest, the holy Hill, vnto which none can ascend but *hee that hath cleane hands*, which none can haue, but by that one and that strong way, of making them cleane, in the blood thy Sonne *Christ Iesus. Amen.*

38.15: "What shall I say? he hath both spoken vnto me, and himself hath done it: I shall go softly all my years in the bitterness of my soul."

This verse is held by many commentators to reflect Hezekiah's re-counting of the sins of his past years and his resolve to do so throughout the future years granted to him by God.[94] His examination and confession are brought about, says Lapide, "not from obligation, but from devotion," so that he gained from God greater grace and favor.[95] Moreover, he recounts his sins not generally but by years: "And so all these years, sinful years, have passed."[96] A great part of the *Devotions*, of course, is given to Donne's self-examination for sin, but no one, to my knowledge, has pointed out that this procedure is an actual preparation for sacramental confession, as Donne relates in the twentieth Expostulation:

O *Lord*, I decline not that *method* in this *physicke*, in things that burthen my *conscience*, to make my *confession* to *him*, into whose hands thou hast put the *power* of *absolution*. I know that *Physicke may be made so pleasant, as that it may easily be taken; but not so pleasant as the vertue and nature of the medicine bee extinguished*; I know, I am not submitted to such a *confession* as is a *racke* and *torture* of the *Conscience*; but I know I am not exempt from all. If it were meerely *problematicall*, left meerely indifferent, whether we should take this *Physicke*, vse this *confession*, or no, a great *Physitian* acknowledges this to haue beene his *practise, To minister many things, which hee was not sure would doe good, but neuer any other thing, but such as hee was sure would doe no harme*. The vse of this spirituall *Physicke* can certainly doe no *harme*; and the *Church* hath alwaies thought that it might, and doubtlesse, many humble *soules* haue found, that it hath done them *good*. *I will therefore take the cup of Saluation, and call vpon thy Name*; I will fill this *Cup* of *compunction*, as full as I haue formerly filled the *Cups* of worldly *confections*, that so I may scape the *cup of Malediction*, and ir-recouerable destruction that depends vpon that. And since thy blessed and glorious *Sonne*, being offered in the way to his *Execution*, a Cup of *Stupefaction*, to take away the sense of his paine, (a charity afforded to condemned persons ordinarily in those places, and times) refused that *ease*, and embraced the whole *torment*, I take not this *Cup*, but this *vessell* of mine owne *sinnes*, into my *contemplation*, and I powre them out here according to the *Motions* of thy *holy Spirit*, and *any where*, according to the ordinances of thy *holy Church*.

38.16: "O Lord, by these things men live, and in all these things is the life of my spirit: so wilt thou recover me, and make me to live."

[94] Lapide, *commentaria in Isaiam*, pp. 477–78.
[95] Ibid., p. 481.
[96] Ibid.

The latter part of this verse gives rise to interesting interpretations, for the Hebrew for "corripies me" can be translated as "give me sleep," and Lapide, echoing Vatablus and Forerius, maintains that the king was unable to achieve normal sleep in his illness. He points to John 11.12, where it is said of Lazarus: "Domine, si dormit, salvus erit."[97] The Expostulation of Devotion 15 (entitled "*Interea insomnes noctes ego duco, diesque,*" "I sleep not day nor night") cites the same verse:

> *Thou giuest thy beloued sleepe.* Shall I lacke that *seale* of thy *loue? You shall lie downe, and none shall make you afraid*; shal I bee *outlawd* from that *protection*? Ionas *slept in one dangerous storme,* and *thy blessed Sonne in another.* Shall I haue no vse, no benefit, no application of those great *Examples? Lord, if hee sleepe, he shall doe well,* say thy *Sonnes Disciples* to him, of *Lazarus*; And shall there bee no roome, for that *Argument* in me? or shall I bee open to the contrary? If I sleepe not, shall I not bee well, in their sense?

Given the connection of the figure of Hezekiah with sleep and contemplation, Donne's use of the quotation from John here is intriguing, for what follows is the great dream vision of Devotions 16 through 18.

38.20: "The Lord was ready to save me: therefore we will sing my songs to the stringed instruments all the days of our life in the house of the Lord."

According to Isaak Walton, his first biographer, Donne composed "An Hymn to God the Father" on his sickbed and, moreover, "caused it to be set to a most grave and solemn tune, and to be often sung to the organ by the choristers of St. Paul's Church, in his own hearing."[98] The weight of scholarly opinion now falls on Donne's illness of 1623–1624 as the occasion of the Hymn's composing, as well as of the composing of "Hymne to God my God, in my sicknesse," which begins with the lines

> Since I am comming to that Holy roome,
> Where, with thy Quire of Saints for evermore,
> I shall be made thy Musique; As I come
> I tune the Instrument here at the dore,
> And what I must doe then, thinke here before.

---

[97] Ibid., p. 482.
[98] "The Life of Dr. John Donne," in *Lives* (London, 1670), p. 62.

38.21: "For Isaiah had said, Let them take a lump of figs, and lay it for a plaister ypon the boil, and he shall recover."

Perhaps to the point, at that moment of his illness when Donne's physicians feared heart failure (Meditation 11: "Therefore doth the *Phisician* intermit the present care of *Braine*, or *Liuer*, because there is a possibilitie, that they may subsist, though there bee not a present and a particular care had of them, but there is no possibilitie that they can subsist, if the *Heart* perish"), they applied an electuary of egg to his breast. This was a plaster containing countervenoms, heart stimulants and febrifuges.[99] It was followed by the appearance of the purple rash of typhus upon his torso that identified the nature of his illness and allowed the doctors to plan a rational course of treatment.

38.22: "Hezekiah also had said, What is the sign that I shall go up to the house of the Lord?"

Most commentators note that this verse is radically out of order (indeed, the entire text of Isaiah 38 is in poor condition),[100] and should come after verse 6, since it refers to the sign of the shadow on the Dial of Ahaz. Donne's own sign of recovery was a cloud; that is, a "concoction" in his urine. Expostulation 19 is, in large part, concerned with this sign and its spiritual relevance: "*Seuen dayes*, O my *God*, haue we looked for this *cloud*, and now we haue it; none of thy *Indications* are *friuolous*; thou makest thy *signes, seales*; and thy Seales, effects; and thy *effects, consolation*, and *restitution*, whersoeuer thou maiest receiue *glory* by that way.

. . .

In the ninth Expostulation of the *Devotions* Donne declares his dependence on "thy third *booke*, the *Scriptures*, where thou hadst written all in the *Old*, and then lightedst vs a candle to read it by, in the *New Testament*." Certainly his making use of the close analogy between his and the case of Hezekiah illustrates the extent of that dependence, and through the *Devotions*, he himself becomes a candle by which we may read the story of the biblical king with new insight. But his light is his own. The *Devotions* is no mere paraphrase of Isaiah 38. Rather, Donne approaches the Hezekiah account as a poetic source, one that

---

[99] Frost, "Prescription and Devotion," 414.

[100] *The Jerusalem Bible* (Garden City, N.Y.: Doubleday, 1966), p. 1201, describes Hezekiah's canticle as "alien to the . . . text. It appears to be a psalm of the post-exilic period. The state of the text is poor."

allows his own stunning artistry full rein.[101] His work is not bound
tightly to this model; rather, it is what Lewalski has called a "re-reve-
lation" of Scripture.[102] Indeed, he had praised the Sidneys' translation of the Psalms in just these terms:

> The songs are these, which heavens high holy Muse
> Whisper'd to *David, David* to the Jewes:
> And *Davids* Successors, in holy zeale,
> In formes of joy and art doe re-reveale.
>
>   (31–34)[103]

---

[101] In "A Litanie," Donne recognizes that Scripture as a poetic model is open to mis-
use. He prays of the prophets:

> Those heavenly Poets which did see
> Thy will, and it expresse
> In rythmique feet, in common pray for mee,
> That I by them excuse not my excesse
> In seeking secrets, or Poetiqueness.
>
>   (68–72)

Despite this acknowledgement of ancient and honorable precedents, Donne was reluc-
tant to publish this poem, as he acknowledged in a letter to Sir Henry Goodyer, lest it
provide ammunition for the opposition in the enduring battle with Rome:

> Since my imprisonment in my bed, I have made a meditation in verse, which I call a Litany;
> the word you know imports no other than supplication, but all Churches have one forme of
> supplication, by that name. Amongst ancient annals I mean some 800 years, I have met two
> Letanies in Latin verse, which gave me not the reason of my meditations, for in good faith I
> thought not upon them then, but they give me a defence, if any man; to a Lay man, and a
> private, impute it as a fault, to take such divine and publique names, to his own little thoughts.
> The first of these was made by *Ratpertus* a Monk of *Suevia*; and the other by S. *Notker*, of whom
> I will give you this note by the way, that he is a private Saint, for a few Parishes; they were
> both but Monks, and the Letanies poor and barbarous enough; yet Pope *Nicolas* the 5, valued
> their devotion so much, that he canonized both their Poems, and commanded them for pub-
> like service in their Churches: mine is for lesser Chappels, which are my friends, and though
> a copy of it were due to you, now, yet I am so unable to serve my self with writing it for you at
> this time, (being some 30 staves of 9 lines) that I must intreat you to take a promise that you
> shall have the first, for a testimony of that duty which I owe to your love, and to my self, who
> am bound to cherish it by my best offices. That by which it will deserve best acceptation, is,
> That neither the Roman Church need call it defective, because it abhors not the particular
> mention of the blessed Triumphers in heaven; nor the Reformed can discreetly accuse it, of
> attributing more than a rectified devotion out to doe.   (*Letters*, pp. 32–34)

Interestingly, Donne here forecasts his publication procedure with the *Devotions*: composition during and following an illness of the matter used for meditation during that
illness; a handing-round of the manuscript to friends; and the exercise of great caution
in the decision to publish, or not, based on the effectiveness of the composition in the
struggle with the Roman church. It is also worth noting that Donne was interested in
ancient models of his work, although he does not admit the litanies of Ratpertus and
Notker as direct sources.

[102] Lewalski, *Protestant Poetics*, p. 52.

[103] Ibid., p. 245 (for extended comment on this passage).

This was not a new ploy; Donne had spoken before with the voice of a Scriptural poet—as Moses in the *Anniversaries*, as David and Paul in the sermons, as Jeremiah in "The Lamentations of Jeremy." But the use of Hezekiah as central type reveals that necessary to an understanding of Donne's "high holy muse" is a recognition of the role of Christ, in whom all is fulfilled. Donne participates in the events of salvation history because, bearing the image of God within him, restored by baptism, he participates in the central role of Christ in that history. In Prayer 19 he acknowledges the basic unreliability of a typology that is not centered in Christ: "From that *people*, to whom thou appearedst in *signes*, and in *Types*, the *Iewes*, thou art departed, because they trusted in *them*; but from thy *Church*, to whom thou hast appeared in *thy selfe*, in *thy Sonne*, thou wilt neuer depart; because we cannot trust *too much* in *him*." A year before his illness, Donne had preached an Easter Monday sermon in which he set forth the principle of typology which underlies the *Devotions*:

> Now, it is a penurious thing, to have but one Candle in a room: it is too dim a light to work by, to live by, to have but Rule and Precept alone; Rule and Example together, direct us fully. Who shall be our Example? *Idaea novi hominis Christus Jesus*. If thou wilt be a new Creature, (and, *Circumcision is nothing, uncircumcision nothing*, but onely to be a new Creature) then Christ is thy *Idaea*, thy Pattern, thine Original.[104]

Hezekiah, with his rising on the third day, was a recognized type of Christ suffering and of Christ risen: "Hezekiah, that is, our Redeemer, became ill, as it is written: He bore our infirmities and carried our diseases. . . . It was an illness for him to have assumed the infirmity of flesh in which . . . he labored, and he became tired. And he was ill even unto death, because he carried mortal flesh as long as it took him to reach immortality through death and resurrection."[105] In applying the passion and resurrection of the biblical king to his own sickness and cure, Donne participated most fully in the Passion and Resurrection of Christ. In the *Devotions* he attempts by intense self-analysis to purge his soul of sin and distraction, of whatever does not belong to the image of God implanted at creation, dimmed by the fall of Adam, and restored at baptism. Once discovered, the image of God within the self creates a new, more general sense of selfhood: "I

---

[104] *Sermons*, 4:99.

[105] Hervaeus de Bourg-Dieu, *Commentaris in Isaiam, Pat. Lat.*, 181, col. 361. "Ezechias, id est Redemptor noster aegrotavit, quia scriptum est: 'Ipse infirmitates nostras accepit, et aegrotationes portavit.' Ei namque aegrotare fuit infirmitatem carnis assumpsisse in qua . . . laboravit, et fatigatus est. Et aegrotavit usque ad mortem, quia tandiu mortalem carnem gestavit, donec per mortem et resurrectionem perveniret ad immortalitatem."

am crucified with Christ: nevertheless I live, yet not I, but Christ liveth in me" (Gal. 2.20). Such self-contemplation frees Donne from the onus of overpersonalized display. It also frees a wealth of life data to be used as evidence of God's salvific activity.

Once one has become accustomed to the typological language of the *Devotions*, it is difficult to object, as does Eliot, to Donne's first person singular. When Donne seems most to be representing himself, he is intentionally representing the human condition. His presentation of himself in the *Devotions* is, as it was later to be on his deathbed, emblematic. He incarnates for his reader the Christian struggle for justification. Although the posing in his shroud has come under heavy fire—he has been accused of creating the striking and unique life-image even to the last moment[106]—yet when one considers the emblematic self-display of Abelard and Augustine, as revealed in their autobiographies, and of Francis of Assisi in his deliberately constructed life situations, one remembers that Christ himself is depicted as leading a demonstrably emblematic life and that, in imitation of him, we are all called so to teach and preach by the events of our own very daily lives. In the historical Christ we may contemplate and imitate either his external life or the spiritual content of its events. This we may do collectively, as members of his church, through public prayer, preaching, and sacraments, or privately as individual members of his body.

As a poet, Donne could take the matter a step further by making public the memoir of his imitation of the suffering Christ. But in any case, the Christian is obligated to turn his eye inward, for knowledge of himself as a child of God, as a member of God's body, with his interior face the very face of Christ, will lead to knowledge of God, so that the whole self will open up, not in mere display, but in attraction toward God as transcendent being and incarnate Christ.[107] The result is neither self-denial nor egocentricity, but rather a newly defined self which goes beyond the individual and the particular and participates, with all redeemed humanity, in the imitation of Christ.

Thus Donne certainly is, in the words of Joan Webber, "vastly and precisely interested in himself," and justifiably so. But I question whether his literary self-consciousness is really "a peculiarly seventeenth-century phenomenon."[108] Rather, it is an artistic pose as old as Paul or for that matter, Hezekiah. The blurring of the boundary between art and life certainly occurs with Augustine and Dante, and

[106] Bottrall, *Every Man a Phoenix*, p. 25.

[107] Goldberg, "Not Unto Death: The *Devotions* of John Donne" (Ph.D. diss., Columbia University, 1971), p. 133.

[108] Webber, *The Eloquent I*, p. 3.

almost obsessively so with Petrarch. That this highly artificial self, at the same time intimate and formally structured, should be both private and public is neither a contradiction nor an indication of bad taste: It is a necessary requirement of Christian spiritual autobiography.

Chapter IV

DONNE AND THE TRADITION OF
NUMBER SYMBOLISM

Our Creatures Are Our Thoughts

THE LONG TRADITION of spiritual autobiography, marked as it was by the use of typology, fictive devices, and deliberate structure, was inevitably affected by the intellectual and scientific changes that stemmed from the Renaissance and radically altered the face of Western culture. Chief among these was the so-called Copernican revolution: No longer could the individual place himself within a coherent moral and spiritual structure; no longer could he see his life played out on a recognizable stratum of the universal hierarchy; no longer was one's very physical existence reflected in and magnified by the speculum of correspondences that composed the late-medieval cosmos.

Moreover, the Protestant revolution, perhaps equally determinant of change, at least for English literature, inexorably moved the writer's focus toward the subjective. Changes in political and social structure opened the possibility of autobiography to the unlearned or at least to groups that were decidedly not of the establishment. (By the end of the seventeenth century, even women were penning their lives and spiritual struggles.)[1]

All of these initiated considerable change within the genre—most obviously, it grew increasingly secular. But somehow in the seventeenth and eighteenth centuries, it changed so radically that critics today throw doubt on the existence of "real" autobiography much before then. One can certainly demonstrate that the major change in poetics that followed the Renaissance has a great deal to do with our diminished ability to treat the literature of the period on its own terms.

[1] See especially the recent essays by Cynthia S. Pomerleau, "The Emergence of Women's Autobiography in England," and Carol Edkins, "Quest for Community: Spiritual Autobiographies of Eighteenth-Century Quaker and Puritan Women in America," in *Women's Autobiography: Essays in Criticism*, ed. Estelle C. Jelinek (Bloomington: Indiana Univeresity Press, 1980).

However, equally responsible was the major change in perception and in reading habits after the invention of the printing press and the immense explosion of information which followed upon its heels. Much of our problem of confronting Donne's *Devotions* and of identifying it as part of the long tradition of spiritual autobiography stems from our modern habit of discursive reading, a habit governed by our perception of the periodic sentence as the dominant unit of meaning. As a result, modern critical appraisal of the genre has often been fragmented and overly subjective.

In recent years, aided by a great deal of patient scholarship, we have moved away from the perception of Donne as the brilliant rake with a hyperactive ego. In some sense, however, the pendulum has swung in the opposite direction, and unfortunately, this most articulate of poets has been condemned to an Augustinian "rhetoric of silence."[2] Along with increased understanding of the mature Donne has come a misunderstanding of his use of divine poesy, one that relegates his complex poetics to the realm of mere rhetoric.[3] Its aim, persuasion to holiness, achieved, the artifact (in this case the *Devotions*) has no further use and is to be abandoned, or, according to Stanley Fish, it "self-destructs." Fish perceives Donne as a divine dialectician. But there is a catch:

> A dialectical presentation succeeds at its own expense; for by conveying those who experience it to a point where they are beyond the aid that discursive or rational forms can offer, it becomes the vehicle of its own abandonment. . . . The reader's self (or at least his inferior self) is consumed as he responds to the medicinal purging of the dialectician's art, and that art, like other medicines, is consumed in the working of its own best effects. The good-physician aesthetic, then, is finally an anti-aesthetic, for it disallows to its productions the claims usually made for verbal art—that they reflect, or contain or express Truth—and transfers the pressure and attention from the work to its effects, from happening on the page to what is happening in the reader.[4]

---

[2] Joseph A. Mazzeo, "St. Augustine's Rhetoric of Silence: Truth vs. Eloquence and Things vs. Signs," in *Renaissance and Seventeenth-Century Studies* (New York: Columbia University Press, 1964), pp.1–28.

[3] The distinct borderline between Renaissance rhetoric and poetic has been defined most clearly by W. S. Howell in his "Poetics, Rhetoric, and Logic in Renaissance Criticism," in *Classical Influences on European Culture, AD 1500–1700*, ed. R. R. Bolgar (Cambridge: Cambridge University Press, 1976), pp. 158 ff., and in his defense of that borderline, "The Two-Party Line: A Reply to Kenneth Burke," *Quarterly Journal of Speech* 62 (1976): 69–77.

[4] *Self-Consuming Artifacts: The Experience of Seventeenth-Century Literature* (Los Angeles: University of California Press, 1972), pp. 3–4.

In his study Fish addresses not the *Devotions* but *Death's Duell*, and in particular one rather long sentence from that last of Donne's sermons. Significantly, he addresses himself as well to "what is happening on the page": The reader's experience is sequential and linear; it can be stopped in midair or slowed in action like a film. Indeed, Fish draws just such a parallel.[5]

It is not my intent to take on Professor Fish in this study, but I do feel compelled to agree in large part with the recent objection of Dame Helen Gardner that reading is a "process by which the past incessantly moves into the future. To concentrate on our power to expect while ignoring our power to retain is to destroy the enchainment of past and future in mental experience."[6] Moreover, when Fish goes on to maintain that the artifact in question "signifies most successfully when it fails, when it points *away* from itself to something its forms cannot capture," and that it is "concerned less with the making of better poems than with the making of better persons"[7] and is thus by implication superior to mere art, I must take strong issue. This kind of thinking should be applied to premodern literature with great caution, for it undervalues the very real dependence of the early writer on the tools of rhetoric, as Barbara K. Lewalski has recently pointed out,[8] and it avoids consideration of the artifact first as artifact, a dangerous avoidance for even the most loosely crafted work in the Renaissance. The artist and his reader might ultimately be reduced to silence before divine truth, but the artifact was intended to remain a means to that silence, a step in the process of quiescence, as long as time lasted—very much alive, speaking, intrinsically mimetic, and permanent in the intention of its stucture.

The problems that arise from applying the techniques of affective stylistics to the work of a poet like Donne are multifold, and many of these stem from imposing the modern frame of mind on a work conceived by a premodern writer for a premodern audience. The modern reader is likely to perceive Donne in terms of the dialect of opposites where the space separating poet from reader—or reader from God—is vast and demands synthesis, rather than in the hierarchical and essentially conjunctive mode in which Donne and his age perceived themselves and imitated an accepted reality. D. W. Robertson

[5] Ibid., p. 389.

[6] *In Defence of the Imagination* (Cambridge: Harvard University Press, 1982), p. 88. Her chapter "Readers and Reading," from which this quotation is drawn, provides a particularly cogent answer to Professor Fish.

[7] Fish, *Self-Consuming Artifacts,* p. 4.

[8] *Donne's "Anniversaries" and the Poetry of Praise: The Creation of a Symbolic Mode* (Princeton: Princeton University Press, 1973), p. 217.

has discussed extensively the gap between modern and premodern perception and has identified the source of that gap as our "consciousness of an internal discord which renders [the ideal of natural harmony] impossible; and hence the endeavor of poetry is to reconcile these two worlds [of matter and spirit] between which we find ourselves divided, and to blend them indissolubly together."[9] Poetry becomes the meeting ground between magnified sense impression and "the indescribable intuitions of the soul."[10] But such a process applied to premodern poetry distorts our perceptions, and "we turn history into a mirror which is of significance to us only insofar as we may perceive in it what appear to be foreshadowings of ourselves arising from reconstructions of the evidence based on our own values."[11]

Hence, the modern reader is open to numerous pitfalls: a partial or skewed vision of the inherent didacticism in Renaissance poetry, the tendency to read only in excerpt (what Professor Gardner, drawing on the ancients, calls "trying to sell a house by showing a brick"),[12] the assumption that the work in question is a spontaneous projection of the author's psyche, what John Steadman terms "an intuited Gestalt"[13] to be sought for itself alone—by which means "a subjectivity enters a subjectivity"[14]—or to be used to bring to bear directly on our own present concerns, to be made "relevant."[15]

Moreover, the affective response of such a reader is often a reaction to the sequential and hence temporal ordering of the words on the page and all too often to the mere physical stimulus of image.

[9] *A Preface to Chaucer: Studies in Medieval Perspectives* (Princeton: Princeton University Press, 1962), p. 31.

[10] Ibid.

[11] Ibid., p.3. He enlarges this argument in his "Some Observations on Method in Literary Studies," in *Essays in Medieval Culture* (Princeton: Princeton University Press, 1980).

[12] Gardner, *In Defence of the Imagination,* p. 90.

[13] *The Lamb and the Elephant: Ideal Imitation and the Context of Renaissance Allegory* (San Marino: The Huntington Library, 1974), p. 199.

[14] Gardner, *In Defence of the Imagination,* p. 169.

[15] Regarding "relevance," Gardner (p. 38) labels as "a damaging assumption" the idea "that we can only find relevance in the works of the past by radical reinterpretations and new readings, by which they can be made to bear directly on our present needs and concerns, so that we can find in them, as modern readers, what we expect to find in modern poems and novels." She goes on (p. 41) to identify the "slightly different, but equally disabling, approach" of "the exaggeration of the truth that we are persons of the twentieth century who cannot divest ourselves of the immense changes in knowledge, thought and sensibility that separate us from men of past ages to 'follow an antique drum,' into the idea that we must inevitably read the literature of the past with the demands and expectations we bring to the literature of our own age."

The result, it seems to me, is an actual alienation of the reader from the text, and I find it not surprising that much current criticism, succumbing to our century's pervasive nominalism, ends in chipping the text away into nonexistence, so that poetry exists neither in what has been called "hot zone" of communication nor in the "cool zone" of artifact.[16] Although Donne was poised on the crux of the seventeenth century, when the cosmological assumptions that underlay Renaissance poetics were giving way to those which were ultimately to produce the modern perception of literature, nevertheless, as an examination of the *Devotions* will show, his was a literary practice where communication and artifact could exist together in a not uneasy balance, where, despite his protest in "The First Anniversarie," coherence yet remained.

The rationally ordered world of the Renaissance artist was one that demanded a like aesthetic response. The order of his poetic creation was not one primarily reflective of his personal experience—that is, he was obliged to impose not a human order on experience but one in which individual experience mirrored the divine order, and the object of his creation, the literary microcosm of his poem, reflected the perfection of the cosmos itself. The artifact he created was yet a product of his imagination, for it presented this vision in forms which attracted the reader to the underlying idea of his invention and elicited admiration for his facility in composition and the learning by which he had achieved his vision. According to Stephen Greenblatt, it stemmed from "an art that constantly calls attention to its own processes, that includes within itself framing devices and signs of its own createdness," so that the artifact "announces its status as art object at every turn."[17]

To understand such a work entails skills and habits rather different from those generally employed by the modern reader, for one must subordinate one's custom of deriving primary meaning from sequential order to a comprehensive overview of the work, an overview that may entail a schematic perception of the piece and, very often, a perception made in terms not of sequential time but of eternity. The modern reader, accustomed to scanning the semantic line quickly, is at a disadvantage unless she is willing to add to her reading techniques a meditative stance aimed at continually revealing the essentially corresponding aspects of the cosmic image generated by the ar-

[16] Alastair Fowler, *Conceitful Thought: The Interpretation of English Renaissance Poems* (Edinburgh: Edinburgh University Press, 1975), p. 21.

[17] Stephen Greenblatt, *Renaissance Self-Fashioning, from More to Shakespeare* (Chicago: University of Chicago Press, 1980), p. 190. See also John Buxton, *Elizabethan Taste* (London: Macmillan, 1963).

tifact. For the full meaning of the work is revealed only when the parts are viewed in the light of the whole and when the implications of the whole are brought to bear on each of its parts.

Hence, the very process of reading a Renaissance poem must be reconsidered. In recent years, a number of scholars have bent their efforts toward this end. Among them, Father Walter Ong has demonstrated the close ties between text and spatial illustration in Renaissance printed books, Alastair Fowler has drawn our attention to spatial constructions in the poetry of the age, and S. K. Heninger has explored the implications of models of the cosmos.[18] Such investigations can result in exciting approaches to the reading of Renaissance literature. For example, in her study of the symmetrical structures of Milton's "Nativity Ode," Maren-Sofie Røstvig has demonstrated convincingly that the reader who approaches the meaning of the poem from the *center*—that is, who reads the first stanza with the circular completion of the last stanza in mind, the second with the penultimate, and so on until he reaches the center—will achieve a rare aesthetic moment when "after the centre the balance is changed, and that which was remembered becomes the experience of the moment, while that which was experienced regresses and becomes memory."[19] Hence, reading in such a fashion becomes more than "a process by which the past incessantly moves into the future." Past, present, future exist simultaneously within the eternal framework of the poem,

[18] Father Ong's chief contributions to our study of the spatial character of Renaissance thought are to be found in *The Barbarian Within and Other Fugitive Essays and Studies* (New York: Macmillan, 1962), ch. V, "System, Space and Intellect in Renaissance Symbolism," and in his essay "From Allegory to the Diagram in the Renaissance Mind," *The Journal of Aesthetics and Art Criticism* 17 (1969): 423–40. His thinking is extended by Norman K. Farmer, Jr., "Renaissance English Title-Pages: Visual Introductions to Verbal Texts," *Literature and the Other Arts,* Proceedings of the Ninth Congress of the International Comparative Literature Association (Innsbruck, 1979), 61–65, and in a recent dissertation: P. S. Weibly, " 'To Any That Will Read It': Michael Drayton's *Poly-Olbion* as Monument, Emblem, and Myth" (Ph.D. diss., University of Texas, 1982). Professor Fowler's contributions to the growing field of number symbolism criticism are many; the one that should chiefly interest the reader concerned with spatial constructions is *Triumphal Forms: Structural Patterns in Elizabethan Poetry* (Cambridge: Cambridge University Press, 1970). Of greatest assistance are Professor Heninger's two studies: *Touches of Sweet Harmony: Pythagorean Cosmology and Renaissance Poetics* (San Marino: The Huntington Library, 1974) and *The Cosmographical Glass: Renaissance Diagrams of the Universe* (San Marino: The Huntington Library, 1977). A study of particular interest to students of modern literature is Joseph Frank's *The Widening Gyre* (New Brunswick, N.J.: Rutgers University Press, 1963), which is concerned in part with the meaning of spatial form.

[19] "Elaborate Song: Conceptual Structure in Milton's 'On the Morning of Christs Nativity,' " in *Fair Forms: Essays in English Literature from Spenser to Jane Austen,* ed. Maren-Sofie Røstvig (Cambridge: D. S. Brewer, 1975), p. 81.

and the sentence as a unit of meaning, devoted as it is to linear time, is revealed as a frail reed.

Such a "spatial" reading negates impressionism in the reader and cultivates a habit of verbal recognition that is unfamiliar to the modern eye.

That Donne's *Devotions* is so ordered and should be so read is the contention of the next chapter of this study, and I shall demonstrate there the amplitude of its schematic construction. I shall also demonstrate that such construction was an essential element of the early spiritual autobiography and that its falling into disuse after the seventeenth century has generated the great gap between early and modern branches of the tradition. It is necessary first, however, to examine the poetics that underlie the devices of spiritual autobiography and, in particular, Donne's own acquiescence in theory and in practice to their tenets. What follows will not be an exhaustive treatment of Renaissance poetic theory. That is a subject of extreme complexity, as is freely admitted by those who have with varying degrees of success attempted its cataloging and elucidation. Rather, I will examine those aspects of Renaissance literary theory that allowed, or even encouraged, the use of numerical and spatial construction. This will be followed by Donne's own statements on the subject and a brief examination of his use of number symbolism and spatial construction.

The very act of reading a printed book of the Renaissance differs from the experience of contemporary reading. Frontispiece and title page (they are often the same), dedications, epistles, digressions, and envois—all must be considered for the relationship they bear to the "text" itself. Moreover, the connection between author and reader via the printed page may not be so immediate as some suppose, for the Renaissance artifact acts not so much as a direct stimulator or affector but rather as a reflector, and hence spontaneity must give way to craft.

Sidney is a case in point: His acquiesence to the old saw *orator fit, poeta nascitur* is self-acknowledged, for, as he says in the *Defence*, "a poet no industry can make, if his own genius be not carried into it."[20] But even the "high-flying wit" needs his Daedalus "to bear itself up into the air of due commendation."[21] For Sidney, the wings of Daedalus are art, imitation, and exercise, and he recognizes them for the

---

[20] *Miscellaneous Prose of Sir Phillip Sidney,* ed. Katherine Duncan-Jones and Jan Van Dorsten (Oxford: Clarendon Press, 1973), p. 111.

[21] Ibid., pp. 111–12.

necessary encumbrances they are when he describes the sometimes wobbly flight of poetic practice:

> Exercise indeed we do, but that very forebackwardly: for where we should exercise to know, we exercise as having known; and so is our brain delivered of much matter which never was begotten by knowledge. For there being two principal parts, matter to be expressed by words and words to express matter, in neither we use art or imitation rightly. Our matter is *quodlibet* indeed, though wrongly performing Ovid's verse, *Quicquid conabor dicere, versus erit;* never marshalling it into any assured rank, that almost the readers cannot tell where to find themselves.[22]

Sidney assumes here a necessary relation between word and underlying reality, one obviated by that *quodlibet:* The reader's response is to be neither individual nor primarily affective; rather it is more of a remembering, a renewed intellectual recognition of the linkage between particular and universal, stimulated by the *speculum* of the poem. The poem itself remains intact, "a speaking picture—with this end, to teach and delight."[23]

Until rather recently, criticism has emphasized Sidney's participle rather than the noun that it qualifies. But spontaneous speaking from the simple stimulus of nature was not held in highest esteem by the age. (Panofsky, for example, has pointed out that Caravaggio, whose naturalism is so prized by modern collectors, was criticized by his contemporaries as "uninventive, unintellectual, and completely subject to the natural model.")[24] As every schoolboy knew, such was not acceptable practice: Imitation, at its lowest a slavish aping of themes and ornament, was the daily drill. Image and pattern, incident and plot, were copped—in the best cases, internalized—from the greats, often from a variety of ponies, commonplace books, and florilegia. From the rhetorical storehouse of Scripture, the ancient world, the Middle Ages, and his own era, the budding poet was expected to select tropes, figures, and schemes and to turn a prose framework into lilting verse. At its worst, the practice produced a Benedick, who could think of no rime for "lady" but "baby." At its best, it produced Shakespeare and his contemporary, John Donne.[25] But the process presup-

---

[22] Ibid., p. 112.

[23] Ibid., p. 80.

[24] *Idea: A Concept in Art Theory,* trans. Joseph J. S. Peake (Columbia: University of South Carolina Press, 1968), p. 104. He is actually quoting here from Scaramucci's *Le finezze de'Pennelli Italiani* (1674), p. 76: "Per finirlo è stato quest' Huomo un gran Soggetto, ma no Ideale, che vuol dire non saper far cosa alcuna senza il naturale avanti."

[25] The English poet who followed the advice of Horace to imitate his predecessors found enhancement of both his own personal authority and that of the English poetic

posed an initial framework, what Sidney calls "the fore-conceit of the work."[26] This, he explains, is the connection (he demonstrates it in terms of the fictive universal Cyrus and the many particular Cyruses awakened in readers) between the universal that the poet attempts to re-create and the particular that he awakens in his reader—between, in other language, the macrocosm and microcosm, the poet's inspired vision of the golden world and the brazen world of individual experience.

What results is a two-handed engine, an artifact that is at the same time instrument and monument. In the first sense, poetry becomes, in the words of John Steadman, a handmaiden of philosophy or theology, a servant of church or state that, "embodying the ideas of virtues and vice—intelligible but invisible essences—in sensuous images capable of striking the imagination and impressing the memory. . . may simultaneously delight the sense, instruct the understanding, and move the will."[27] It is a ladder by which the reader ascends from the level of mere sensuous particulars to the plane of the universal. But it is at the same time, by virtue of its very linkage of sensuous particulars with abstract universals, an enduring monument, for the

---

tradition—and Sidney's early voice attests well to the desire that the national literary voice be heard loudly on the Continent. The practice of imitation provided real tools for the poet as well: a common poetic vocabulary; firm rules for poetic creation (whether the poet used his sources as guides or stereotypes was a matter of his ability and often his doom); a rich body of models–classical and Biblical tradition (each enhanced with commentary); English and continental medieval tradition; and even the fund of material provided by the wit combats of contemporary coteries. Nonetheless, there was ample room for poetic invention. The poet could apply a poetic tradition to fresh material, as in Jonson's "Carey-Morison Ode"; he could deliberately combine traditions for effect, as in Milton's "Lycidas"; he could also, given sufficient ambition, erudition, and genius, attempt the virtuosity of Donne's *Anniversaries,* where imitation and invention combine in an explosive display, the individual elements of which are indistinguishable to all but the most erudite. That Donne himself was, despite his often seamless virtuosity, aware of the imitative process of selection, reinterpretation, and improvement (often represented by the figure of the bee that from the nectar of many flowers produces its honey) is attested to in several of his works. Harold O. White points out that in addition to his early satires—which imitated more or less freely Horace, Persius; and Juvenal, even before the publication of Hall's *Virgidemiarum*—Donne voiced his adherence to the traditional practice of imitation in *Satire III,* the Preface to *The Progresse of the Soul,* and *Essayes in Divinity.* See H. O. White, *Plagiarism and Imitation During the English Renaissance: A Study in Critical Distinctions* (New York: Octagon, 1973), pp. 127–28. For a lucid explanation of the general practice of imitation, see Steadman, *The Lamb and the Elephant*; of imitation of the classical tradition in particular, G. W. Pigman, "Versions of Imitation in the Renaissance," *Renaissance Quarterly* 33 (1980): 1–32.

[26] *Miscellaneous Prose*, p. 79.

[27] Steadman, *The Lamb and the Elephant*, p. xvi.

poem as it most perfectly embodies truth beyond time frees itself from the bondage of sequential and linear time and partakes of eternity. The poet, stamping his matter with the accident of his own wit and style, had thus a very real claim, along with the artifact he produced, to immortality. It was an immortality, however, that depended not on enduring reader appreciation but on participation through mimesis in the unfading moment of Creation.

It is this essentially fictive element of poetry that Sidney insists on, stressing repeatedly the function of poetry as mimesis. Poetry teaches and delights—indeed, the operations of the aesthetic and the didactic upon the reader are inextricably intermingled—but the rhetorical figures that convey the activity of poetry themselves function within a mimetic framework, conveying to it a dimension which outstrips rhetoric. The role of poet also exceeded that of the orator, for he functioned as an *alter deus,* creating from "the zodiac of his own wit" the minicosmos of the poem, as God had created the framework of the universe.

The concept was hoary with age, stemming both from Greek and Hebrew sources and, as with so much of Christian tradition, flowing through the watershed that was Augustine. In the second book of *De libero arbitrio,* he speaks of the world as God's poem, created, according to the book of Wisdom (11.21) in "measure, number, and weight."[28] The poet—and Augustine, like Sidney, here calls to mind Moses and David, those conduits of divine inspiration—practices mimesis, but not of mere human experience and concerns. Rather, he mimes the creative process of God himself. In his attempt to explain the call of the will to attain perfect good, Augustine uses (more than metaphorically, I think) the concept of God as divine artificer and man's chief good emulation of that artifice:

Hold on to indestructible loyalty to such an extent that nothing is good for you in either feeling, understanding, or thinking in any way which is not from God. For nothing living exists which is not from God. When you see measure, number, and order, do not hesitate to attribute everything to God the Artificer. If you have subtracted those things [measure, number, and weight] in excess, nothing will remain because, although some incipient form will remain where you find neither measure, number, nor weight (because these things are everywhere), form is perfect; it is necessary that you take away those very beginnings of form

---

[28] His chapter 11 of that book is entitled Sapientia et numerus ad idem, an alterum ab altero vel in altero existat. *Pat. Lat.* 32, cols. 1257–58.

which seem to underlie form itself as a material to be perfected by the Artificer.[29]

The poetics Augustine advocates requires a fore-conceit: an intellectual preconception that would ordain that the end product be created in measure, number, and weight like the universe itself. The argument of course is Platonic: All acts of creation require a preconceived design. Donne, in a sermon preached to King Charles in April 1629, echoed the concept, applying it to the creation of the individual Christian: "We are made to an Image, to a pattern; and our obligation [is] to set a pattern before us, in all our actions."[30] He goes on to apply the concept to the work of Moses and to Creation at large:

> God appointed *Moses* to make all that he made according to a pattern. God himselfe made all that he made according to a pattern. God had deposited, and laid up in himselfe certaine formes, patternes, *Ideas* of every thing that he made. He made nothing of which he had not preconceived the forme, and predetermined in himselfe, I will make it thus. And when he had made any thing, he saw it was good; good because it answered the pattern, the Image; good, because it was like to that.[31]

He concludes that the Christian must "propose good patterns to thy selfe; and thereby become a fit pattern for others."[32] The individual, as he conformed more perfectly to the pattern of Creation, partook in that perfection and reflected it to others. More than that, Moses had made "all that he made" according to a pattern—and for the churchmen of Donne's day, Moses had penned the account of the six days of Creation.

Hence Augustine was able to infuse the Platonic Idea with new relevance and vitality by allying it with the allegory of the hexaemeron, a figure which paralleled Plato's six-step process of creation, thus identifying the Mosaic week with the lambda formula for cosmic har-

---

[29] Ibid., cols. 1269–70. Tu tantum pietatem inconcussam tene, ut nullum tibi bonum vel sentienti, vel intelligenti, vel quoquo modo cogitanti occurrat quod non sit ex Deo. Ita enim nulla natura occurrit quae non sit ex Deo. Omnem quippe rem ubi mensuram et numerum et ordinem videris, Deo artifici tribuere ne cuncteris. Unde autem ista penitus detraxeris, nihil omnino remanebit: quia etsi remanserit aliqua formae alicujus inchoatio, ubi neque mensuram neque numerum neque ordinem invenias, quia ubicumque ista sunt, forma perfecta est; oportet auferas etiam ipsam inchoationem formae, quae tanquam materies ad perficiendum subjacere videtur artifici.

[30] *Sermons*, 9:73.

[31] Ibid., 73–74. Donne here is very likely thinking of Exodus 25.40: "And look that thou make them [the plan and furnishings of the tabernacle] after their pattern, which was shewed thee in the mount."

[32] Ibid., 75.

mony.[33] By paralleling the Mosaic poem of Creation with the divine creation of the universe, he set a formal standard for poetry that was to persist until the cosmos itself gave way to Copernican mathematics. Functioning as a mirror of the mind of God, the poem could thwart mutability. It was intrinsically resistant to self-destruction, for it held within itself the formula for mundane, cosmic, and divine harmony, and thus as much permanence as the farthest limits of time would allow. At its most inspired, it could outlast marble and gilded monuments, laying claim even to eternity.

But of course no human creation could hope to mirror adequately the divine archetype; hence Aquinas identified the foreconceit as a "quasi-idea."[34] That is, although the foreconceit is essentially a parallel action to the original idea immanent in the mind of God, from which God created the world, it differs essentially in that it is individual and not universal, and more particularly, it is dependent upon sensory experience. Nevertheless, it is at the same time evidence of the image of God in man, for the artist can "bring forth a new, intelligible cosmos," and thus can "compete with Nature."[35] Donne's contemporaries show no real disagreement on this point, and indeed the concept persisted into the eighteenth century, when it was abandoned along with much of the impedimenta of the Ptolemaic universe. Thus Scaliger, for example, on whom Sidney drew so heavily, can give specific directions that the writer of epithalamia take into consideration the whole of the cosmos in the fabrication of his poem: "Wherefore, in the tempest after the separation of Chaos, the nuptials of Heaven and Earth are celebrated. And then by their conjunction all species were created, and by imitation of this generation were multiplied, that where matter prevented, immortality of souls was to be obtained through ordered succession."[36]

[33] Plato's description of the creation of the world soul in the *Timaeus* had been explicated by Macrobius, in his commentary on the *Dream of Scipio*, in the form of the Platonic lambda: "With the monad located on the apex, two sets of three numbers each descended on either side, on one the even, on the other the odd: that is, after the monad we had on one side two, four, and eight, and on the other three, nine, and twenty seven; and the mixture arising out of these seven numbers brought about the generation of the World-Soul at the behest of the Creator." *Commentary on the Dream of Scipio*, ed. W. H. Stahl (New York: Columbia University Press, 1952) p. 109. The formula, represented diagrammatically, resembled the Greek letter, hence its name. For Augustine's thought on the subject, see *De Genesi ad litteram*, 4:7, 14.

[34] *Quodlibitales*, 4:1.1.

[35] *Summa Theologica*, 1:1.15.

[36] *Poetices libri septem . . . apud Petrum Santandreanum* (1594), pp. 382–83. "Qua tempestate post digestum Chaos, Caeli terraeque sunt nuptiae celebratae. Quorum coniunctione & tunc species omnes productae sunt: & ad eorum imitationem generando

The poet, then, was an *alter deus* in a double sense. As a man and a Christian, he was created in the image of God and bore within his soul the divine image, marred by the Fall and restored through the Redemption. This state, which could be claimed by all Christians, proved a fertile subject for the practice of literary typology, one in which Donne's proficiency has been amply demonstrated. But as a poet, Donne could also create, like God, in measure, weight, and number. He could explore the workings of God in the cosmos in several ways. These have been identified by Leonard Barkan as principally, "the chemical geocosm, envisaging a world composed of the four elements; the astral geocosm, presupposing a heavenly cosmos that is both physical and spiritual; a numerical geocosm made up of abstract mathematical relations; and a natural geocosm comprised of the objects of the world as immediately beheld by the senses."[37] In the *Devotions* Donne displays a knowledgeable skill in exploiting the poetic possibilities of all these. As he plays with the system of correspondences of the natural geocosm, so he explores the elemental imbalance of the humors within his own body, an imbalance which reflects the basic flawed nature of the fallen world in which he comes to represent sinful man, the weakest link in the chain of being. Finally, he has embodied this brilliant play, as we shall see in Chapter 5, in a structure numerically patterned according to the calendar of the year, the ages of the world, and the progression of his own life.

The modern habit of reading in anthological excerpts does not serve the reader of the *Devotions* well, for Donne's book cannot be understood, certainly cannot be talked about successfully, in excerpt. At most, the practice achieves a partial abstraction of the work in its totality, but it is hardly a reading. Taken by themselves, the Meditations present a far different picture than the less anguished Prayers, and either of these will differ from a reading of an individual Devotion with its triadic structure of Meditation, Expostulation, Prayer. Each Meditation, for example, presents a veritable onslaught of data from the Book of the Creatures: soil, snow, chemical experiments, beds, governments, geography, vapors, time, sleep, bells, university degrees, books, money, continents, houses, rivers, the sea, seasons, gardens, armies, statues, the liberal arts, the new cosmology, farming, fire, and executions, as well as a bewildering array of plants, animals, angels, and astral manifestations.

In his recent study of the cosmos and the human body, Barkan (by

---

propagatae: ut quod materia prohibebat, formarum ordinata successio adipisceretur immortalitatem."

[37] *Nature's Work of Art* (New Haven: Yale University Press, 1975), p. 140.

consideration of these Meditations alone) finds Donne manifesting a massive insecurity in perceiving so many levels of creation between himself and God. In turning to the "Humane condition," as perceived in his own sick body, Barkan says, Donne faces God alone in a "terror of doubt" occasioned by implications of multiplicity inherent in man's nature that would disqualify him from seeking within himself the one God and by the advent of modern empirical science, which threw all in doubt.[38]

A reading of the Meditations excerpted from the body of the *Devotions* would seem to confirm Barkan's opinion. In particular, two Meditations demonstrate Donne's preoccupation with multiplicity and decay. From the fourth Meditation:

> It is too little to call *Man* a *little World;* Except *God,* Man is a *diminutiue* to nothing. Man consistes of more pieces, more parts, then the world; then the world doeth, nay then the world is. And if those pieces were extended, and stretched out in Man, as they are in the world, Man would bee the *Gyant,* and the world the *Dwarfe,* the world but the *Map,* and the man the World. If all the *Veines* in our bodies, were extended to *Riuers,* and all the *Sinewes,* to *vaines of Mines,* and all the *Muscles,* that lye vpon one another, to *Hilles,* and all the *Bones* to *Quarries* of stones, and all the other pieces, to the proportion of those which correspond to them in the *world,* the *aire* would be too litle for this *Orbe* of Man to moue in, the firmament would bee but enough for this *star;* for, as the whole world hath nothing, to which something in man doth not answere, so hath man many pieces, of which the whole world hath no representation. Inlarge this Meditation vpon this *great world, Man,* so farr, as to consider the immensitie of the creatures this world produces; our *creatures* are our *thoughts, creatures* that are borne *Gyants:* that reach from *East* to *West,* from *earth* to *Heauen,* that doe not onely bestride all the *Sea,* and *Land,* but span the *Sunn* and *Firmament* at once; My thoughts reach all, comprehend all. Inexplicable mistery; I their *Creator* am in a close prison, in a sicke bed, any where, and any one of my *Creatures,* my *thoughts,* is with the *Sunne,* and beyond the *Sunne* in one pace, one steppe, euery where. And then as the other *world* produces *Serpents,* and *Vipers,* malignant, & venimous creatures, and *Wormes,* and *Caterpillars,* that endeauour to deuoure that world which produces them, and *Monsters* compiled and complicated of diuers parents, & kinds, so this world, our selues, produces all these in vs, in producing *diseases, & sicknesses,* of all those sorts; venimous, and infectious diseases, feeding & consuming diseases, and manifold, and entangled diseases, made vp of many seuerall ones. . . . Call back therefore thy Meditations again, and bring it downe; whats

[38] Ibid., p. 53.

> become of mans great extent & proportion, when himselfe shrinkes him-
> self, and consumes himselfe to a handfull of dust; whats become of his
> soaring thoughts, his compassing thoughts, when himselfe brings him-
> selfe to the ignorance, to the thoughtlesnesse of the *Graue?*

Donne here enunciates the full scope of his human and, incidentally, his poetic power: He is diminutive to none save God; his
thoughts, his creatures, are giants; himself, their creator, a giant; the
world, a dwarf. But all is in vain: a great prince in prison lies, and it
is the prison of that very body that exceeds the universe.

Donne's second great disquisition on the Book of the Creatures,
the tenth Meditation, forgoes even the opening optimism of the
fourth Meditation. All tends to multiplicity and decay:

> This is *Natures nest of Boxes;* The *Heauens* containe the *Earth,* the *Earth,*
> *Cities, Cities, Men.* And all these and *Concentrique;* the common *center* to
> them all, is *decay, ruine;* only that is *Eccentrique,* which was neuer made;
> only that place, or garment rather, which we can *imagine,* but not *dem-*
> *onstrate,* That light, which is the very emanation of the light of *God,* in
> which the *Saints* shall dwell, with which the *Saints* shall be appareld, only
> that bends not to this *Center,* to *Ruine,* that which was not made of *Noth-*
> *ing,* is not threatned with this annihilation.

He goes on to catalog the mutability of the heavens, with their
"*Comets* and *blazing starres,*" with their "*dropsie,* the flood," of common-
wealths and states, threatened mortally by "a few *whisperers,* and secret plotters in corners," of the human soul, plagued with "secret dis-
obediences, secret repugnances" against the will of God, which are
"the most deadly, the most pernicious." Finally, he brings the matter
home: "and it is so to, with the *diseases* of the *body;* and that is my
case." Thus he moves down the great ladder of Creation, progressing
through the heavens to the earth, to the state, the tribe, and, finally,
his own individual condition. One is reminded of that other great
paean on degree: "O when degree is shak'd, / Which is the ladder of
all high designs, / The enterprise is sick. / . . Take but degree away,
untune that string, / And hark what discord follows."

But Donne's enterprise is sick, his string untuned not through any
inherent flaw in the multiplicity of the cosmos nor even (I would argue with Professor Barkan), through man's containing "a cosmic
wholeness within himself which is at the same time a war with himself."[39] The enterprise is sick because, as Donne insists in the very first
Expostulation, the human condition is sinful: "I fall sick of sin, and
am bedded and bedrid, buried and putrified in the practice of sin."

[39] Ibid., p. 57.

But a reading of the Meditations alone is apt to confuse one about the cause of Donne's anguish, and concentration on the first sections of Donne's triads, to the exclusion of the Expostulations and Prayers, allows Barkan to identify the poet's illness as one "largely without moral implication."[40]

A reading of each Meditation, however, as the first step of a three-part unit, with each unit a step in the larger twenty-three-part whole, presents evidence to the contrary. To read the *Devotions* successfully, one must proceed from the totality of the work to the significance of its individual parts, their relationships to each other and to the whole. With a grasp of the work's total pattern, the reader can proceed to the understanding of that pattern in the light of its individual parts.

In recent years, several attempts have been made to identify the pattern of the *Devotions,* the most notable being that of Joan Webber, who saw the work as a progression from negation (in the Meditations) through questioning (in the Expostulations) to affirmation (in the Prayers).[41] Although the overall pattern is far more complex than this, Webber was correct in assuming that no coherent statement can be made about Donne's book without taking into account the framework of Meditations, Expostulations, and Prayers *in toto*—and to them I would add *"Stationes"* and "Epistle Dedicatory."

These considered, a structure emerges patterned both autobiographically and temporally by the use of number symbolism. The term *numerology* today has primarily a pejorative meaning for most readers. We no longer subscribe to the world vision that made its use important to the composition of great poetry, and our own removal from the tradition has caused its dubious association with obscure mysticism rather than with the extremely rational approach to reality that was its hallmark.

The world of the Renaissance artist was ordered by reason, one that demanded a like aesthetic response. It was not for the artist to impose an individual and thus particular and to some degree irrational order on his creation but rather to reveal to his audience the inherently logical order of the cosmos, thus both turning their gaze to the Creator and eliciting admiration for the skill with which the poet's framework was constructed. The history of the arithmetical tradition is yet to be written, and perhaps it will never be, for it is both extraordinarily complex and very old, drawing its most ancient literary roots

---

[40] Ibid.

[41] "The Prose Style of John Donne's *Devotions Upon Emergent Occasions," Anglia* 79 (1961): 141. This essay, in expanded form, constitutes chapter 7 of her later book *Contrary Music: The Prose Style of John Donne* (Madison: University of Wisconsin Press, 1963).

from the Pythagoreans and the Hebrews, maintaining itself in the underpinnings of medieval literary tradition, and enjoying a late efflorescence through the efforts of the humanists to delve into those ancient roots in their search for the sources of ancient poetry.[42]

On the one hand, the number lore of classical tradition was confronted early on by Augustine in a series of treatises that brought it into harmony with Christian exegesis and influenced Christian poet-

[42] As a working guide to the use of number symbolism in the literature of the English Renaissance, see: Douglas Brooks and Alastair Fowler, "The Structure of Dryden's *Song for St. Cecilia's Day,* 1687," *Essays in Criticism* 17 (1967): 434–47; Marianne Brown, " 'Finely framed, and strongly trussed vp together': A Structural Approach to Edmund Spenser's *The Shepheardes Calendar*" (Ph.D. diss., University of Oslo, 1978); Christopher Butler, *Number Symbolism* (London: Routledge & Kegan Paul, 1970); R. T. Eriksen, "The Forme of Faustus' Fortunes: A Structural and Thematic Analysis of Christopher Marlowe's *The Tragicall Historie of Doctor Faustus* (1616)" (Ph.D. diss., University of Oslo, 1976); Alastair Fowler, *Conceitful Thought* (ed.), *Silent Poetry: Essays in Numerological Analysis* (London: Routledge and Kegan Paul, 1970), *Spenser and the Numbers of Time* (London: Routledge and Kegan Paul, 1964), and *Triumphal Forms*; Antonia Gransden, "Silent Meanings in Ranulf Higden's *Polychronicon* and in Thomas Elmham's *Liber metricus de Henrico Quinto,*" *Medium Aevum* 46 (1977): 231–40; S. K. Heinger, Jr., "Some Renaissance Versions of the Pythagorean Tetrad," *Studies in the Renaissance* 8 (1961): 7–33, *Touches of Sweet Harmon*; A. Kent Hieatt, "A Numerical Key for Spenser's *Amoretti* and Guyon in the House of Mammon," *Year of English Studies* 3 (1973): 14–27, Review: *Conceitful Thought, Renaissance and Reformation,* n. ser. 4 (1980): 110–15, *Short Time's Endless Monument: The Symbolism of the Numbers in Edmund Spenser's "Epithalamion"* (New York: Columbia University Press, 1960); Vincent Foster Hopper, *Medieval Number Symbolism: Its Sources, Meaning, and Influence on Thought and Expression* (New York: Columbia University Press, 1938); R. V. LeClerq, "Crashaw's *Epithalamium*: Pattern and Vision," *University of Wisconsin Literary Monographs* 6 (1975): 71–108; J. Leath Mills, "Spenser and the Numbers of History: A Note on the British and Elfin Chronicles in *The Faerie Queene,*" *Philological Quarterly* 55 (1976): 281–87; C. A. Patrides, "The Numerological Approach to Cosmic Order During the English Renaissance," *Isis* 49 (1958): pp. 391–97; Gunnar Qvärnstrom, *The Enchanted Palace: Some Structural Aspects of "Paradise Lost"* (Stockholm: Alqvist & Wiksell, 1967), *Poetry and Numbers: On the Structural Use of Poetic Numbers,* Scripta Minora Regiae Societatis Humaniorum Litterarum Lundensis, 2, 1964–1965 (Lund: C.W.K. Gleerup, 1966); Maren-Sofie Røstvig "*Ars Aeterna*: Renaissance Poetics and Theories of Divine Creation," in *Chaos and Form,* ed. Kenneth McRobbie (Winnipeg: University of Manitoba Press, 1972), pp. 101–19, (ed.) *Fair Forms: Essays in English Literature from Spenser to Jane Austen* (Cambridge: D. S. Brewer, 1975), "A Frame of Words: On the Craftsmanship of Samuel Daniel," *English Studies* 60 (1979): 122–37, *The Hidden Sense,* Norwegian Studies in English, 9 (Oslo, 1963), "Images of Perfection," in *Seventeenth-Century Imagery: Essays on the Use of Figurative Language from Donne to Farquhar,* ed. Earl Miner (Berkeley: University of California Press, 1971), "*In ordine di ruota*: Circular Structure in 'The Unfortunate Lover' and 'Upon Appleton House,' " in *Tercentenary Essays in Honor of Andrew Marvell,* ed. Kenneth Friedenreich (Hamden, Conn.: Shoe String Press, 1978), pp. 245–67, "Milton and the Science of Numbers," *English Studies Today* 4 (1966): 267–88, "Renaissance Numerology: Acrostics or Criticism?" *Essays in Criticism* 16 (1966): 6–21, "*The Shepheardes Calendar*—A Structural Analysis," *Renaissance and Modern Studies* 13 (1969): 49–75.

ics for centuries to come.[43] Keeping in mind the basic harmony of the diapason and its striking analogy in the Mosaic hexaemeron,[44] Augustine referred all material beauty back to the rational order of the universe, to the reign of proportionate number. But this harmonious disposition of parts that constitutes the universe exists only as shadow to the carnal perceiver, and the means to its perception lies not in sense but intellect: We perceive, he says in *De vera religione,* "not by means of the fleshly eye nor of any of the senses, but by the conceptual intellect."[45] The latter, in the very process of turning from the mutable *many* embodied in the artifact to the unchangeable *one,* from multiplicity to unity, occasions a regeneration of the soul.

Augustine tied this intellectual perception of abstract beauty via numerical proportion directly to the Christian tradition by means of a series of striking proof texts. Wisdom 8.1: "She reacheth therefore from end to end mightily, and ordereth all things sweetly"; 11.21: "But thou hast ordered all things in measure, and number, and weight"; Romans 1.20: "For since the creation of the world his invisible attributes are clearly seen—his everlasting power also and divinity—being understood through the things that are made"; Hebrews 11.3: "By faith we understand that the world was fashioned by the word of God; and thus things visible were made out of things invisible"; 2 Corinthians 4.16–18: "Wherefore we do not lose heart. On the contrary, even though our outer man is decaying, yet our inner man is being renewed day by day. For our present light affliction, which is for the moment, prepares for us an eternal weight of glory that is beyond all measure; while we look not at the things that are seen, but at the things that are not seen. For the things that are seen are temporal, but the things that are not seen are eternal."

These texts call us to turn away ultimately from the carnal works we perceive through the eyes of the flesh to the spiritually harmonizing art which underlies them, so that we may contemplate the beauty that gives the name to all that is beautiful. The act of reading literature thus becomes a means of regeneration, inasmuch as literature is imbued with the harmonies of the divine universe.

Whether every Christian author sought thereafter to build into his work such an infusion is another matter, although there is ample evidence that many of them attempted the feat.[46] Nevertheless, the tra-

---

[43] See especially *De ordine* 2, *De vera religione* 30, *De musica* 6, as well as *De libero arbitrio* 2, *De doctrina christiana* 16, and *De trinitate* 4.

[44] *De vera religione* 30, 1v.

[45] *Pat. Lat.* 34, col. 146.

[46] See Butler, *Number Symbolism,* ch. 2. "The Early Medieval Period: Biblical Exegesis and World Schemes."

dition persisted, and Augustine's theorizing emerges periodically and persistently in such authors as Bonaventura, Landino, Ficino, Pico, and Giorgio.[47] On the other hand, Hebrew poetry had its own numerological tradition, perceived and interpreted for the Christians as early as Philo and Origen, who added their own theological accretions, and complicated further by the cabbalists and rabbinical commentators of the Middle Ages. Moreover, the astronomical, astrological, seasonal, and liturgical convergences of the calendar contributed to an increasingly complex body of temporal numerology, which gained its masters in Dante and Petrarch and its zenith in the late English Renaissance. Finally, a relatively "pure" and obscure Pythagorean system was "rediscovered" by the humanists and had much to say to the philosophers, architects, and budding scientists of the Renaissance—who in turn had much to say that further obscured the matter.[48]

By Donne's day a threefold tradition, through which Augustine's poetics reverberated, was established: a cosmological science of creation by number; a tradition of biblical exegesis in which numbers were endowed with symbolism; and a late-developing (albeit from early roots) tradition of occult arithmology connected with astrology and magic. It made available to the artist an extraordinarily rich, if sometimes conflicting, collection of numerical premises from which he often worked in a thoroughly syncretistic and ahistorical fashion.

If the twentieth-century eye, habitually following the sequential line, falters before the concept of numerical form, it is to be pardoned. But Donne, Sidney, and their like were the inheritors of two millenia of schematically ordered verse, even as they stood poised on the edge of the intellectual crevasse that was to swallow the Ptolemaic cosmos and with it the rationale for arithmetical ordering of relationships within a poem. For them, the literary artifact could in truth mirror the structure of reality, often in bewildering complexity. At its simplest, the numerological scheme could serve as an organizational framework upon which the work was literally hung,[49] but at its best, it reinforced spatially even the most subtle complexities of content.

---

[47] Bonaventura, *Collationes in Hexaemeron, Collation IV, 16*, trans. Wilhelm Nyssen *Das Sechstagewerk* (Dormstad, 1964); Cristoforo Landino, *Comedia del divino poet a Florentino Dante Aleghieri col commento di Christoforo Landino* (Venice, 1484); Marsilio Ficino, "Commentarium in Timaeum," *Opera* (Paris, 1641), *Theologia Platonica*, 12, v, xii, and 2, vi, xxxii; Francesco di Giorgio, *Harmonia mundi* (Venice, 1525).

[48] Heninger, *Touches of Sweet Harmony*, pp. 234–55.

[49] See Elizabeth K. Berry, "Henry Ferrers, an Early Warwickshire Antiquary, 1550–1633," *Dugdale Society Occasional Papers* 16 (Oxford, 1965): 30, for a description of such planning framework.

One has only to look at Spenser's *Amoretti* and "Epithalamion" for evidence.[50]

For the modern reader, an appreciation of number symbolism can open whole new vistas of understanding and delight. It may, however, be a delight hard won against ingrained prejudice, for the practice belonged to what Bacon calls "parabolic" poetry,[51] which translates (most often pejoratively) as "mystical" or "irrational." But in a rationally, (that is, mathematically) ordered universe, the very structure of the soul corresponded to the order of the universe, and the creation of mathematically ordered poetry was the natural movement of that soul in imitation of its maker. Hence, in English poetry of the sixteenth and seventeenth centuries, we find the use of number symbolism in the work of Wyatt, Surrey, Sidney, Spenser, Shakespeare, Chapman, Jonson, Fletcher, Wither, Milton, Cowley, Marvell, and, as we shall see, John Donne.

It is this aspect of Donne's literary practice that warrants some prefatory remarks, both in explanation of a poetic tradition still too little known and in demonstration of Donne's employment of it throughout his literary career. In the oft-quoted nineteenth Expostulation of his *Devotions,* Donne draws an extended analogy between God as poet and his own poetic efforts:

> [T]hou art a *figuratiue,* a *metaphoricall God* too: a *God* in whose words there is such a height of *figures,* such *voyages,* such *peregrinations* to fetch

[50] Spenser's *Epithalamion* and *Amoretti* have yielded rich treasures to Hieatt, *Short Time's Endless Monument,* and to Fowler, "Numerical Composition in *The Faerie Queen,*" *Journal of the Warburg and Courtauld Institutes (JWCI)* 24 (1961): 199–239, and *Spenser and the Number of Time.* Maren-Sofie Røstvig and S. K. Heninger have both contributed essays on the numerology of the *Shepheardes Calendar:* her "The Shepheardes Calendar—A Structural Analysis," *Renaissance and Modern Studies* 13 (1969): 49–75, and his "The Implications of Form for the Shepheardes Calendar," *Studies in the Renaissance* 8 (1961): 7–33. Most interesting, it seems to me is the recent investigation of the so-called arithmological stanza of Book 2.ix.22, which describes the proportions of the House of Alma. Although Sir Kenelm Digby was the first to comment on Spenser's preoccupation with numbers in this stanza, modern critics have thrown increasingly bright light on its complexities; see, for example, Carroll Camden, "The Architecture of Spenser's House of Alma," *Modern Language Notes (MLN)* 58 (1943): 262–65; R. H. Chapman, "The Body as a Triangular Structure in Spenser and Chapman," *MLN* 64 (1949); R. M. Cummings, "A Note on the Arithmological Stanza: *The Faerie Queen,* II.ix.22," *JWCI* 30 (1967): 410–14; Vincent Hopper, "Spenser's House of Temperance," *PMLA* 55 (1940): 958–67; Jerry Leath Mills, "Spenser's Castle of Alma and the Number 22: A Note on Symbolic Stanza Placement, "*Notes & Queries (N & Q)* 212 (1967): 456–57. My own observations on the problem can be found below in chapter 5.

[51] *The Twoo Bookes of Francis Bacon. Of the proficience and aduancement of Learning, diuine and humane.* London, 1605, sig. Ee2v.

remote and precious *metaphors*, such *extentions*, such *spreadings*, such *Curtaines* of *Allegories*, such *third Heauens* of *Hyperboles*, so *harmonious eloquutions*, so *retired* and so *reserued expressions*, so *commanding perswasions*, so *perswading commandements*, such *sinewes* euen in thy *milke*, and such *things* in thy *words*, as all *prophane Authors*, seeme of the seed of the *Serpent*, that *creepes*, thou art the *doue*, that flies.

Such a metaphorical God emboldens Donne to copy the figurative method of the Fathers

whose delight it was to write after thy *Copie*, to proceede the same way in their *expositions* of the *Scriptures*, and in their composing both of *publike liturgies* and of *priuate prayers* to thee, to make their accesses to thee in such a kind of *language*, as thou wast pleased to speake to them, in a *figuratiue*, in a *Metaphoricall language;* in which manner I am bold to [speak].

Donne's own language will strive to be like God's, and God spoke his Creation in figures of number, weight, and measure. Nevertheless, in the light of statements by Thomas Carew and Drummond of Hawthornden—among the very few contemporary critical appraisals of Donne's work—we must question whether Donne also speaks in *poetical* numbers. Carew points out that Donne's method included the use of strong lines and the adoption of a normal and stringently intellectual English diction:

> The Muses garden with Pedantique weedes
> O'rspread, was purg'd by thee; The lazie seeds
> Of servile imitation throwne away;
> And fresh invention planted. . . .
>
> The subtle cheat
> Of slie Exchanges, and the jugling feat
> Of two-edg'd words, or whatsoever wrong
> By ours was done the Greeke, or Latine tongue,
> Thou hast redeem'd, and open'd Us a Mine
> Of rich and pregnant phansie, drawne a line
> Of masculine expression. . . . [52]

Moreover, he has rejected classical deities as allegorical types and as decoration, along with the allegorical framework which underlies such a method:

[52] "An Elegie upon the death of the Deane of Pauls, Dr. John Donne," Grierson, p. 347, ll. 25–29, 33–39. See Ruth Wallerstein, *Seventeenth-Century Poetics* (Madison: University of Wisconsin Press, 1950), p. 72.

> But thou art gone, and thy strict lawes will be
> Too hard for Libertines in Poetrie.
> They will repeale the goodly exil'd traine
> Of gods and goddesses, which in thy just raigne
> Were banish'd nobler Poems, now, with these
> The silenc'd tales o'the'Metamorphoses
> Shall stuffe their lines, and swell the windy Page,
> Till Verse refin'd by thee, in this last Age
> Turne ballad rime, Or those old Idolls bee
> Ador'd againe, with new apostasie. . . . [53]

Drummond, on the other hand, censures Donne as among those who have abandoned traditional ornament for metaphysics and obscurity: "In vain have some Men of late (Transformers of every Thing) consulted upon [Poesy's] Reformation, and endeavoured to abstract her to *Metaphysical* Idea's, and *Scholastical* Quiddities, denuding her of her own Habits, and those Ornaments with which she hath amused the World some Thousand Years."[54] Donne himself in his sermons had overtly rejected softness and decoration. Did he, then, in his repudiation of traditional forms, also repudiate the use of numerological construction? The evidence indicates the contrary.

Donne's own remarks on numbers in Book 2 of *Essayes in Divinity* (which book he seems to have been rereading in the days before his illness)[55] reveal his knowledgeable acquaintance with the art. Indeed, his statement shows at least some of his study to have been derived from the Fathers and from the Italian Neoplatonists. In the first section, "Of Number," he justifies God's creation of man in number, pointing especially to the Book of Numbers "in which Saint *Jerom* saith are contained *totius Arithmeticae Mysteria*."[56] In the section "Variety in the Number," at the beginning of which he wryly comments that "Numbring is so proper and peculiar to man, who only can number, that some philosophical Inquisitors have argued doubtfully, whether if man were not, there were any Number," he embarks on a long digression on the number 70 as a composition of the two perfect numbers 7 and 10, questioning "whether any Mystery reside in that chosen Number; the rather because very many remarkable things, and passages in History, seeme to me to have been limited in that Number, which therefore seems more Periodick then any other." His

---

[53] "An Elegie," ll. 61–70.

[54] *The Works of William Drummond of Hawthornden* (Edinburgh, 1711), p. 143.

[55] Janie Mueller, "The Exegesis of Experience: Dean Donne's *Devotions Upon Emergent Occasions*," *Journal of English and Germanic Philology* (*JEGP*) 67 (1968): 9.

[56] *Essayes in Divinity* (Oxford: Clarendon Press, 1952), p. 53.

apology for this digression indicates his thorough knowledge of the art of number symbolism:

> But because any overcurious and Mysterious consideration of this Number 70. though it be composed of the two greatest numbers (for *Ten* cannot be exceeded, but that to express any further Number you must take a part of it again; and Seven is ever used to express the infinite,) be too Cabalistick and Pythagorick for a vulgar Christian, (which I offer not for a phrase of Diminution or Distrust, that such are unprovided of sufficient defences for themselves, or are ignorant of any think required in such as they, for salvation; But that there is needed also a Meta-theology, and super-divinity, above that which serves our particular consciences, in them, who must fight against Philosophers and Jews) because I am one, and in a low degree, of the first and vulgar rank, and write but to my equals, I will forbear it, as mis-interpretable; since to some palates it may taste of Ostentation; but to some of distraction from better contemplations, and of superstition to others: yet, we may, as well with reverence to the things, as respect to the Number, rest a little upon those works of God, or his Servants, which this Number, at least, reduces to our memory.[57]

He proceeds to point out that there were 70 patriarchs, 70 elders, 70 kings slain by God's vengeance, 70 years of Babylonian captivity, and finally, 70 years allotted to man's life, based on the life of David. The number 7 in particular held significance for Donne, generally in its relation to the framework of Creation as evidenced in the hexaemeral tradition. In the series of sermons on the Penitential Psalms delivered in the two years before his illness, he repeatedly alludes to 7 (and, one might add, to the figure of Hezekiah as a type of penitence and conversion).[58] His sermon on Colossians 1.19–20, preached Christmas Day 1622, is particularly elaborate in its elucidation of the number's meaning:

> If God had given over at his second daies work, we had had no sunne, no seasons; If at his fift, we had had no beeing; If at the sixt, no Sabbath; but by proceeding to the seventh, we are all, and we have all. *Naaman*, who was out of the covenant, yet, by washing in Jordan seven times, was cured of his leprosie; seaven times did it even in him, but lesse did not.

[57] As Maren-Sofie Røstvig has recently pointed out ("*Ars Aeterna*," p. 117) Donne's reference to Pico's *Heptaplus* and Giorgio's *De harmonia mundi* here in the *Essayes* indicates his probable acquaintance with the two works and their number lore through the one-volume French translation of 1579, which indicates as well his probable acquaintance with the preface of their translators, Guy and Nicolas le Febre de la Boderie, which dwells on the relevance of cosmic structure to poesie. *Essayes*, p. 53.

[58] See especially *Sermons*, 17:349.

The Priest in the Law used a seven-fold sprinkling of bloud upon the Altar; and we observe a seven-fold shedding of bloud in Christ; In his Circumcision, and in his Agony, in his fulfilling of that Prophesie, *genas vellicantibus,* I gave my cheeks to them, that plucked off the haire, and in his scourging; in his crowning, and in his nayling, and lastly, in the piercing of his side. These seven channels hath the bloud of thy Saviour found. Poure out the bloud of thy soule, sacrifice thy stubborne and rebellious will seaven times too; seaven times, that is, every day; and seaven times every day; for so often a just man falleth; And then, how low must that man lie at last, if he fall so often, and never rise upon any fall? and therefore raise thy self as often, and as soone as thou fallest. *Iericho* would not fall, but by being compassed seaven dayes, and seaven times in one day. Compasse thy selfe, comprehend thy selfe, seaven times, many times, and thou shalt have thy losse of bloud supplied with better bloud, with a true sense of that peace, which he hath already made, and made by bloud, and by his owne bloud, and *by the bloud of his Crosse,* which is the last branch of this second part.[59]

His statement comprehends the hexaemeral tradition: Based on the seven days of Creation, the history of the world was divided into 7 ages, as was the life of man; as the week was divided into 7 days, so was the day divided into 7 canonical hours. Donne calls on his congregation to repent daily, 7 times daily, a course followed by the Church since its earliest days. The hexaemeral tradition seems to have fascinated Donne. It was at least as ancient as Augustine's *City of God* and had received its most recent and complex manifestation in the *Sepmaine* of Du Bartas (Englished by Joshua Sylvester as the *Devine Weekes*).[60] Donne pays homage to it in some of his major work: the "Holy Sonnets,"[61] the *Anniversaries,*[62] and at least three sermons.[63] He consistently applies the days of Creation and their Sabbath to the life of the individual Christian, and he reiterates that analogy in the last public statement of his life, *Death's Duell:* "That which we call life, is but *Hebdomada mortium, a week of deaths,* seaven dayes, seaven peri-

---

[59] *Sermons,* 4:295. See also 5:312.

[60] *La Semaine, ou Creation du Monde* (1578), *La Seconde Semaine, ou Enfance du Monde* (1584), in U. T. Holmes, Jr., et al., *The Works of Guillaume De Salluste Sieur Du Bartas,* 3 vols. (Chapel Hill: University of North Carolina Press, 1935–1940); *Bartas: His Devine Weekes and Workes* (1605, fascm. ed., Gainesville, Fla.: Scholars' Facsimiles & Reprints, 1965).

[61] Gardner, Divine Poems, p. xl; Hughes, *The Progress of the Soul, the Interior Career of John Donne* (New York: Morrow, 1968), pp. 184, 207.

[62] Hughes, *The Progress of the Soul,* p. 200.

[63] Ibid.; Gale H. Carrithers, *Donne at Sermons: A Christian Existential World* (Albany: State University of New York Press, 1972), pp. 137–39.

ods of our life spent in dying, *a dying seaven times over;* and there is an end. *Our birth dyes* in *infancy,* and our *infancy* dyes in *youth,* and *youth* and all the rest dye in *age,* and *age* also dyes, and *determines all.*"[64]

The evidence of Donne's verse also shows him to be widely conversant with the tradition of numerical composition. On some occasions, for example in "The Primrose," he employs substantive numerology. There he exploits the symbolic implications of the numbers 4, 5, 6, and 10 in relation to the nature of woman and of man's proper love for her, concluding that the number 5 most properly belongs to women (as imperfect men): "Ten is the farthest number; if halfe ten / Belonge unto each woman, then / Each woman may talke halfe us men . . ." (ll. 25–27). Here we see Donne's familiarity with the symbolism of ordinal numbers: he is aware that "Ten is the farthest number," that 4 stands for the four elements and the first solid body, and that 6 is a number of perfection.[65]

More prevalent, however, is his employment of what may be called "calendar numerology," the exploitation of the multitudinous connections between calendrical and actual time, both secular and liturgical, which reached its dazzling epitome in the English Renaissance. "Elegy XII," with its fifty-two couplets, is concerned with the passing of the year; *"La Corona"* proceeds through the church year, beginning at Advent.[66] "The Computation" plays with the twenty-four hours of the day; "The Autumnal," with the personal zodiac and its implications with the passage of life from youth to old age.

A recent study by Alastair Fowler of Donne's three epithalamia demonstrates just how deeply the poet was committed to the tradition of temporal numerology.[67] For example, the Valentine's Day "Epithalamion" of 1613, celebrating the marriage of Princess Elizabeth to Count Palatine, mimes both the date of the wedding in its fourteen-line stanzas and the eight hours of the day in their numbering. More complexly, the epithalamion composed for the wedding of the earl of Somerset and the countess of Essex (also 1613) contains a nuptial song that consists of eleven numbered and titled eleven-line stanzas, deliberately playing on the wedding date of December 26 and the imminent demise of the old year, then of course, in its eleventh hour.

[64] *Sermons,* 10:234.

[65] See Edward D. Cleveland, "Donne's *The Primrose,*" *Explicator* 8 (October 1949); Gary A. Stringer, "Donne's *The Primrose*: Manna and Numerological Dalliance," *Essays in Renaissance Culture* 1 (1974): pp. 23–29.

[66] For the association of "La Corona" with the Advent liturgy, see Gardner, *Divine Poems,* pp. 57–58, and Barbara K. Lewalski, *Protestant Poetics and the Seventeenth-Century Religious Lyric* (Princeton: Princeton Univ. Press, 1979), p. 258.

[67] Fowler, *Triumphal Forms,* pp. 160–61.

The renewal of the sun's dying light by the love of the bridal couple during the five days remaining in the year is reflected in the sixth and central stanza (constituting another witty play on the number 11):

> Now from your Easts you issue forth, and wee,
>   As men which through a Cipres see
>   The rising sun, doe thinke it two,
> Soe, as you goe to Church, doe thinke of you. . . .

(160–63)

Moreover, a change in the variable refrain after this stanza signals the new era of the couple's love. Finally, the "Epithalamion at Lincoln's Inn," probably composed as early as 1594, divides its structure into nocturnal and diurnal action, so that light and darkness in the stanzas equal their actual proportion in the natural day (a device Donne was to employ again in the *Devotions*).[68] Fowler has also explored the intricacies of the "Ecclogue at the Mariage of the Earle of Somerset" and those of "The Ecstasy,"[69] intricacies that should lead the student of Donne to approach the "Holy Sonnets" and the longer poems, such as the *Satyres* and the Prince Henry Elegy, with curiosity and care.

Donne's divine poems, especially, offer a rich mine for the study of number structures. These include, in particular, two sequences which appear to draw on the liturgical calendar and on the hexaemeral tradition: The "Holy Sonnets" form an incomplete septad, and "*La Corona*," with its opening address to Magdalene Herbert and its emphasis on Mary Magdalene as a witness to the Resurrection, comprises eight poems in all. Both "*La Corona*" and the "Holy Sonnets" deserve analysis in the light of number patterns that inform the tradition of the sonnet sequence. The three hymns, each occasional and highly autobiographical, along with the equally occasional and autobiographical "Good Friday, Riding Westward," demonstrate Donne's application of temporal number symbolism to his own life pattern. The latter, comprising forty-two lines, was written in Donne's forty-second year, a major climacteric, when he was deep in the process of the decision that was to take him two years later into holy orders. The former, each written on the occasion of near (or presumed near) death, must be analyzed in the light of a long tradition of musical number symbolism. Finally, "Resurrection, Imperfect," with its twenty-three lines and deliberate emphasis on incompleteness,

---

[68] Ibid., p. 160.
[69] Ibid., pp. 71–74.

smacks strongly of the structure of the *Devotions* and deserves study in this light.

However, little critical attention has been paid to this aspect of Donne's knowledge and poetic practice. Considering the tantalizing evidence offered by such lyrics as "Love's Growth," with its interesting arrangement of long and short lines; "A Valediction Forbidding Mourning," with the suggestion of complete circularity built into the numbering of its lines; "The Computation," with its play on the number 24 (possibly imitated by Cowley's "The Long Life");[70] and "A Lecture Upon the Shadow," with its strong suggestion of the demarcations of a sundial, students of Donne's verse might do well to explore possible schema in the whole corpus of his work. The crucial places, it seems to me, are the obviously structured long poems such as "Metempsychosis" and the *Anniversaries*. My guess is that much of the perplexity engendered by these troublesome poems will be alleviated once we perceive the deliberate and meaningful structures that inform them.

But perception of such structures entails new habits of reading. No longer can the image or the periodic sentence claim place as the dominant unit of meaning. Rather, our improved skills as readers of schematically constructed artifacts will reveal a new criteria for coherence, and the conceit, the theme, the image, the period, will take their places in the complex process of relating part to whole that reveals meaning in premodern literature. Our response as readers will also change. We will read less often in excerpt, and our perceptions will perhaps be less fettered to the subjective instant, more given to meditative and rational study.

Moreover, the questions we ask of Donne will differ as we observe the thin and often vanishing line between mere wit and substantive meaning. Some opinion of his work may need to be revised—lyrics praised for their sharp spontaneity and modern psychological insight may need reexamination in terms of less-than-spontaneous internal

---

[70] *The Complete Works in Verse and Prose*, ed. Alexander B. Grosart (1881; reprint, Hildesheim: G. Olds, 1969) 1:112. "The Long Life," like Spenser's *Epithalamion*, mimes the length of day and night at the summer solstice by internal verbal echoes which divide the poem's lines into groups of 8 and 16. Fowler (*Triumphal Forms*, pp. 14–15) has demonstrated an interesting reversal of the pattern: the lover equates the shortest night of absence (midsummer night) with the longest night (winter solstice), inverting the Spenserian format to 8 line-hours + 16 line-hours, rather than 16 stanza-hours + 8 stanza hours. In addition, Cowley puns on the shortness of days at the end of his poem. No one seems to have pointed out, as far as I can see, that Cowley's poem is the twenty-fifth in the sequence *The Mistress*, an unremarkable fact were it not that the fifth poem in the sequence was "Written in Juyce of Lemon" and thus was invisible. Hence, "The Long Life" can be thought of as a full day or, more wittily, as the *longest* day.

crafting. And the question of genre, so complex with Donne, may be better elucidated, or at least better framed, in the light of his numerological practice and its antecedents. All of this, however, must stem from the reader's conception that, for Donne, the poetic artifact was not essentially futile in its attempt to communicate truth intrinsically. Rather, it functioned as an endless monument to the eternal verities embodied by his Creator in the fragile construct of short time.

Chapter V

STRUCTURAL SIGNIFICANCE
IN THE *DEVOTIONS*

An Eternity of Threescore and Ten Years

THAT DONNE'S BOOK is more than casually structured has been attested to by both its author and at least one of his contemporaries. In his letter accompanying the proofs sent to Sir Robert Carr, Donne announced his intention of putting "the meditations had in my sicknesse, into some such order, as may minister some holy delight."[1] The "Epistle Dedicatory" to the *Devotions* and the correspondence accompanying presentation copies of the book indicate the directions in which the reader might look to discern that order. Moreover, that Donne was in the habit of paying studious attention to the structure of at least his religious works is witnessed by Walton, who draws attention to his "many divine sonnets, & other high, holy & harmonious composures."[2] Closer in time (actually within a month of its publication), the *Devotions* was noted by the Jacobean letter writer John Chamberlain, who praised it for its "many curious & daintie conceits, not for common capacities, but surely full of pietie and true feeling."[3]

Some four years after his illness (the *Devotions* had just passed through its third edition, one example of which may have been Donne's personal copy),[4] in a sermon on James 2.12, Donne approached the subject of submitting his private devotions to the exigencies of form:

> Now, your *conversation is in heaven*; and therefore *loquimini Deo*, first speak to him that is in heaven, speak to God. Some of the Platonique Philosophers thought it a profanation of God, to speak to God; They thought, that when our Thoughts were made Prayers, and that the

[1] *Letters to Severall Persons of Honour* (London, 1651), sig. Kkr.

[2] "The Life and Death of Dr. Donne, Late Deane of St. Pauls, London," in *LXXX Sermons* (London, 1640), sig. B2r.

[3] *The Letters of John Chamberlain*, ed. N. E. McClure (Philadelphia: The American Philosophical Society, 1939) 2:545.

[4] Geoffrey Keynes, *A Bibliography of Dr. John Donne* (Oxford: Clarendon Press, 1973), p. 87.

Heart flow'd into the Tongue, and that we had invested and apparel'd our Meditations with words, this was a kinde of Painting, and Dressing, and a superfluous diligence, that rather tasted of humane affections, then such a sincere service, as was fit for the presence of God; Onely the first conceptions, the first ebullitions and emanations of the soul, in the heart, they thought to be a fit sacrifice to God, and all verball prayer to be too homely for him. But God himself, who is all spirit, hath yet put on bodily lineaments, Head, and Hands, and Feet, yea and Garments too, in many places of Scripture, to appear, that is, to manifest himself to us: And when we appear to God, though our Devotion be all spiritual, as he is all spirit, yet let us put on lineaments and apparel upon our Devotions, and digest the Meditations of the heart, into words of the mouth. God came to us *in verbo*, In the word; for Christ is, The Word that was made flesh. Let us, that are Christians, go to God so, too, That *the words of our mouth*, as well as *the Meditations of our heart*, may *be acceptable to him*.[5]

The lineaments with which he clothed his *Devotions*, as we shall see, exceed mere "Painting, and Dressing," and we shall find as well that they are "not for common capacities."

Modern critics of the *Devotions* have found varying degrees of structural complexity in the work. John Sparrow, its first editor in this century, maintained that it "pretends to be nothing but a collection of musings, divided up into a series of '*Meditations*,' '*Expostulations*,' and '*Prayers*,' without any singleness of plan or idea."[6] Recent evaluations, however, have predicated a more deliberate arrangement of material. According to N.J.C. Andreasen, who based her identification of the structure on its thematic concern of assent to the divine will, the twenty-three individual Devotions may be arranged in four sections: Devotions 1 through 5 presenting the frailty of the human condition; 6 through 12 asserting the hope of recovery from sin; 13 through 18 forming the climax (with 17 the thematic pivot), and 19 through 23 proclaiming the achievement of spiritual and physical health. Within this larger structure, each single Devotion "follows a pattern of assent on a small scale, just as it is followed on a larger scale through the plot; each can be used in isolation, as an independent devotional exercise."[7]

[5] *Sermons*, ed. G. F. Potter and Evelyn Simpson, 10 vols. (Berkeley: University of California Press, 1953–1962) 8:338–39.

[6] *Devotions Upon Emergent Occasions* (Cambridge: Cambridge Univ. Press, 1923), p. xviii.

[7] N.J.C. Andreassen, "Donne's *Devotions* and the Psychology of Assent," *Modern Philology* 62 (1965): 210.

Taken as well with the idea of plot, Jonathan Goldberg sensed a narrative framework "which purports to be self-revelatory and sequential," but one that is actually neither: "Thematic concerns form the basis for self-understanding, and a series of topics rather than a series of events accounts for the narrative structure."[8] And, he adds, this lack of overtly event-structured narrative disqualifies the work as autobiography.[9]

Finally, the recent vogue for identifying Jesuit meditative form as the predominant contemporary influence has allowed the latest editors of the *Devotions* to accept the Ignatian meditation as Donne's model.[10] The first of these, Sister Elizabeth Savage, who sees within individual devotions the influence of "circular" Ignatian method, emphasizes that influence by dividing the entirety of the work into five thematic sections, reflecting the five-part Ignatian form.[11]

To my knowledge, only one critic has approached the question of the numerical arrangement of the *Devotions*: Clara Lander, after questioning the meaning of the number 23 itself (she proposes the Elizabethan coming of age, the twenty-third psalm, and the Pythagorean progression of the prime numbers),[12] relates the number to the supposed twenty-three-day course of typhus, with each three-part Devotion corresponding to the "Morning, Afternoon, and Evening Services of the Book of Common Prayer."[13] Lander's theory is under-

[8] "Not Unto Death: The *Devotions* of John Donne" (Ph.D. diss., Columbia University, 1971) 85.

[9] Ibid.

[10] Sr. Elizabeth Savage, S.S.J., ed., *John Donne's "Devotions Upon Emergent Occasions": A Critical Edition with Introduction and Commentary*. 2 vols. (Salzburg: Institut für Englische Sprache und Literatur, 1975); Anthony Raspa, ed., *Devotions upon Emergent Occasions* (Montreal: McGill-Queens University Press, 1975).

[11] Savage groups the Devotions thus: Devotions 1 through 4 form the Ignatian preparatory unit; 5 through 12, 13 through 15, 16 through 18, and 19 through 22 the matter of the exercise, and 23 the conclusion (1:lxiv–lxxi).

[12] "Per Fretum Febris: "A Study of the Relationship Between Theme and Form in John Donne's *Devotions Upon Emergent Occasions, and Several Steps in My Sicknes*" (Ph.D. diss., Univ. of Manitoba, 1968) 94–95.

[13] "A Dangerous Sickness which turned to a Spotted Fever," *Studies in English Literature 1500–1700* 11 (1971): 93–94. The reference to the "Afternoon" service is perplexing. Despite its promotion by John Cosin, whose *Notes on the Book of Common Prayer* were published only in 1710 in William Nicholls' *Comments on the Book of Common Prayer and the Administration of the Sacraments*, public prayer at all the rung canonical hours was almost nonexistent in early-seventeenth-century London. Stow's *Survey of the Cities of London and Westminster* (1633) lists ninety-seven churches within the city walls (exclusive of St. Paul's) in which by the close of the century there was: daily Morning Prayer at forty-six churches from 6:00 to 11:00 A.M., at eighteen from 6:00 to 9:00, and the majority at 11:00 A.M.; daily Evening Prayer in forty-two churches, ranging from 2:00 to 8:00 P.M., the majority at 3:00 P.M.; Holy Communion every Sunday at seven

mined by the doubtful historicity of her evidence, but as we shall see, her perception of an underlying framework to the *Devotions* that is based on symbolic number and the progression of time is accurate.

Let us review the arrangement of the *Devotions*: an "Epistle Dedicatory," followed by a poem in hexameters entitled "*Stationes*," followed by twenty-three three-part Devotions, each preceded by a fragment of the Latin poem. Immediately we are confronted with the question of what part the introductory material—the "Epistle" and the "*Stationes*"—plays in the whole structure. The inclusion of such matter in a consideration of the work in its entirety has ample precedent,[14] and we must decide how much of it may have been designed by Donne to figure in the framework of the whole. External evidence—the letter to Sir Robert Carr—demonstrates that the "Epistle Dedicatory" was not formally integral (indeed, probably had not been composed) at the time of the work's completion, although it gives evidence of some of the *Devotions'* thematic and structural concerns. The case for the "*Stationes*," however, is different. First, Donne draws attention to the integral role of the poem and to its progressive nature through its distribution in the text. A twenty-two-line metrical preface was not unique,[15] and the number was often used for structural composition because of its association with the books of the Bible and the letters of the Hebrew alphabet, a structure reflected in Psalm 118, the Book of Lamentations, and in Jerome's manipulation of the books of the Old Testament to achieve the total number of letters in the Greek alphabet.[16] The imputation of the structure of the alphabet to the Bible assured its circularity, for God is the Alpha and Omega, as the beginning and end of Revelation demonstrates. To adopt such a structure for one's own creative use was no blasphemy: Augustine had done so with *De Civitate Dei*, which is organized into twenty-two books, and Donne showed his awareness of the tradition in his metrical paraphrase of Lamentations. Certainly, the

---

churches, generally at noon, others holdings the service every other Sunday, every second and third Sundays, and monthly. At Donne's own St. Paul's, Morning Prayer was at 6:00 and at 10:00 A.M. (this probably in choir), with Evening Prayer at 3:00 P.M. There was Holy Communion every Sunday at 11:00 A.M. On Sundays, Evening Prayer was accompanied by a sermon. Although these times corresponded generally with the rung canonical hours, the content of service and its timing was removed from the ancient practice significantly.

[14] Alastair Fowler, *Triumphal Forms: Structural Patterns in Elizabethan Poetry* (Cambridge: Cambridge University Press, 1970), pp. 1–8.

[15] For example, both Thomas Whythorne's autobiography and Fletcher's *Christ's Victorie and Triumph* were accompanied by twenty-two-line metrical prefaces.

[16] Fowler, *Triumphal Forms*, p. 7; Maren Sofie-Røstvig, *The Hidden Sense*, Norwegian Studies in English, 9 (Oslo, 1963), pp. 10ff.

use of the number in the "*Stationes*" does not jar with Donne's general play on the symbolic circular, both in the *Devotions* and elsewhere in his work. Moreover, a syllable count of the poem reveals a total of 359 Latin syllables, one short of the number of perfect circularity.

But the alphabetic tradition was not the only one available to Donne. The number 22 is also associated with the soul. In the *Timaeus*, twenty-two terms compose the "double interval" series involved in the formation of the soul, and the number, says Professor Fowler, became connected with "the Soul, and with the principle of order informing the cosmos."[17] Fowler makes his point in exploring the various complexities in the body-soul relationship exemplified in Spenser's Castle of Alma. But the Castle of Alma is the House of Temperance, an allegory of the perfectly tempered and ordered human body. In this connection, the number takes on interesting significance, for it is also in common medieval tradition an indicator of temperance itself. Isidore of Seville, among other encyclopedists, derives the symbolism from the ancient Hebrew measure of grain, the *modius*, which was fixed at the quantity of twenty-two sextarii. Stephen Bateman, in his late-sixteenth-century redaction of Bartholomaeus Anglicus's *De Proprietatibus Rerum*, explained the association thus:

> *Modius* hath that name, for it is perfect of his manner, & is the measure of 44 li. that maketh 22 Sextaris, and is therefore figure and token of perfect workes of six dayes. God did make 22. workes within six dayes. . . . And 22. generations were from Adam to Iacob, of whose seede came all the people of Israel. And there be 22. bookes of the olde Testament unto Hester, and 22 letters of A.B.C. by whom all the lore of Gods law is written. Then by these ensamples, the measure *Modius* containeth 22. Sextarius, by Moses lore: and *Modius* hath that name of *Modus*, for it is a moderate measure, as Isid. saith.[18]

The divergence in the tradition—22 as symbol of the formation of the soul and the tempering of the body—is confusing unless one recalls the pre-Cartesian vision of soul and body as inextricably linked. Call it "subtle gumph" or what you will, the link between them posited a strong effect upon the soul when the body was disordered or distempered, as a contemporary writer bears witness: ·

[17] *Spenser and the Numbers of Time* (London: Routledge and Kegan Paul, 1964), p. 286.

[18] Steven Bateman, *Batman vppon Bartholome* (London, 1582), sigs. 417v–418r. For the exploration of this symbolism in relation to the Castle of Alma, see Jerry Leath Mills, "Spenser's Castle of Alma and the Number 22: A Note on Symbolic Stanza Placement," *Notes & Queries* (*N&Q*) 212 (1967): 456–58.

FIGURE 1. The "Dial" of Ahaz. Paris, Bibliothèque Nationale, ms. lat. 11560 (Bible moralisée), fol. 120v. Photo: Bibliothèque Nationale.

FIGURE 2. Christ, Hezekiah, and the "Dial" of Ahaz. Oxford, Bodleian Library, ms. Bodl. 270b (Moralized Bible), fol. 183v. Photo: Bodleian Library.

FIGURE 3. Temperance. Detail from the Tabernacle of Orcagna. Florence, Orsanmichele. Photo: Alinari/Art Resource.

Figure 4. Temperance. Detail from the Allegory of Good Government, Palazzo Pubblico, Siena. Photo: Istituzioni e Beni Culturali.

FIGURE 5. Temperance. Paris, Bibliothèque Nationale, ms, fr. 9186 (J. de Courtecuisse [Martin de Broga], *"Seneca" on the Virtues*), fol. 304r. Photo: Bibliothèque Nationale.

FIGURE 6. Temperance. Paris, Bibliothèque Nationale, ms. fr. 606 (Christine de Pisan, *Othea*), fol.2v. Photo: Bibliothèque Nationale.

FIGURE 7. Temperance. Brussels, Bibliothèque Royale, ms IV, iii (*Horloge de Sapience*), fol. 13v. Copyright Bibliothèque Royale Albert Ier.

FIGURE 8. Solomon as Temperance. Paris Bibliothèque Nationale, ms. fr. 455, fol. 9. Photo: Bibliothèque Nationale.

FIGURE 9. Humoral calendar. Frontispiece, Thomas Walkington, *The Optik Glasse of Humors* (1631). Photo: Humanities Research Center, The University of Texas at Austin.

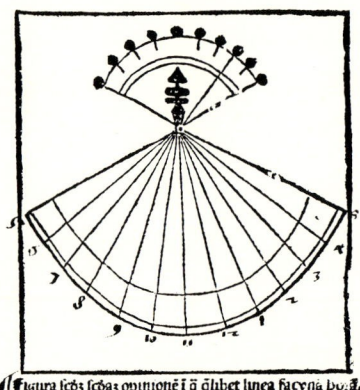

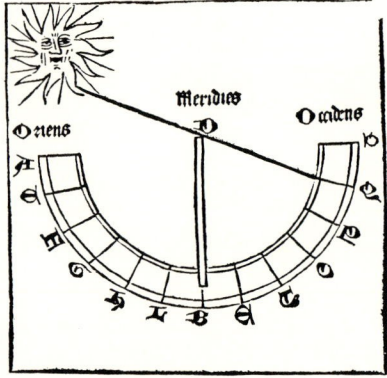

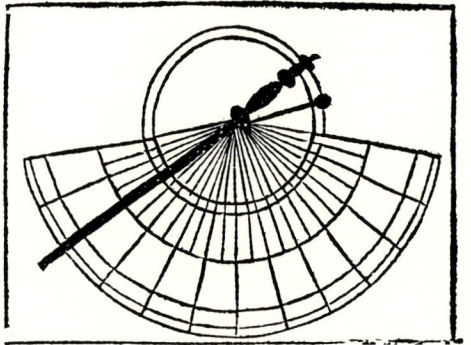

FIGURE 10. Sundials. Nicholas of Lyra and Paul of Burgos, *Postilla Super Totam Bibliam* (Strasburg, 1492).

AETERNA HOMINVM NATVRA.

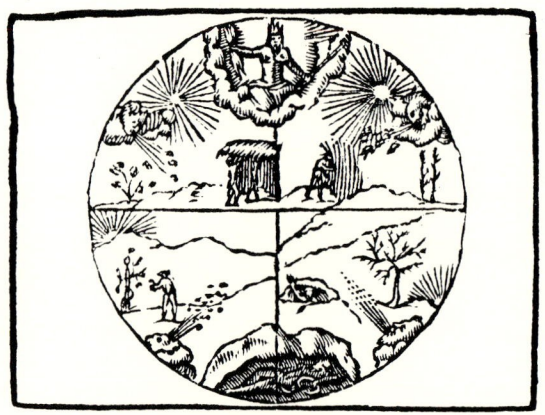

VER, *Aestas, Autumnus, Hyems, Hæ quattuor annis*

FIGURE 11. "The Undying Nature of Man." Barthelmy Aneau, *Picta Poesis* (1552). Photo: The Huntington Library.

FIGURE 12. Title page. John Case, *Lapis Philosophicus* (1599). From the Art Collection of the Folger Shakespeare Library.

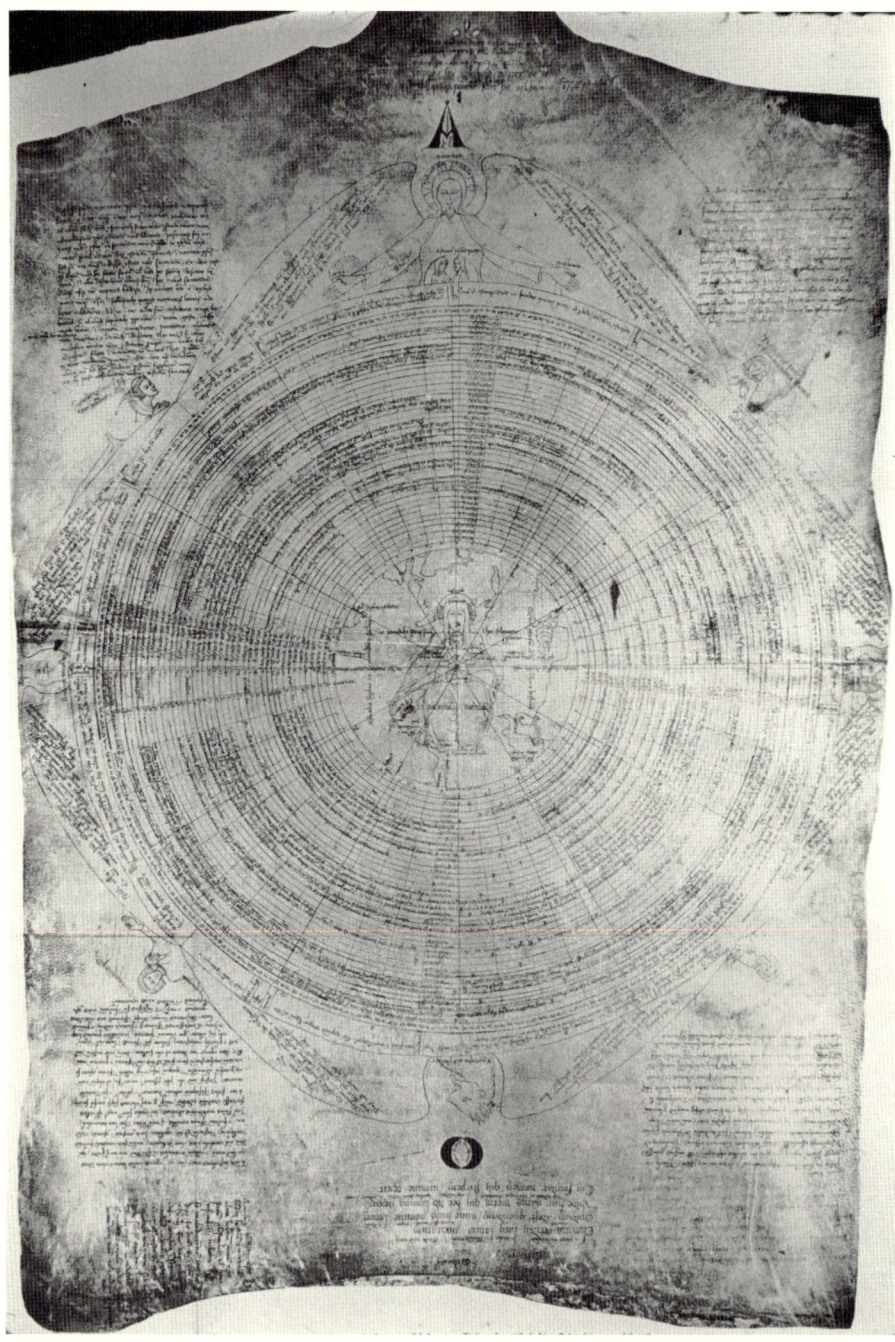

FIGURE 13. Autobiographical chart of Opicinus de Canistris. Rome, Biblioteca Apostolica Vaticana, cod. Vat. lat. 1993. Photo: Biblioteca Vaticana.

The infection of the aire, as in the extinguishing of some blazing comet, the eructation of noysome vapours from the bosome of the earth, the disastrous constellation or bad aspect of some malevolent planet, the dampting fumes that the Sun elevates from bogges and fennish grounds, the inflammation of the aire by the intense heat of the sun, ... this infection causeth our bodies first to be badly qualified, and tainted with a spice of corruption, and so by consequent our very soules to be ill affected.[19]

Both of these connections with the number 22 are interesting for their further linkage to the figure of Hezekiah. His story, it will be remembered, appears four times in the Vulgate Old Testament: 2 Paralipomenon 32.24–33; 4 Kings 20.1–20; Isaiah 38.1–22; and Ecclesiasticus 48.20–28.[20] The accounts of 4 Kings and Isaiah are generally the fullest, each supplying what the other omits from the story (the rising on the third day is omitted from Isaiah, and 4 Kings gives Hezekiah a choice in the matter of the direction, forward or back, of the shadow on the Dial of Ahaz). In general, the order of events is rather garbled, owing to the state of the texts, but commentators were able to weave some whole cloth from the divergent accounts, admitting enough variation for the joy of arguing, say, over the cause of the king's illness or the nature of the impostume which laid him low.[21]

His place in Christian tradition is an interesting, if less than major one: It consists of the usual commentaries, a rather sketchy iconographic shorthand, and the use of Isaiah 38.15 ("Recogitabo tibi omnes annos meos et in amaritudine animae meae") by the authors of autobiographical and confessional literature. Augustine, for example, paraphrases it ("et requiescebam in amaritudine"; "in amaritudine recogitationes meae") in his *Confessions*;[22] Jacopo Passavanti (1300–1357), the renowned trecento Dominican preacher, employs it in his *Lo specchio de' peccati*;[23] Bernardino of Siena (1380–1444) takes the text for a sermon on confession;[24] and Giovanni da Ravenna, disciple of Petrarch, inaugurates his *Vita* with it (upgrading the *recognito* to the more classical *excutio*).[25] Eventually, the phrase made its way

---

[19] Thomas Walkington, *The Optick Glass of Humours* (London, 1607), sig. C1v.

[20] The corresponding references in the King James Version are 2 Chronicles 32.24–26; 2 Kings 20.1–21; Isaiah 38.1–22. Ecclesiasticus is included only in the Apocrypha.

[21] See, for example, the *Glossa Ordinaria*, *Pat. Lat.* 113, cols. 624–25.

[22] *Confessions*, 4.6; 2.1.

[23] *Lo specchio di vera penitenza* (Florence, 1925), p. 102.

[24] *Le prediche volgari inedite* (Siena, 1935), p. 469.

[25] Remigio Sabbadini, *Giovanni da Ravenna* (Como, 1924), p. 127; Balliol College,

into the Tridentine canon *de poenitentia*: "Si quis dixerit, eam contritionem, quae paratur per discussionem, collectionem et detestationem peccatorum, qua quis recogitat annos suos in amaritudine animae suae. . . ."[26] Perhaps the major use of the figure of the king is by Dante in the *Commedia*, where Hezekiah is found (in *Paradiso* 2:49–54) in the eyebrow of the eagle with Trajan, "a type," says A. C. Charity, "of Dante, in that [Hezekiah] descended into hell and yet was ultimately saved."[27]

The iconographical tradition of Hezekiah gains substantial interest as it changes from a general visual shorthand to a complex involvement with the developing technology of time measurement. Earliest representations—like the possibly pre-ninth-century fresco in Santa Maria Novella[28]—depict the king, crowned and robed, reclining in the standard head-on-hand attitude of the sick patient, contemplative, or dreamer. He is flanked by the figure of Isaiah and by the Dial of Ahaz, the depiction of which ranges from a series of steps, to a sundial, to (by the late medieval period) a twenty-four-hour astrological clock. (A variation of this iconography occurs when Hezekiah takes his place with the ancestors of Christ, as in the glass of the southwest transcept of Canterbury Cathedral, where he is depicted enthroned, bearing a sundial in his right hand.)[29] The Moralized Bible of the early thirteenth century, however, presents the conservative portrayal of the king—in Isaiah 38 he reclines as usual beside the prophet, who points to the sun as it prepares to ascend the Dial of Ahaz (here a staircase with fifteen steps; fig. 1). In 4 Kings 20, a new technological wrinkle, the king is depicted as reclining in an architectural setting (perhaps the royal palace) accompanied by Christ, who indicates the sun rising beside a waterclock which pours its contents into a vessel beneath (fig. 2).

MS. 288, fol. 1r. I am indebted to Prof. T. C. Price Zimmerman for making a photocopy of this manuscript available to me.

[26] *Conc. Trid.*, t. 7, actorum pars. 4, vol. 1, p. 358, sess. 14.

[27] *Events and Their Afterlife: The Dialectics of Christian Typology in the Bible and in Dante* (Cambridge: Cambridge University Press, 1966), pp. 23ff. Charity also demonstrates the similarity of Dante's "nel mezzo del cammin" to Isaias 38:10: "In dimidio dierum meorum vadam ad portas inferi." Robert Hollander, *Allegory in Dante's Commedia* (Princeton: Princeton University Press, 1969), p. 299, agrees with Charity, pointing to the heading of chapter 38 in the Vulgate—"Canticum Ezechiae a morte liberati"—"words," he says, "that apply with rigorous exactitude to Dante's situation in Inferno I and II."

[28] W. de Gruneisen, *Sainte-Marie-Antique* (Rome: M. Bretschneider, 1911), p. 162.

[29] Bernard Rackham, *The Ancient Glass of Canterbury* (London: Lund, Humphries, 1949), pl. 8c, p. 39. A similar presentation may be found in the depiction of St. Matthew and the ancestors of Christ in Dublin, Trinty College, MS. 53, fol. 7v, where Hezekiah holds the sundial to his breast.

As this iconographical tradition develops, it accrues astrological significance. The mid-fourteenth-century *Concordantiae caritatis* of Ulrich of Lilienfeld, for example, illustrates Isaiah 38.8 with a personified sun and astrological signs,[30] and much later, the sixteenth-century fresco entitled "Astrologia" in the Escorial Library presents the recumbant Hezekiah, complete with sundial, as a reigning figure of that art.

The connection of the Hezekiah iconography with time, particularly astrological time, became conflated with the iconography of Temperance, an intriguing association. The earliest representations of that virtue are twofold, largely because of its association with measure and proportion. In the first case, Temperance is portrayed—for example, on the portal of Or San Michele in Florence—as holding up to view the compasses usually associated with the creating divinity (fig. 3). In the second instance—for example, in a fresco in the Palazzo Pubblico in Siena—she holds what appears to be a cup but is actually, as Lynn White has proved, the earliest representation yet to be found of a sandglass (fig. 4).[31] Now neither of these illustrations of the virtue seems to fall much within the Macrobian tradition of the bridled Temperance, with her eyeglasses and windmill, who gave birth to such homely daughters as Verecundia, Abstinentia, Castitas, Honestas, Moderatio, Parcitas, Sobrietas, and Pudicita (fig. 5).[32] White has also pointed out that the winecup of Temperance, into which she pours diluting water from a jug, is an iconographical device dating at least from the eleventh century. Its likeness to the sandglass of the Palazzo Pubblico fresco makes the transition from cup to timepiece understandable.

Less comprehensible, however, is the Temperance who, in two early fifteenth-century manuscripts of Christine de Pisan's *Othea*, bears neither compasses nor sandglass, but rather fiddles with the works of a large mechanical clock (fig. 6). White, who demonstrates that such iconography became the standard in illustrated editions of *Othea*, has shown the availability to Christine, daughter of the Parisian court astrologer Thomas de Pisan, of the illustration from the Moralized Bible, which depicts Christ regulating a weight-driven water-

[30] Antonius Rampigollis, *Aureum bibliae repertorium* (Koln; ca. 1478).

[31] "The Iconography of Temperentia and the Virtuousness of Technology," in *Action and Conviction in Early Modern Europe*, ed. Theodore Rabb and Jerrald Seigel (Princeton: Princeton University Press, 1969), especially p. 210, figs. 7 and 8.

[32] Rosamund Tuve, "Notes on the Virtues and Vices. Part I: Two Fifteenth-Century Lines of Dependence on the Thirteenth and Twelfth Centuries," *Journal of the Warburg and Courtauld Institute* 26, nos. 3 and 4 (1963): 264–303, on the multiplicity of streams of tradition in the iconography of Temperance.

clock that pours into a basin (fig. 2).[33] He attributes her approval of the Temperance/clock device (the manuscripts were illustrated under her supervision) to an amalgamation of the Christ/Temperance/Wisdom iconographies, in part due to the influence of Henry Suso's *Horologium Sapientia*. Christine herself illuminates her choice of iconography:

> Temperance should be called a goddess likewise. And because our human body is made up of many parts and should be regulated by reason, it may be represented as a clock in which there are several wheels and measures. And just as the clock is worth nothing unless it is regulated, so our human body does not work unless Temperance orders it.[34]

Temperance here is a virtue which draws on some meanings of the word *temper* nearly forgotten to us: to modify; to mix; mingle, blend together; to keep, conduct, or manage in just measure; to regulate; to control; to tune, adjust the pitch of (a musical instrument); to bring into harmony, attune; to regulate (as a clock).[35] And the word might just as easily be applied to the humoral balance of man's body, as did Sir Thomas Elyot in the sixteenth century, speaking of the effect of eating meats: "they be in the highest degree of heate and drithe, aboue the iuste temperaunce of mannes bodie."[36]

Hezekiah's association with this Temperance tradition seems rather tenuous at first, although his ever-present sundial is a well-accepted, if rather primitive, device for measurement of time. Indeed, an illustration of the French *Horloge de sapience*, which White has shown to stem from the Temperance/clock iconographical tradition, shows Sapientia-Temperance conversing with its author, Blessed Henry Suso, to whose *Exemplar* I have alluded in chapter 2, amid what White calls "the finest exhibition of time-measuring devices surviving from the fifteenth century," including the "first indisputable evidence of a spring-driven *fusee*-regulated mechanism" (fig. 7).[37] Hanging from the table in this illustration is a quadrant—a portable sundial used both for temporal and spatial measurement—and atop the table is a small sundial. The gear-driven twenty-four-hour clock that the lady adjusts is astronomical in function; hanging below its face is an instrument for calculating planetary time.

[33] White, "The Iconography of Temperentia," 210.

[34] *L'Epitre d'Othea*, Br. Mus., Harley MS 4331; Bibl. Nat., ms fr 606; quoted in Tuve, "Notes on the Virtues," 289.

[35] *The Compact Edition of the Oxford English Dictionary* (Oxford: Oxford University Press, 1971) 2:3254–55.

[36] *The Castle of Helthe* (1541), sig. D1r.

[37] White, "The Iconography of Temperentia," 212.

A similar illustration replaces Sapientia-Temperance with Solomon himself, who does not regulate but repairs the mechanism of the clock, his tools scattered at his feet (fig. 8). White maintains, I think correctly, that the clock has become "the icon of the Christian life."[38] We, with our twelve-hour digital clocks, may find it difficult to comprehend that the invention of the mechanical escapement in the fourteenth century did not immediately affect humanity's ability to measure time in a linear fashion, moment by moment. Rather, in a vertical fashion, it demonstrated visually the order of the cosmos. Pre-Copernican time was far more "cosmic" than our own; some of the earliest Christian sundials, for example, bear the image of the creating God, compasses poised.

For us, to feel the effects of time is to feel merely the biological signs of growth and decay as they are measured against the forward movement of the clock and the calendar. For pre-Copernicans, those signs were not only measured but to a large extent determined by that movement. In the tenth chapter of the second book of *De generatione et corruptione*, Aristotle ascribed all change on earth to the diurnal motion of the heavens: The perfect motion of the fixed stars from east to west constituted the principle of permanence and growth; the motion of the planets in their irregularly paced annual courses from west to east athwart the movement of the fixed stars constituted the principle of earthly change. The tradition had been preserved by Macrobius and Chalcidius and popularized by Albumasar. The doctrine held medical science in an iron grip for centuries, for the harmonious fabric of the heavens—what Boethius called *musica mundana*—was repeated in the human body whose harmonies, *musica humana*, had to be brought into accord, however imperfectly, with the larger cosmos. The body was an instrument to be tempered.[39] Thus, the astronomical clock and the musical instrument were apt symbols. One reflected the silent, the other the aural, harmonies of the universe.

The very act of tuning his instrument gave man a place in the cosmic orchestra (although the chairs varied). The elements within the body, delicately reflecting the structure of their external environment, in turn affected, in their balance or lack of it, the workings of the human soul. Thus, the connection of moral well-being with the

---

[38] Ibid., 213.

[39] The theory had popular credence in Donne's day. For example, according to *The Optick Glasse of Humours*, "the body is like an instrument of musicke, that, when it hath a discordancie in the strings, is wont to jarre, and yeelds no melodious & sweete harmony, to goe vnto the Philosophers owne simile," sig. E3v.

workings of the universe was a very real one, a familiarly held theory
to which John Swan's *Speculum Mundi*, a late-seventeenth-century en-
cyclopedia, attests:

> For God, besides delight and contemplation that we enjoy by this great
> work abundantly, hath created all things for use; and hath made all
> plants, Seas, Rivers, Mettals, Jewels, Stones, and all things else that are
> dug forth of the earth, or adorn the superficies of it, and distinguish it
> with variety, and very bodies of men, and the humours in them, to the
> Stars: So that from the Stars they feel some motion, impulsion, and ef-
> fects. But the Spirit of God onely doth move and agitate the minds of
> men that are loose and free from all mortall concretion, and were in-
> spired by Him, and they have no commerce or society with the Stars,
> unless perhaps sometimes they are drawn aside to corporeal delights by
> consent and conspiring with the body (when reason is against it) whose
> ministery and help every mans mind and Soul is forced to make use of.[40]

Few created men were "loose and free from all mortall concretion,"
hence the extraordinary importance for the physician of the system
of astrological *electiones* that determined the propitious moment for
undertaking medical treatments.[41]

[40] (Cambridge, 1635), sig. Mm4r. Sylvester, in his version of DuBartas's Fourth Day,
goes to some length to demonstrate the effect of the heavens on the human body, part
of which reads:

> I'le ouerpasse how Sea doth Ebb and Flow,
> As th'Horned Queene doth eyther shrinke or grow:
> And that the more she *Fills* her forked Round,
> The more the Marrow doth in bones abound,
> The bloud in Veines, the sap in Plants, the moisture
> And lushious meat, in Creuish, Crab, and Oyster:
> That, Oake and Elme, and Firr and Alder, cut
> Before the *Crescent* haue her Cornets shut,
> Are neuer lasting for the Builders turne,
> In Ship or House, but rather fit to burne,
> And also, that the Sicke, while shee is filling,
> Feele sharper Fitts through all their members thrilling.
> So that, this Lampe alone approues, what powers
> Heau'ns Tapers haue euen on these soules of ours:
> Temp'ring, or troubling (as they be inclinde)
> Our minde and humours, humours, and our minde:
> Through Sympathie, which, while this Flesh we carie,
> Our Soules and Bodies doth together Marrie.

>   (Sigs. L1v–L2R)

[41] Theodore Wedel, *The Mediaeval Attitude Toward Astrology, Particularly in England*
(New Haven: Yale University Press, 1920), p. 55. Paracelsan medicine, for example,

Bringing the human body into a state of "temper" depended on a knowledge of one's own humoral physiology, a considerable reverence for the forces of nature, and often the skill of a physician who possessed not only that necessary reverence but a good deal of knowledge about how those natural forces operated. Although the balancing of the humors could be achieved by the individual, as the multiplicity of self-help manuals of the day attests, it was a delicate affair. Says *The Opticke Glasse of Humours*:

> Wee must know that all naturall bodies haue their composition of the mixture of the elements, fire, ayre, water, earth: now they are either equally poisd according to their weight, in their combination, as just so much of one element, as there is of another, throughout the quaternion or whole number: as imagin a duplum, or quadruplum or decuplum of earth, so much iust of fire, as much of ayre, and the like quantity of water and no more, then they bee truly ballanced one againe another in our vnderstanding: when there are as many degrees of heat as of cold, of drinesse, as of moisture, or they bee distemperate or vnequall, yet measured by worthinesse, whereone hath dominion over another.[42]

The reference to the quaternion was not a casual one, for in numerological thought, the soul was number and the tetrad "an ideogram for the creation *in toto*."[43]

Thus, the balancing of the humors brought the individual into harmony with the universe, and temperance became much more than a mere restriction of appetite. Again, the contemporary medical manuals give evidence of the correspondence:

> And as in Musical Instruments there is perceived a certaine accord of tunes and a sweet agreeable harmony in striking the strings, that no unpleasant discord or bungling jarre dislike the curious eare of the hearer: so likewise in a temperate habit of the body there is an apt and convenient mixture and temperature of the Elements and qualities, insomuch

---

despite its revolutionary use of chemicals, was bound to the correspondence between the macrocosm and microcosm. According to Paracelsus, the disease possessed its own "cosmos," which confronted the individual microcosm. In the individual, each aspect of the anatomy had a "planetary cycle" whose motion in correspondence with the macrocosm kept the body in health. Interruption of these cycles by the anti-cosmos resulted in sickness.

[42] Sig. F1v.

[43] S. K. Heninger, *Touches of Sweet Harmony: Pythagorean Cosmology and Renaissance Poetics* (San Marino: The Huntington Library, 1974), p. 79. Almost the *locus classicus* of this concept was the Third Canto of *De harmonia mundi* by Francesco Giorgio, whom Donne had called (referring specifically to the *Harmonia*) "that transcending Wit" (*Essayes in Divinity*, pp. 10–11).

that no one quality can by it selfe be shewed, but a constant, absolute, and perfect composition, and mingling of the qualities and Elements all together.[44]

Translated into physiological language, the preservation of equable temperature in terms of heat and cold merited first attention, for the body's natural heat could be overcome, especially in the northern latitudes, by cold, which was "no manner of utility or helpe, touching the conservation and maintenance of the body,"[45] especially in matters of digestion and blood strength. Hence, "it is good and expedient by all wayes and meanes to stir up and cherish naturall heat with nourishment and exercise convenient, that it be not through cold, oppressed and trodden down."[46] Cold was the great enemy, and thus, of all the temperaments, the sanguine was to be preferred "because it coms nearest vnto the principles & groundworks of our life, which stands in an attempered heat & moisture."[47]

The melancholic, on the other hand, was "the most vnfortunate and greatest enemy to life, because his qualities being cold and drie do most of all disagree from the lively qualities, heat and moisture: either with his coldnes extinguishing naturall inherent heate, or with his drines sucking vp the natiue moisture."[48] The unfortunate melancholic—by virtue of innate disposition or old age, which is cold and dry—must pay special attention to diet and "ayre." Indeed, he who through intemperance increased the cold and dry humors inordinately might be brought to premature old age and death: "For death is nothing else, but the extinction of nature, that is to say, of the naturall heat, and naturall humour. In which two things life consisteth, to which extinction and end many are brought sooner then they should be, either through want and defect of nourishment, or through untemperate life."[49] John Swan advised that the truly temperate man maintain the mechanism of his body through moderation—of meat, drink, exercise, and "Venus"—and also through regulation, for he was obliged to consider the action of the heavens upon his physiology, hourly, daily, by the lunar month, and in the progression of the planetary years:

[44] Levinus Lemnius, *The Touchstone of Complexions*, trans. Thomas Newton (London, 1576), sig. H1v.
[45] Ibid., sig. O1v.
[46] Ibid.
[47] Walkington, sig. H4r.
[48] Ibid., sig. I2v.
[49] Lemnius, *The Touchstone*, sig. G2v.

The Stars, the Elements, the Sea, the times of the year, and the Skies of Heaven have their motions, and changes, and move by a certain order. The humours are under the like law, for they have certain motions, and effects and periods in mans body, that every humour keeps its turn according to the variety of the four parts of the year, and exercises its faculties and forces on mans body, so it is that the blood in the spring is in force, and breeds feaver and diseases of its own nature; so choler every other day in summer with cholerick burning causeth a tertian Flegm, corrupting in the winter quarter, causeth a quotidian intermitting, and melancholly when Autumn comes, makes a quartan.[50]

The human body, and indirectly the soul, was affected by the movement of the heavens, by the rising and falling of the tides, and the seasonal changes of the green earth, even by the fluctuating hours of the days.[51] The system had a certain native practicality: Prominence among the bodies of the heavens was given to the sun, especially in its seasonal activity, for with its heat and drying qualities, it regulated the temperature of the earth itself, and thus of men. According to Swan, in the winter, when the sun is low in the sky, the sky is "clowdy and dark, and the aire grosse and thick." Men's humors, directly affected by the condition of the air they breathe, then are "sad and sour countenanced, and sleepy." But come spring, the air changes, the humors warm, and "men are cheerfull, and lightsome, and very much given to mirth."[52]

The sanguine temperament was associated with spring, the choleric (hot and dry) with summer, the melancholic with autumn, and the phlegmatic (cold and moist) with winter (fig. 9). But the analogy of the tetrad to the human body extended even further: Just as the four humors reflected the intrinsic structure of the cosmos and reflected the seasonal activity of the sun, so man's life span itself mirrored the seasons:

---

[50] John Swan, *Speculum Mundi* (London, 1635), sig. L4r.

[51] The twenty-four hours of the day could be perceived both as equal units of time when, as sidereal hours, they were clocked against the movement of the stars, and as temporal hours when they were clocked against the seasonal movement of the sun. In the latter case, the hours of the day and night equaled those of the sidereal day and night only at the equinoxes, at all other times lengthening and shortening with the seasons. That this disparity was used as a literary device has been perceived by A. Kent Hieatt, *Short Time's Endless Monument: The Symbolism of the Numbers in Edmund Spenser's "Epithalamion"* (New York: Columbia University Press, 1960), pp. 32ff, and by Alastair Fowler, *Spenser and the Numbers of Time* (London: Routledge and Kegan Paul, 1970), pp. 215ff.

[52] Swan, sig. V3v.

[F]or as the Year changeth by the twelve months, into twelve divers man-
ners, so doth Man change himself twelve times in his Life, by twelve
Ages, and every six-times six maketh thirty six, and then man is at the
best, also the highest; and twelve times six maketh threescore and twelve,
and that is the Age of Man. Thus you may count and reckon for every
Month six Years, or else it may be understood by the four Quarters and
Seasons of the Year, so Man is divided into four Parts, as to Youth,
Strength, Wisdom and Age.[53]

The year could be reckoned either from January or, as the Year of
Grace, from March 25 and the sign of Aries. The author opted for
the former, but the same scheme was normally applied so that, after
fifty years, man entered the sign of Capricorn, often called the Gate
of Death. From there, he passed through the water signs, Aquarius
and Pisces, the Houses of the Dead. This was an ancient tradition,
which found its *locus classicus* in Macrobius's commentary on *The
Dream of Scipio*:

> The Milky Way girdles the zodiac, its great circles meeting it obliquely so
> that it crosses at the two tropical signs, Capricorn and Cancer. Natural
> philosophers named these the "portals of the sun" because the solstices
> lie athwart the sun's path on either side, checking farther progress and
> causing it to retrace its course across the belt beyond whose limits it
> never trespasses. Souls are believed to pass through these portals when
> going from the sky to the earth and returning from the earth to the
> sky.[54]

Donne approached the gate of Capricorn both literally and figuratively in that winter of 1623, for he was fifty-one. Like Hezekiah, he
stood at the gates of the grave. Like Hezekiah, he returned.

Hezekiah's place in the temperance tradition hinges on his association with the winter solstice. For him, literally, the sun had stood still
and had even moved in the retrograde motion characteristic of its
activity in the Tropic of Capricorn. But for exegetes this posed a
problem, and since the iconography of the Hezekiah story is so
deeply embedded in Donne's *Devotions*, it is one which must be explored, at least in its major outlines.

The controversy swirled around the relation of the empirical to the
marvelous in Scripture. For example, was the retrogression of the

---

[53] Godfridus, *The Knowledge of Things Unknown: Showing the Effects of the Planets and
other Astronomicall Constellations* (London, 1707), sig. D1r. It is notable that the author
of this astrological manual sets aside December 13 as a "Perillous Day" (sig. B3v), and
identifies the numbers 21, 22, and 23 with the sign of Capricorn (sig. D3v).

[54] *Commentary on the Dream of Scipio*, ed. W. H. Stahl (New York: Columbia University Press, 1952), p. 134.

sun a miracle or merely the solsticial "dancing" of the sun? If actually marvelous, was the sign a private one, or was it intended for all the world? And how did the extended day of Hezekiah square with the account in Joshua 10.13–14, where "the sun stood still in the midst of heaven, and hasted not to go down the space of one day"? There were those who held that the event was explained by the solstitial movement, but they were roundly condemned for their inability to stretch their faith from the merely empirical to the miraculous: "when therefore they [the commentators] denigrate troubling statements that the sun changed its course, they overturn all careful work that [the commentators], reconciling Scripture with philosophy, should join together the truth of philosophy with faith in the miraculous."[55] More hotly debated was the private or public nature of the miracle, for even the *Glossa Ordinaria* interpreted the later visit to Hezekiah by the Babylonians (Vulgate 4 Kings 20.14) as a type of the Epiphany, they having seen the sign in the heavens as did the later Magi.[56]

The weight of opinion held that the movement of the sun was indeed a sign to all nations, both of the righteousness of Hezekiah, who had restored the worship of the true God in his temple, and of the eventual coming of the Messiah.[57] But from this point on, opinion fragmented, for the problem of the exact length of Hezekiah's day was one with delicate theological implications. At the siege of Gabaon, the very heavens had stood still, and the author of the book of Joshua explicitly comments on the uniqueness of the event: "There was not before nor after so long a day" (Joshua 10.14). The controversy lay with the Dial of Ahaz, for if the sun indeed moved ten degrees, whether backward or forward, and even if it began its motion at noon (as nearly all the commentaries agreed), if each degree on the dial equalled one hour, the shadow would inevitably move into the hours of darkness, when it would of course no longer be a shadow.

The resultant scrambling to interpret the passage led to a great deal of talk about sundials, their construction, and the matter of Palestinian latitudes and day lengths. The practice of counting each of the degrees on the dial as an hour resulted in a thirty-two-hour day for Hezekiah, since the sun in its backward and forward movement

[55] *Commentaria in Isaiam Prophetam*, vol. 19 of *Commentaria in Scripturum Sacrum* (Paris, 1866), p. 474: "cum enim illi animadvertissent incommoda sententiae eorum qui solem ipsum vertisse cursum aiunt, omnem verterunt curam ut Scripturam cum philosophia conciliantes, veritatem historiae simul cum miraculi fide componerent."

[56] *Pat. Lat.* 113, col. 625.

[57] Lapide, *Commentaria in Isaiam*, pp. 475–76.

had added twenty hours to the normal twelve-hour day. The theory did not gain numerous advocates, however, not only because of its inherent logical problem but also because it seemed obviously to controvert the Joshua story (although among various explanations, at least one pointed out that since the event had occurred at the winter solstice as commonly accepted, even a thirty-two-hour day could not equal the day of Joshua since the solar hours were naturally shorter). The main bodies of opinion divided on the twenty-seven and twenty-two-hour days.

The first school held that the sun had actually slowed in its returning course, taking five hours to retrogress the ten degrees and ten hours to retrace its route to the meridian. The resulting twenty-seven-hour day mirrored, in its addition of fifteen hours to the twelve-hour day, the addition of fifteen years to the life of Hezekiah.[58]

But another body of opinion held out for the twenty-two-hour day, explained by counting each degree of the Dial of Ahaz as a *half* hour, so that the day was augmented not by twenty but by ten hours.[59] To this end Nicholas of Lyra in his commentary on Isaiah 38, and Paul of Burgos in his postillum to Lyra, spent much time and graphic effort (fig. 10) in demonstrating that such a dial, coupled with the presence of the noon meridian and the event of the winter solstice, explained the miracle and neatly avoided any contradiction of Scripture.[60]

Hezekiah's place in the temperance tradition, connected as it is with the winter solstice and his miraculous extension of life, now begins to make sense. I am inclined to think that this rich tradition was in Donne's mind as he suffered through the days of early winter in 1623. Certainly his physicians were exerting every effort at tempering the wayward humors of his body. They administered a broad spectrum of cooling nostrums, including diaphoretic antimony, oil of scorpions, mercury enemas, and the usual cupping, blistering, and venesection (probably of the hemorrhoids).[61] Moreover, Donne himself was rich in the knowledge of physic.[62] His writing gives ample

[58] Ibid.

[59] Ibid.

[60] Nicholaus de Lyra, *Postilla Super Totam Bibliam*, 4 vols. (Strasburg, 1492; facsm. ed. Minerva GmbH., Frankfurt/Main.: *Unveränderter Nachdruk*, 1971, sigs. Uubr-Uubv.

[61] Kate Frost, "Prescription and Devotion: The Reverend Doctor Donne and the Learned Doctor Mayerne—Two Seventeenth Century Records of Epidemic Typhus Fever", *Medical History* 22 (1978): 408–16.

[62] Walton attests to this in "An Elegie upon Dr Donne": "Spake he all *Languages*?

evidence of it, and we know that his stepfather, John Syminges, president of the Royal College of Physicians, practised from his house in Trinity Lane and held meetings of the college there during Donne's adolescence.[63]

Donne's own association with the winter solstice is most interesting. Richard Hughes has pointed out that he seems to have accepted December 13 as his *natalia* (and the feast of the Nativity of St. John, six months preceding, on midsummer's day, as his name day).[64] His announcement of his decision to take orders is dated December 13, as is his will. Moreover, his sermons of that date reflect concerns relevant to the *Devotions*. In a sermon preached before the queen on December 14, 1617—four months almost to the day, after the death of his wife—he repeated substantially and at greater length the matter of her commemorative sonnet, especially his turning, through her, to the love of God: "for, for the love of other creatures, it is but a secondary love; if we love God, we love them for his sake; if we love our selves, we love them for our sakes."[65] This sermon is replete with allusions to the passing of the short, dark solstitial day, as is a sermon of December 12, 1626, preached at the funeral of Sir William Cokayne, where Donne brings together types of the Resurrection; the metaphor, so prominent in the *Devotions*, of the body and the library; the structure of the arch; and the hexaemeral day of death as the day of the Resurrection.[66] Both of these sermons share with the *Devotions* a thematic concentration on bodily health, youth and old age, the nature of prayer, and the movement and position of the sun. The latter, of course, he had already exploited wittily, and negatively, in "A Nocturnall upon S. Lucies Day."

Given Donne's interest in the winter solstice, the events surrounding the writing of the *Devotions* can only be called extraordinary. He fell ill at the end of November 1623; probably he was bedridden by November 30, the First Sunday in Advent, when the liturgy began its great four-movement symphony of darkness and light. The Collect

---

knew he all *Lawes*? / The grounds and use of Physicke; but because / 'Twas mercenary wav'd it?" (Grierson, *Poems*, 2.577.45–47). Donne's medical expertise has received the attention of D. C. Allen, "John Donne's Knowledge of Renaissance Medicine," *Journal of English and Germanic Philology (JEGP)* 42 (1943): 322–42.

[63] I am indebted to T. H. Robb-Smith, retired, formerly of the Royal College of Physicians, for drawing this information to my attention.

[64] *The Progress of the Soul: the Interior Career of John Donne* (New York: Morrow, 1968), p. 214.

[65] *Sermons*, 1:242.

[66] *Sermons*, 7:257ff.

for that Sunday, when Donne lay in the throes of fever surrounded by the music from St. Gregory's and the noise of its bells, combined this imagery with that of the Second Coming:

> Almighty God, give us grace that we may cast away the works of darkness, and put upon us the armour of light, now in the time of this mortal life (in the which thy Son Jesus Christ came to visit us in great humility;) that in the last day, when he shall come again in glorious majesty to judge both the quick and the dead, we may rise to the life immortal through him. . . .[67]

The Epistle was drawn from Romans 13: "This also, we know the season, how that it is time, that we should now awake out of sleep; for now is our salvation nearer, than when we believed. The night is passed, the day is come nigh: let us therefore cast away the deeds of darkness, and let us put on the armour of light. . . ." And the Gospel related the triumphal entry of Christ into Jerusalem. A week later, when Donne had just passed the near-fatal crisis of his illness, the Gospel for the second Sunday in Advent (which began the solstitial week in 1623) repeated the great apocalyptic passage from Luke 21: "There shall be signs in the sun and in the moon, and in the stars." The daily lessons for December 12 and 13 are drawn from Isaiah 37–40, so that the entire story of Hezekiah is played out at the time of the winter solstice. Donne, privately following or at the very least aware of the liturgy from his sickbed, was conversant with the rich tradition connecting the biblical king to the Advent liturgy and perceived both parallels and applications of that tradition to his own case.

The formal expression of that case shows strong evidence that Donne did indeed apply the Hezekiah episode to himself in the *Devotions*, both typologically and structurally. I have already examined at some length the connection between the traditions of temperance and the sun's seasonal tempering of the human body. However, the twenty-two *"Stationes"* take on a real significance as waystations in Donne's moral journey when one recalls that, including their title, they comprise 359 hexameter feet, the first of a series of "short time" units which will characterize the formal construction of the whole work. The number reflects the diurnal movement of the sun, for while the celestial sphere completes its 360-degree revolution around the earth in somewhat less than twenty-four hours, the sun during

---

[67] *Liturgies and Occasional Forms of Prayer Set Forth in the Reign of Queen Elizabeth* (Cambridge: Cambridge University Press, 1847), pp. 78ff.

the same time completes only 359 degrees of its circle, and thus, daily "hanging back" by 1/360 of a circle, takes 365 days to complete its annual course, forming the solar year.

The 359-degree movement of the sun in a sidereal day creates both the length of day and night and the points at which the seasons change, and on it, as A. Kent Hieatt has demonstrated, "the year, with all the variety of its seasons and the whole rhythm of organic life, depends, for without it the sun could not forge along its rising and falling eastward path of the zodiac."[68] Hieatt has explored exhaustively the use of this data in Spenser's "Epithalamion," where the 359th long line of the poem occurs at the end of the twenty-third stanza, one of a series of formal devices which illustrate "short time," or, as Hieatt puts it, "time caught short," in an attempt to express symbolically the inability of either poet or his song to express the joy and perfection of his wedding day. "The poem," he says, "is a monument to short time in the sense that it celebrates the cyclical measures of time created by the sun—the day, the year, and their divisions; and in the sense that it celebrates short time over against Eternity."[69] This play on numbers to denote imperfection or excess (for example, Augustine gives 11 as the number of sin, since it exceeds by one the number of the Decalogue) was a common one, and it is not surprising to find Donne adapting the device for his own purpose. Thus the 359 feet of the "*Stationes*" are spread over the twenty-three Devotions, an arrangement echoing that of Spenser's "Epithalamion." Moreover, when one considers the implications of both numbers with the imminent finality of the day, the connection with the eschatalogical tradition of Hezekiah is exciting, for we await with Donne the advent of the *sol iustitiae*.

Spenser had made much of his wedding day's falling at the summer solstice, when the day was sixteen and one-quarter hours in length and the night seven and three-quarters. At the winter solstice, the situation was exactly reversed. In midwinter, when the earth is at the diametrically opposite side of its orbit around the sun, the North Pole points 23 degrees away from the solar direction. Thus the sunrise and sunset appear in the southeast and southwest in midwinter London, a phenomenon that, given the location of St. Paul's deanery, Donne was probably able to witness during his residence there.[70]

To the naked eye, the sun had reached the southernmost point in

[68] Hieatt, *Short Time's Endless Monument*, p. 4.

[69] Ibid., p. 47.

[70] The deanery, according to Stow, was located to the southwest of the cathedral.

its journey along the zodiac, slowing as it neared the apogee in the apparent retrograde motion characteristic of the solstice. (Chapman exploits this movement in "The Amorous Zodiack," where he mimes the daily retardations in the sun's course around the ecliptic, and in its twenty-third stanza draws attention to the solsticial hesitation of the sun by himself deviating from his structure of zodiacal progression.)[71] The turning back of the sun at Capricorn was connected to a symbolism that may go far to explain some heretofore puzzling passages in early spiritual autobiographies, especially in Dante. The cosmographer Sacrobosco defines the sign thus: "Capricorn is truly said to be a tenfold sign because, even as the Goat raises himself from pasturing, so also the Sun from the southern hemisphere ascends toward our hemisphere. Whence this Tropical sign is called, so to speak, a turning point. For this is the winter solstice, and from thence the sun is turned to us."[72]

The emphasis on conversion in connection with the number 23 is reinforced by the literature of spiritual autobiography. The twenty-third chapter of the *Vita Nuova* and the same chapter of Suso's *Exemplar* both present intense conversion experiences, as does the twenty-third of Petrarch's *Rime*. My estimation is that 23 is a traditional number of conversion—a turning back along the ecliptic course of one's life. Hence it plays an important structural part in the early spiritual autobiography, concerned as the tradition is with the turning of the individual from earthly to heavenly love.

But the evidence to bear this out, at least in the commentaries, is rather sparse. Rather, most commentators associate the number with justice and especially with the final justice of the Second Coming,[73] although, given the association of that event with the winter solstice, the connection with conversion is logical. The scholarship available on the subject is tantalizing but not always directly enlightening. Most points to the use of the number in conjunction with the zodiac or with the vertical structure of the universe, or with the consummation of the salvation of man and the final defeat of Satan.[74] There are other

[71] Fowler, *Triumphal Forms*, pp. 140–46.

[72] *De Anii ratione* (Antwerp, 1551), sig. Biir. Capricornus; Decimum vero signam Capricornus dicitur, quia quaemadmodum Caper in pascendo erigit se, ita Sol tunc ab inferiori hemisphaerio versus nostrum hemisphaerium ascendit. Unde hoc signum Tropicum, *quasi conversuum dicitur*. Est enim tunc solstitium hyemale, & de caetero sol conuertitur ad nos. (Emphasis added.)

[73] A representative case can be found in Pietro Bongo, *Mysticae Numerorum Significationes Liber* (Bergamo, 1484) 2:sig. E3r.

[74] See, for example, Fowler, *Triumphal Forms*, pp. 136, 145, 168, 192n, and Gunnar

possibilities, of course. One should consider both the pentad and hexad, for example, for the number 23 may be considered as either the sum or the product of its integers. Interpreted as $2 + 3$, the resulting pentad could be a marriage number or a number of justice. As 2×3, the number, as the hexad, was a marriage number as well, the particular property of the Lucretian Venus, whom Martianus Capella terms, "the Mother of Harmony."[75] Or, as I have already mentioned, the number can be considered as one of a procession of prime integers, indicating its indivisibility. Finally, it has been associated with the coming of age and with the twenty-third Psalm.[76]

There is, however, a more directly applicable interpretation of the number, for it is associated in the commentaries with 1 Corinthians 10.8: "Neither let us commit fornication, even as some of them committed fornication, and there fell in one day twenty-three thousand." The verse refers to the twenty-fifth and fourteenth chapters of Numbers, where the children of Israel are struck down for fornicating with Canaanite temple prostitutes and murmuring against the land apportioned to them, a situation which Donne recalls in Devotion 5. Peter Bongo's *De Numeris Mysticis*, one of the few extant Renaissance treatises on numbers, represents 23 as a number signifying God's judgment on sinners coupled with his eventual mercy:

> The number twenty-three is prime and irregular, unpropitious according to Pythagorus. Now, twenty-three lacks the foundation of the perfection of numbers, likewise, five, eleven, and seventeen. Wherefore, according to Moses, it signifies Divine vengeance over sinners. The twenty-three-thousand constructing the calf were ordered slain down to the last one by Moses. Paul, writing to the Corinthians, refers to the twenty-three-thousand dying on a day who defiled themselves with the Madianite women. It is possible by this number to represent the fullness of human salvation, and especially that perfection of righteous belief which is maintained by good works. Sound faith is denoted by three, which mystically contains the belief in the Divine Trinity. The perfection of works is manifested in the observation of God's commands, which is expressed by the regular number twenty in its doubly repeating the

Qvarnström, *The Enchanted Palace: Some Structural Aspects of "Paradise Lost"* (Stockholm: Alqvist & Wiksell, 1967), pp. 81, 84, 104, 105–7, 118–19nn, 156–57, 176.

[75] Fowler, *Spenser and the Numbers of Time*, especially ch. 5 and 6; *De nuptiis Philologiae et Mercurii*, ed. Adolfvs Dick (Stutgart: B. G. Teubnari, 1969) sect. 737, p. 372: "totius harmoniae toni sunt sex . . . unde Venus Harmoniae mater perhibetur."

[76] Lander, *"Per Fretum Febris,"* p. 193.

decalog, transmitted by the Old Testament and fully revealed in the New. And three joined to twenty completes this apt number.[77]

Bongo's definition has recently brought some light to Milton studies, for it seems to illuminate the central structure of *Paradise Lost*, the segment of Book 6 that Gunnar Qvarnström, in his most recent study of the poem's structure and time frame, calls "the Enthronement."[78]

Qvarnström noticed early that the arrangement of the central book depended on the number 23:

> Milton has placed God's almighty "chariot," that formidable "thunder" (clumsily aped by Satan's artillery), in the midst of his epic. The textual process around the mid-point is the following: Christ speaks to God in *23* anti-satanic lines; forth rushes the chariot; *Christ, divine love, ascends*, at his right hand, *Victorie* herself; the troops summoned anew, Christ speaks to them—once more in 23 anti-satanic lines. Then Satan is driven to hell, conquered, as God says just before, already in the moment where Christ "Ascended, at his right hand Victorie": because *in that moment love becomes almighty.*[79]

In his early study, Qvarnström pointed to the twenty-third canto of the *Paradiso*, which contains the joint ascensions of Christ and the Virgin, and questioned whether the number might have connection with patterns of ascent. There is sufficient evidence—the positioning of Dante's arch of life in the twenty-third chapter of the *Convivio*, the exploitation of the number in the Ascension portal of Chartres, the twenty-three-degree *scala* of Gansfort—for us to question whether the number may be associated with the movement of the sun through the zodiac as it progresses along the great arch from Cancer to Capricorn and back again, or whether it refers to the ascending structure of the universe: hell, earth (with its four elements), the nine planetary spheres, and the nine choirs of angels, through all of which Christ progressed after the harrowing of hell.

As Qvarnström points out in *The Enchanted Palace*, his later and much fuller investigation of the poem, immediately after his triumph, Christ pursues Satan to hell as the bringer of divine justice,

---

[77] Bongo, *Mysticae Numerorum*, sig. E3r, here has to fudge the Old Testament text to argue that the number killed for adoring idols and for fornicating with the daughters of Moab was not 24,000 but 23,000. The number 23 thus takes on overtones both of vengeance upon sinners and of fornication. Qvarnström demonstrates its use in the later sense in *Paradise Lost*, p. 106n.

[78] Qvarnström, *The Enchanted Palace*, p. 56.

[79] *Poetry and Numbers*, Scripta minora Regiae Societatis Humanorum Literrarum Londensis, 1964–1965 (Lund, 1966), pp. 93–94.

and returns to Paradise, rising through the structure of the created universe, a device which bears out Qvarnström's perception of the number as signifying the ascension of divine love. More than this, however, he sees a direct reflection of Bongo's association of the number with justice and mercy in the rhetorical structure of the central book where Christ's twenty-three-line "justice" speeches are themselves flanked by twenty-three-line "justice" speeches are themselves flanked by twenty-three-line "mercy" speeches, which may be represented as the following diagram shows:

lines	23	23	101	23	23
theme	Mercy	Justice		Justice	Mercy
source	III, 144	VI, 723		VI, 800	XI, 22

For Qvarnström, this structure, at the exact center of the epic, indicates "Christ's role as executor of the divine will, divine *Justice* preparing the way for divine Grace by effecting the complete overthrow of Satan."[80]

But Milton has built into this structure an emphasis which, I think, Qvarnström has somewhat neglected. There are, as he points out, actually five, not four, twenty-three-line speeches in *Paradise Lost*, the fourth (at 10.914) that of Eve wherein she sets forth the concepts of mercy and justice as they apply to the human condition. That there are five such speeches and, as is evident, that the narrative episode which they frame itself consists of fifty-five lines, draws attention to the association of the number 23 with the pentad in its function as a number of justice, an association which bears directly, as we shall see, on the *Devotions*. The principal association of the pentad was (no surprise) with justice. Hear Sir Thomas Browne's famous disquisition on the number:

> To enlarge this contemplation unto all the mysteries and secrets, accommodable unto this number, were inexcusable Pythagorisme, yet [we] cannot omit the ancient conceit of five surnamed the number of justice; as justly dividing between the digits, and hanging in the centre of Nine, described by square numeration, which angularly divided will make the decussated number. . . . And might be the originall of that common game among us, wherein the fifth place is Soveraigne, and carrieth the chief intention. The Ancients wisely instructing youth, even in their recreations unto virtue, that is, early to drive at the middle point and Cen-

tral Seat of justice. . . . The Ancients have named it the Divisive Number, justly dividing the Entities of the world.[81]

That 5 is the number of justice and the number of sovereignty has been amply documented elsewhere,[82] and much of the documentation ends with the query whether the number is used to indicate mathematical relationships between the cycles of the universe and those in the life of man—a question, again, that will have strong bearing on Donne's plan for the *Devotions*, for we are once more concerned with the movement of the planets, the course of the sun, and the change of the seasons in their effect on the "Humane Condition."

Interestingly, some of this association with the periodical cycles of the cosmos is reflected in *Paradise Lost*, for the person of the Son of God has been inextricably linked, thematically and structurally, with the entity of the sun. In a parody of the later enthronement episode, as Qvarnström points out, Satan arrives at the sun at or about noon of the twenty-third day of action in the poem. The description of the sun explicitly calls up the image of Aaron's breastplate, an image which is to dominate the description of the ascendant Christ of Book 6. There, "Hee in Celestial Panoplie all armd / Of radiant Urim, work divinely wrought, / Ascended; at his right hand Victorie / Sate Eagle-wingd. . . ." (4.760–73). It is the center of the epic, "dominated by the image of the Sun in its highest dignity, that is by that Sun which is the Messiah, the personification of Christian Victory."[83] For the *urim*, as Qvarnström demonstrates, was alchemically significant of the philosopher's stone, "believed capable of giving to the Sun its supernatural light and power, but also divine Grace or Christ, and hence also the Sun itself."[84] Moreover, the creation of the sun on the seventeenth day of the epic action (the first day of Creation), the center of actual time in the poem, provides an exact parallel to the enthronement scene, which is located at the numerical center of the epic. The sun is created on the first day of creation, the Son on the first day of epic action. The identification, even were we not familiar with the habitual punning of Renaissance poets—Donne certainly not the least—its complete.

But there is a further implication of the number 23 that is exploited in *Paradise Lost*: its association with the Last Judgment. Paul

[81] *The Garden of Cyrus*, ed. J. Carter (Cambridge: Cambridge University Press, 1958), p. 108.

[82] Fowler, *Triumphal Forms*, pp. 26, 69, 70, 113, 178ff.; *Spenser and the Numbers of Time*, pp. 34ff, 204.

[83] Qvarnström, *The Enchanted Palace*, p. 64.

[84] Ibid., p. 63.

had directed attention to the slaughter of the twenty-three thousand as "a type . . . written for our correction, upon whom the final age of the world has come" (1 Cor. 10.11), and the number took on, as a result, the symbolic connotation of judgment and the "eleventh hour" of the world before the Second Coming and the eighth day of eternity. (Henry Suso, for example, in the conversion episode which occupies the twenty-third chapter of the *Exemplar*, replies to the angel who, appearing to him after he is struck down with a malady like Hezekiah's, urges him to join the angelic singing: "The only kind of music I feel like accompanying is a funeral dirge, because my life's clock points to half past eleven.")[85] When one recalls the astronomical clock of Figure 7, it is clear that he does not refer to his life's zenith. Qvarnström points to the God-Christ dialogue of Book 3 (containing the first of the Son's twenty-three-line speeches), where the Father ends the discussion—and the twenty-third day of epic action—with a seventy-line speech. Says Bongo: "Now, as for the period of seventy years, the course of the whole human life is figured, when, the time completed, at last we are called home by our King Jesus Christ." Now Augustine explicated this rich mystery fully in his commentary on Psalm 125. Seventy years signifies all time, that is brought full circle in seven days. However, when all time will have passed, then we return to our homeland, in the same manner as the people after seventy years returned from the Babylonian captivity. Babylon certainly is this world. Likewise he expressed the same idea in the commentary on Psalm 147.[86]

And indeed Augustine had, in *De doctrina christiana*, explicitly associated the number 70 with the ages of the world, one-thousand-year episodes that formed a cosmic week of seven days, mirroring the Days of Creation. The association of this number (of which the *Devotions'* sixty-nine prose units fall one short) with the number 23, expanded by thousands as well, calls to mind the eschatological prophecy of Daniel about the twenty-three hundred days. Here the mind

[85] *The Exemplar: Life and Writings of Blessed Henry Suso, O.P.*, ed. Nicholas Heller, trans. Sister M. Ann Edward, O.P. (Dubuque: The Priory Press, 1962) 1:64. James Bobrick, "The Structure of Giles Fletcher's *Christs Victorie and Triumph*," *Texas Studies in Literature and Language* 21 (Winter 1979): 544, attributes the eschatological significance of the number to its symbolizing the joint operation of justice and mercy: "This is exactly the operation that Christ in the center of heaven will perform on the day of Judgment, sorting the saved from the damned, dividing those on his right hand from those on his left—an operation prefigured by his earlier victories in heaven and in the desert. By reason of its double significance, 23 itself had overtones of the 'eleventh hour' of the world, before the eighth day of eternity in which God would come to judge men."

[86] Bongo, *Mysticae Numerorum*, sig. E3r.

boggles, for the amount of ink expended on this one verse of scripture (much of it crackpot and all of it intriguing) far exceeds my powers of scholarship. Nevertheless, the association was made, even in
Donne's time, for, as I have already mentioned, the year 1623 was
regarded by some as a fulfillment of those days and hence as a likely
one for the Second Coming.[87]

Gunnar Qvarnström's scholarship has enriched greatly our knowledge of *Paradise Lost*, but for the purposes of this study, it has even
more greatly enhanced our ability to understand Donne's use of numerological structure in his *Devotions*, and in particular his use of the
number 23 as the most obvious formal division of his book. The number, in summary, had associations with the ecliptic, the sun, the solstice, and conversion; with sovereignty, the central place, and the vertical structure of the universe; with justice and mercy; with the
Advent liturgy, the ages of the world, and the ages of man; with the
Second Coming; and with the immanence of the Last Judgment.

But what has *Paradise Lost* to do with Donne, other than the fact
that Milton was then a schoolboy at St. Paul's and might well have
heard Donne sermonizing? It was December, the solstice, a year of
possible doom; Donne was aging—entering Capricorn on his own zodiac—and sick nearly to death. Most of all, it was Advent. Christmas
and the rising of the *sol iustitiae* were not far away. Hence the *Legenda
Aurea*:

> The whole of this fugitive life is divided into four periods: the period of
> erring, or wandering from the way; the period of renewal, or returning
> to the right way; the period of reconciliation; and the period of pilgrim-
> age. . . . The period of renewal began with Moses and lasted until the
> birth of Christ, for this is the period during which man was renewed and
> called back to the faith through the mouth of the Prophets. It is repre-
> sented, in the Church, by the past of the year which runs from Advent
> until Christmas. Isaias is then recited, because he revealed this divine
> renewal most clearly. . . . These four divisions of the spiritual life are
> comparable to the four parts of the natural year, so that the first is the
> Winter, the second the Spring, the third the summer, and the fourth the
> Autumn, and the meaning of this comparison is apparent. Another com-
> parison may be made with the times of the day, so that the first spiritual
> period is like the Night, the next like the Morning, the third like Noon,
> and the fourth like Evening.
>
> Advent is celebrated for four weeks, to signify that this coming of the
> Lord is fourfold; namely, that He came to us in the flesh, that He came

---

[87] See ch. 3, note 49.

with mercy into our hearts, that He came to us in death, and that he will come to us again at the Last Judgment. The last week is seldom finished, to denote that the glory of the elect, as they will receive it at the last advent of the Lord, will have no end.[88]

Jacobus goes on to associate the state of man and the world with sickness, quoting Augustine ("The great physician came at a moment when the entire world lay like a great invalid") and Bernard ("We suffer from a three-fold sickness: we are easily misled, weak in action, and feeble in resistance. Consequently the coming of the Lord is necessary, first to enlighten our blindness, second to succour our weakness, and third to shield our fragility"). Hence, just before the Nativity, the church sings the seven *O Sapientia* antiphons that recall the variety of human ills and the timeliness of the divine remedy. Thus, when the sun has reached the southernmost point of its annual journey; when the year and, in terms of the understood physiology of the time, the human mechanism are at their lowest point; the Church calls for Christ the physician and announces his coming as "our Teacher, our Redeemer, our Liberator, our Guide, our Enlightener, and our Saviour."[89] As the sun turns to begin its annual climb, bringing light and life and health, so must we turn, convert, to meet the rising *sol iustitiae*.[90]

Donne had used the number 23 structurally before in the twenty-three-line "Resurrection, Imperfect," where he made explicit the analogy between the sun and the *sol iustitiae*. The poem is replete with alchemical imagery, and, given the connection of the sun and the number 23 with the philosopher's stone, its numerological structure may bear some investigation in connection with that art. It ends with the Latin tag: "*Desunt caetera*," which may refer to an unfinished textual state. But the status of 23 as an "incomplete" number, as well as Donne's use of it as the primary structural number of the *Devotions*, throws this into doubt. Rather, the incompleteness of the poem draws attention to the Resurrection in process, for Christ, having "enlightned hell" and "walk'd on earth," is "now Hasting to Heaven," a course which would take him through the twenty-three levels of the created universe.

[88] *The Golden Legend of Jacobus de Voragine*, trans. Granger Ryan and Helmut Ripperger (New York: Longmans, Green, 1941), pp. 1–3.

[89] Ibid., p. 3.

[90] The winter solstice had long been associated with the Nativity. According to Thomas Hill's *The Schoole of Skil* (London, 1599): "The winter solstice in the first beginning of *Olympias* hapned the first day of January, or there about. In the year of Christs byrth it hapned the 15. day of December (in which day at the hour of 12. in the night, they affirme our sauiour to bee born)" (sigs. H8v–I1r).

The *Devotions* thus has some structural precedent in Donne's verse. It remains to be seen, however, whether Donne gives any indication, either in the text of the *Devotions* or in external evidence, of the foreconceit which underlies the work. Several possibilities present themselves. It may be remembered that in the letters accompanying complimentary copies of the *Devotions*, Donne declared his desire that the work be accepted as a type of patience, in the face either of adversity or of death. Moreover, one letter draws attention to possible rhetorical or spatial structure: "To make myself believe that our life is something, I use my thoughts to compare it to something. . . . It is like a sentence, . . .and such a difference as is in styles is in our lives, contracted parentheses, sentences within sentences, so there are lives within our lives."[91] This of course points directly to the "Epistle Dedicatory," where Donne states: "I *Haue had three* Births," relating them to his natural birth, his entrance to the ministry, and to his recovery "*from this* Sicknes."

This autobiographical intent becomes even clearer in the text of the *Devotions*, where Donne frequently draws attention to the composition of the work as an exercise of retrospective analysis, rather like the extended and detailed examination of one's life made before a general confession. He prays to God to enable him "to looke forward to mine end, and to looke backward to, to the considerations of thy mercies afforded mee from the beginning."[92] "I was whipped by thy *rod*, before I came to *consultation*, to consider my state. . . . I haue gone so farre, as to the *consideration* of my selfe."[93] His most direct statement of this self-examination occupies most of the fourteenth Devotion, in particular dominating the Expostulation:

> My *God*, my *God*, wouldest thou cal thy selfe the *Ancient of dayes*, if we were not to call our selues to an account for our *dayes*? . . . When thou reprehendest the *Galatians* by thy Message to them, *That they obserued dayes, and Moneths, and Tymes, and Yeares*, when thou sendest by the same *Messenger*, to forbid the Colossians *all Criticall dayes, Indicatory dayes, Let no Man Iudge you, in respect of a holy day, or of a new Moone, or of a Saboth*, doest thou take away all Consideration, all destinction of *dayes*? Though thou remoue them from being of the *Essence* of our *Saluation*, thou leauest them for *assistances*, and for the *Exaltation* of our *Deuotion*, to fix our selues, at certaine *periodicall, & stationary times*, vpon the consider-

[91] Edmond Gosse, *The Life and Letters of John Donne, Dean of St. Paul's* (London, 1899) 2:208.
[92] Prayer 1, sigs. B8v–B9r.
[93] Expostulation 20, sigs. Z11r–Z11v.

ation of those things, which thou hast done for vs, and the *Crisis*, the *triall*, the *iudgment*, how those things haue wrought vpon vs, and disposed vs to a spirituall recouery, and conualesence. . . . So far then our daies must be *criticall* to vs, as that by consideration of them, we may make a *Iudgment* of our *spiritual health*.

He goes on in this fourteenth Expostulation to equate spiritual with bodily health, "for if the *Soule* be leane, the marrow of the *Body* is but water; if the *Soule* wither, the verdure and the good estate of the *body*, is but an illusion." He then identifies seven "critical" days in his sickness and recovery: first, the day of "thy *visitation* by sicknes"; second, the day of "the *Crisis* and examination of my *Conscience*"; third, "my day of preparing, & fitting my selfe for a more especial *receiuing* of thy *Sonne*, in his institution of the *Sacrament*"; fourth, "the day of my *dissolution & transmigration* from hence"; fifth, "the day of my *Resurrection*"; sixth, "*The day of Iudgement*"; and seventh, "my *Euerlasting Saboth* in *thy rest*."

This week of days—less the seventh—is reflected in the progression of the *Devotions* from the initial onset of Donne's illness in the first Meditation to his acceptance of a final judgment on the state of his soul in the last Prayer, forming, in groups of four thematically related Devotions, an incomplete week (chart 1). Devotions 1–4 present those extended disquisitions on the diseased microcosm for which the work is so famous. Donne is stricken, his senses fail, he takes to his bed, he sends for the physician. "And as I feele thy hand vpon all my body," he says in the third Prayer, "so I may find it vpon all my bedde, and see all my *corrections*, and all my *refreshings* to flow from one, and the same, and all, from thy hand." And in the second Expostulation: "*My God, my God*, why comes thine anger so fast vpon me? Why dost thou melt me, scatter me, powre me like water upon the ground so instantly?"

The second group, Devotions 5 through 8, present the coming of the physician, his fear, his need for consultation, and the arrival of the king's physician. Fear and loneliness and the anguished questioning of God's purpose prevail, as in the fifth Expostulation: "Must I bee concluded with that, that . . . solitarines, & dereliction, and abandoning of others, disposes vs best for *God*, who accompanies vs most alone?"

In the third group, Devotions 9 through 12, as the disease continues its progress, the physicians diagnose and prescribe cordials and the application of the carcasses of doves to his feet. These four de-

CHART 1.

The Hexaemeral Week

DAY 1:   "thy *visitation* by sicknes"
1.   The first alteration, The first grudging of the sicknesse.
2.   The strength, and the function of the Senses, & other faculties change and faile.
3.   The Patient takes his bed.
4.   The Phisician is sent for.

DAY 2:   the *Crisis* and examination of my *Conscience*"
5.   The Phisician comes.
6.   The Phisician is afraid.
7.   The Phisician desires to haue others ioyned with him.
8.   The King sends his owne Phisician.

DAY 3:   "my day of preparing, & fitting my selfe for a more especial *receiuing* of thy *Sonne*, in his institution of the *Sacrament*"
9.   Vpon their Consultation, they prescribe.
10.   They find the Disease to steale on insensibly, and endeauour to meet with it so.
11.   They use Cordials, to keep the venim and Malignitie of the disease from the Heart.
12.   They apply Pidgeons, to draw the vapors from the Head.

DAY 4:   "my *dissolution & transmigration* from hence"
13.   The Sicknes declares the infection and malignity thereof by spots.
14.   The Phisicians obserue these accidents to haue fallen vpon the criticall dayes.
15.   I sleepe not day nor night.
16.   From the bels of the church adioyning, I am daily remembred of my buriall in the funeralls of others.

DAY 5:   "the day of my *Resurrection*"
17.   Now, this Bell tolling softly for another, saies to me, Thou must die.
18.   The bell rings out, and tells me in him, that I am dead.
19.   At last, the Physitians, after a long and stormie voyage, see land; They haue so good signes of the concoction of the disease, as that they may safely proceed to purge.
20.   Vpon these Indications of digested matter, they proceed to purge.

DAY 6:   "*The day of Iudgement*"
21.   God prospers their practise, and he, by them, calls Lazarus out of his tombe, mee out of my bed.
22.   The Physitians consider the root and occasion, the embers, and coales, and fuell of the disease, and seeke to purge or correct that.
23.   They warne mee of the fearefull danger of relapsing.

votions present lengthy examinations of the state of Donne's soul and an anatomizing of his sins, wherein, as in Prayer 10, he catalogs sins

> of *Thought, Word,* and *Deed,* of sinns of *Omission,* and of *Action,* of sins against *thee,* against my *neighbour,* and against *my self,* of sinns *vnrepented,* and sinnes *relapsed* into after *Repentance,* of sinnes of *Ignorance,* and sinnes against the testimonie of my *Conscience,* of sinnes against thy Commaundements, sinnes against thy *Sonnes Prayer,* and sinns against our owne *Creed,* of sins against the laws of that *Church,* & sinnes against the laws of that *State,* in which thou hast giuen mee my station

in preparation for "*Peace,* and *Reconciliation* to thee, by the *ordinances* of thy *Church.*"

The fourth group, which sets the day of "my *dissolution & transmigration,*" brings Donne literally to the door of death, for in Devotions 13 through 16, the rash of typhus appears, and he enters the critical days of his fever, his sleeplessness accompanied by the sound of the passing bell. He closes the episode in Prayer 16: "*Let this praier* therfore, O my *God,* be as my *last gaspe,* my *expiring,* my *dying* in *thee*; That if this bee the houre of my *transmigration,* I may die the *death* of a *sinner,* drowned in my *sinnes,* in the *bloud* of thy *Sonne.*"

The fifth group—the critical, "decretory" day—comprises Devotions 17 through 20 with the three digressive meditations on the passing bell and the decision of his doctors to purge. "I am *dead,* in an *irremediable,* in an *irrecouerable* state for bodily health. . . . *I am dead,* I was *borne dead,*" he says in the eighteenth Prayer. In the nineteenth: "establish me in a *Sabbath,* and *rest* in *thee.*" And in the twentieth Expostulation: "This proceeding to *action* therefore, is a returning to thee, and a *working* vpon *my selfe* by thy *Physicke,* by thy *purgatiue physicke,* a free and entire euacuation of my *soule* by *confession.*"

The final group, Devotions 21 through 23 is, of course, incomplete, for Donne's judgment has not been final—that would come in 1631. In this group, he rises from bed, is given a final purge, and is warned of the danger of relapse. He concludes in the twenty-third Prayer with a final statement on the state of his soul: "thy *Correction* hath brought mee to such a *participation of thy selfe* . . . as that I durst deliuer my selfe ouer to thee this *Minute,* If this *Minute* thou wouldst accept my *dissolution.*" In the closing words of the *Devotions,* Donne acknowledges "those *sinnes,* which I haue *truely repented,* and thou hast *fully pardoned.*" The *Devotions* ends with the sixth day, for the judgment that Donne has received has been that of the Sacrament of Penance. The Sabbath was yet to come, and I doubt not that he is enjoying it now.

Donne's hexaemeral week is the first of several temporal structures underlying the *Devotions* that reflect "certaine *periodicall*, and *stationary times*" (*stationes* if you will) in his illness, both physical and, as he saw it, spiritual. Yet although its episodic form takes the reader through the stations of Donne's experience, there are few explicit temporal references in the text of the *Devotions*, other than the prefatory verse tags that document the progress of the disease. References to time, even those that may reflect the situation or moment of writing, are indirect, ambiguous, or metaphorical. When, for example, the bell tolls for his dying neighbor, Donne focuses our attention on the action and its application, and only perfunctorily on the time or day of passing. The final Meditation speaks of the ringing of curfew, but whether it is the literal evening curfew of London or a metaphorical one is not clear. He mentions events of personal history—his calling to the ministry by the king the most notable—but they are nowhere placed in actual time.

Rather, Donne has created an extended sense of present time; he rarely employs the past tense, and the *Devotions* both begins and ends on the needle's point of a present moment: "this minute I was well, and am ill, this minute" and "I durst deliuer my selfe ouer to thee this *Minute*, If this *Minute* thou wouldst accept my *dissolution*."[94] As a result of this overwhelming sense of metaphorical present time, any references to actual time attract attention. And these are only four in number. In the first and the last Devotions, just mentioned, we began and ended in instants ("this minute") of unidentified time that barely qualify as real time. In addition, the sixteenth Expostulation, part of the three-unit digression on bells, informs us that Donne's neighbor has died, his passing bell rung "yesterday." The seventeenth Meditation provides perhaps the only identifiable reference to actual time when it refers to "this *Bell*, that tolls for our *euening prayer*."

It is interesting that this explicit reference to the coming of night occurs at the beginning of the seventeenth Devotion, paralleled by the movement of actual time, for in December, the sun set at the end of the sixteenth hour—at 4:48 P.M. to be exact. The December sun rose at 8:12 A.M.[95] But, backtracking to the Devotion which corresponds to that hour—the eighth—we may at first be disappointed, for there is no specific time reference which would set up an easy correspondence between the Devotions and actual time. Rather, in the Meditation of Devotion 8, Donne alludes to "*an eternity* of threescore

---

[94] Meditation 1, sig. B1r; Prayer 23, sig. EE2v.
[95] *Liturgical Services, Liturgies and Occasional Forms of Prayer Set Forth in the Reign of Queen Elizabeth* (Cambridge, 1847), p. 455.

& ten yeares," in the Expostulation, to his calling to the ministry by James I as "the twy-light, of that day, wherein thou, thorow him, hast shind vpon mee before," and in the Prayer, to that uncertain moment when "[*thy Son*] comes in the *clouds*." But the reference to twilight is an interesting one, for the term could refer either to the dim light after sunset or to that just before dawn. Moreover, it is the twilight "of that day, wherein thou . . . hast shind vpon mee before," and "the *Eccho* of that voyce, whereby thou . . . hast spoke to mee before."[96] That is, the twilight may be understood as a reflection, or shadow, of James's action. In sending his own physician he offers Donne physical health, just as years before he had offered spiritual health through a calling to the ministry. In this sense, it appears that Donne has given us indeed a "shadowed" day, for the structure of the *Devotions*, in the correspondence of its units to the hours of actual time, imitates the structure of the solstitial day (see chart 2).

Between the dawn of the eighth and the dusk of the seventeenth Devotions, Donne makes no reference, either literal or metaphorical, to the length or time of day, except in the negative. The thirteenth Meditation, for example, coming just after the midpoint of the work (and hence after the noon of Donne's metaphorical day), denies the possibility of dividing time by equal units and also denies that in the apportioning of hours of misery and happiness, man lives "vnder a perpetuall *Equinoctial, night*, and *day* equall." In the fifteenth Meditation he discounts the telling of time altogether: "if I be entring now into *Eternitie*, where there shall bee no more distinction of *houres*, why is it al my businesse now *to tell Clocks*?"

If Donne's metaphorical day, as he maintains, is not equinoctial, then the hours of day and night are uneven, and it may be possible to determine whether their pattern echoes that of the solstice. Yet turning to the time references in the text results in some confusion, for in Meditation 17, at the very moment of evening prayer, although it accords with the time of sunset at the winter solstice, we find three references to dawn and the sun's rising: first, to matins ("*they should ring first that rose earliest*"); next, to his own morning rising ("wee would bee glad to make it ours, by rising early"); and finally, the sun's rising ("Who casts not vp his *Eie* to the *Sunne* when it rises?"). Moreover, in the Expostulation of this seventeenth Devotion, Donne asks: "My *God*, my *God*, Is this one of thy waies, of *drawing light out of darknesse*? . . ." And in the corresponding Prayer: "let the power of thy *Spirit* recompence the shortnesse of time."

These references to dawn rather than to sunset, to drawing light

---

[96] Expostulation 8, sig. I12v.

Chart 2. The Solstitial Day

Hexaemeral Week	Devotion	Hour	
	1	1:00 A.M.	
Day 1	2	2:00	
	3	3:00	
	4	4:00	
	5	5:00	
Day 2	6	6:00	
	7	7:00	
	8	8:00	◄——— December sunrise 8:12 A.M. Expostulation: "The twy-light of that day"
	9	9:00	
Day 3	10	10:00	
	11	11:00	
	12	12:00 M.	
	13	1:00 P.M.	
Day 4	14	2:00	
	15	3:00	
	16	4:00	◄——— December sunset: 4:48 P.M. Meditation: "this *Bell*, that tolls for our *euening prayer*"
	17	5:00	
Day 5	18	6:00	
	19	7:00	
	20	8:00	
	21	9:00	
Day 6	22	10:00	
	23	11:00	

from darkness, to short time, though they may derive some clarity from their reflection in the Hezekiah story with its extended hours of light, are puzzling until we take into consideration Donne's very last time reference in the *Devotions*:

> when wee must *pant* through all those *fierie heats*, and *saile* thorow all those *ouer-flowing sweats*, when wee must *watch* through all those long *nights*, and *mourne* through all those long *daies*, (*daies* and *nights*, so *long*, as that *Nature* her selfe shall seeme to be *peruerted*, and to haue put the *longest day*, and the *longest night*, which should bee *six moneths* asunder, into one *naturall, vnnaturall day*).[97]

[97] Meditation 23, sigs. CC12r–CC12v.

Now the "natural" day in December 1623 was some 7.75 hours long, the night 16.25 hours. At the summer solstice, St. John's Eve, the time was reversed, so that the sun rose at 4:48 A.M. and set at 8:13 P.M.[98] Like Hezekiah, Donne waits through an "unnatural" day of some thirty-two hours (a period, one remembers, accepted by some glossators for Hezekiah's extended day), for the sun which sets at 4:48 P.M. in Capricorn rises at 4:48 A.M. in Cancer. Thus the *Devotions* contains both a "natural" day—patterned after the eight hours of light and sixteen of darkness characteristic of the winter solstice—and an "unnatural" day—the sixteen-hour progression of the winter night already embedded in the structure of the work (see chart 2) upon which is imposed the sixteen-hour pattern of light characteristic of the summer solstice. The resulting pattern, a double day and night, is subtly reinforced by his double mention of "long nights" followed by the puns on "mourne" (see chart 3).

But we must correct ourselves. Just as the day of Hezekiah does not equal that of Joshua, so that of Donne does not equal that of the biblical king, for Donne's is an incomplete day of twenty-three hours, and as the foregoing chart demonstrates, even his "unnaturall" combinations of the two solstices results in a thirty-one-hour period, one short of Hezekiah's. Like Henry Suso, Donne saw the hands of his life's clock approaching the final hour. His posture is one literally forced on him by his illness, one to be applied to his spiritual condition: "But why rather being entring into that presence, where I shall wake continually and neuer sleepe more, doe I not interpret my continuall waking here, to bee a *parasceue*, and a *preparation* to that?"[99] The number 23, with its association with final judgment and the eternal Sabbath, coupled with the typological and structural use of the story of Hezekiah, gives the *Devotions* a decidedly apocalyptic flavor, not in the least diminished by its continued references to James I, the literal and figurative steward who awaits his master's coming in all readiness.

The *Devotions* mirrors the rising of the *sol iustitiae* even in its center, the great discourse on ascent and descent of vapor found in the twelfth Expostulation, where Donne concludes: "So that though our last act be an ascending to glory, (we shall ascend to the place of *Angels*) yet our first act is to goe the way of thy *Sonn, descending*." This as the sun begins its descent through Donne's metaphorical day, which itself reflects the solstitial pattern of the sun.

The association of the number 23 with the eve of the eternal Sab-

98 *Liturgical Services*, p. 455.
99 Meditation 15, sigs. R6v–R7v.

Chart 3. The Naturall, Unnaturall Day

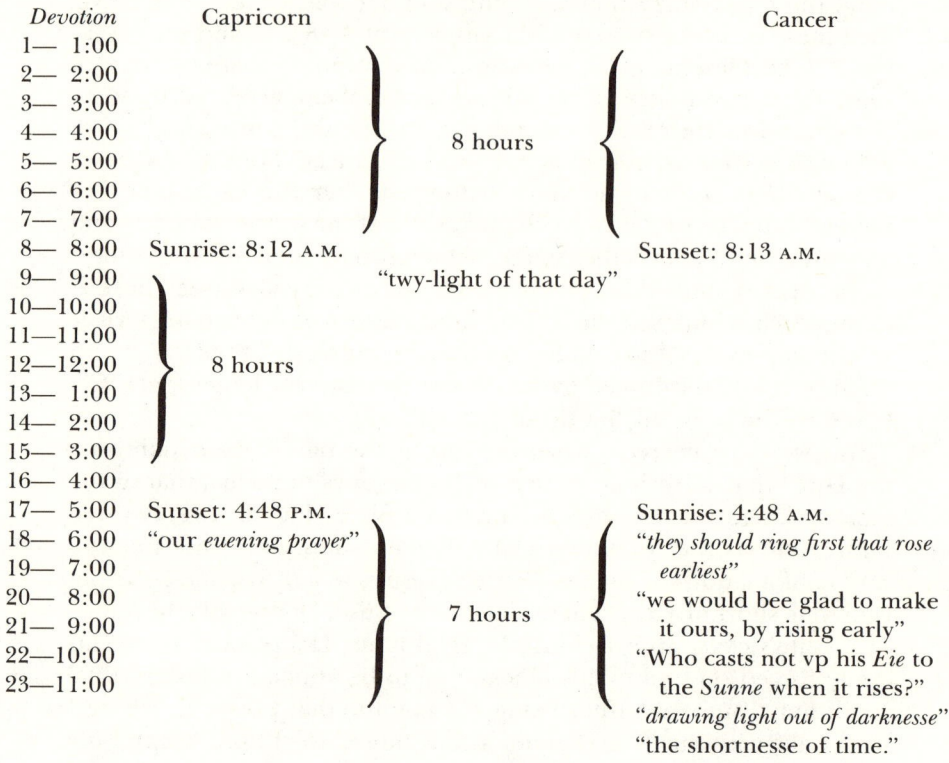

Devotion	Capricorn		Cancer
1— 1:00			

Devotion
1— 1:00
2— 2:00
3— 3:00
4— 4:00
5— 5:00   Capricorn   Cancer
6— 6:00
7— 7:00   8 hours
8— 8:00   Sunrise: 8:12 A.M.   Sunset: 8:13 A.M.
9— 9:00   "twy-light of that day"
10—10:00
11—11:00
12—12:00   8 hours
13— 1:00
14— 2:00
15— 3:00
16— 4:00
17— 5:00   Sunset: 4:48 P.M.   Sunrise: 4:48 A.M.
18— 6:00   "our *euening prayer*"   "*they should ring first that rose earliest*"
19— 7:00
20— 8:00   7 hours   "we would bee glad to make it ours, by rising early"
21— 9:00
22—10:00   "Who casts not vp his *Eie* to the *Sunne* when it rises?"
23—11:00   "*drawing light out of darknesse*"
                                                   "the shortnesse of time."

bath has ancient roots. As early as Philo, the number was held to reflect the sixth day of Creation:

> When, then Moses says, "He finished His work on the sixth day," we must understand him to be adducing not a quantity of days, but a perfect number, namely six, since it is the first that is equal to the sum of its own fractions 1/2, 1/3, and 1/6, and is produced by the multiplication of two unequal factors 2 × 3: and see, the numbers 2 and 3 have left behind the incorporeal character that belongs to 1, 2 being an image of matter, and being parted and divided as that is, while 3 is the image of a solid body, for the solid is patient of a threefold division.[100]

Augustine had echoed Philo almost verbatim, adding: "Sound Scripture commends the perfection of this number to us, especially in this,

[100] Philo Judaeus, *The Allegorial Interpretation of Genesis II, III*, tr. F. H. Colson and G. H. Whitaker (London: Loeb Classical Library, 1929), 1:249.

that God completed his work in 6 days, and made man to the image of God on the sixth day. And the Son of God came in the sixth age of the human race and was made the Son of Man in order to re-form us to the image of God." The sixth age is now in progress, "up to the hidden end of time." It is the age of Advent in which "we have received the sacrament of the renewal in this last age, in order that we may be also renewed in every part at the end of time by the resurrection of the flesh, and thus may be healed from every weakness, not only of the soul but also of the body."[101] The seventh day will be the rest of the saints—now spiritually in progress. Both the sixth and the seventh days will end in the Last Judgment and the eternal regeneration of the eighth day. The last age, then, will renew not only the soul but the body. Augustine, however, went one step further, allying the six ages of the world with the ages of man when in his second discourse on Psalm 29, he condensed the six ages into three "days," concluding that each of us must reenact the sequence of human history during our three "days" of life—youth, maturity, and old age.[102] By the seventeenth century, the conflation of the ages of the world with the ages of man was a commonplace of hexaemeral literature.[103]

The application of the *septmaine* to the life of man gave rise to multiple schemes, that of Palingenius's *Zodiacus vitae* exercising the most influence, for its distribution of contents according to the twelve signs of the zodiac gave rise to numerous imitations, not the least of which was Spenser's *Shepheardes Calendar*. But this was not the only popular scheme. Thomas Tusser, for example, in his *Five Hundred Points of Husbandrie*, offered the reader a choice. The first, "mans age deuided into twelve seauens," presented in awkward couplets the span of life from birth to age eighty-four, divided by seven-year "prentiships."[104] The second scheme was at the same time more simple and more imaginative: "The Ape, the Lion, the Foxe, the Asse, / Thus sets foorth man, as in a glasse." The doggerel is unimproved, however:

[101] *Pat. Lat.* 42, cols. 885ff.

[102] *Pat. Lat.* 36, col. 224.

[103] See Frank E. Robbins, *The Hexaemeral Literature: A Study of the Greek and Latin Commentaries on Genesis* (Chicago: University of Chicago Press, 1912); Raymond Klibansky, *The Continuity of the Platonic Tradition during the Middle Ages* (London: The Warburg Institute, 1950).

[104] In chapter 49: "Mans ague deuided here he haue / By prentiships, from birth to his graue" (pp. 138–39 in the 1573 edition). I have been unable to draw substantially on three excellent studies which have appeared recently: J. A. Burrow, *The Ages of Man: A Study in Medieval Writing and Thought* (Oxford: Clarendon Press, 1986); Mary Dove, *The Perfect Age of Man's Life* (Cambridge: Cambridge University Press, 1986); Elizabeth Sears, *The Ages of Man: Medieval Interpretations of the Life Cycle* (Princeton: Princeton University Press, 1986).

> Like Apes we be toiling, til twentie and one,
> Then hastie as Lions till fortie be gone:
> Then wilie as Foxes, till threescore and three,
> Then after for Asses accounted we bee.[105]

Tusser was drawing here the fourfold division of man's life, a scheme nearly as ancient as that of the hexaemeral ages, which had found its definitive statement in Dante's *Convivio*. Dante's division is outwardly simple: The four ages—adolescence, manhood, age, and decrepitude—are likened to the four horses who draw the chariot of the sun through the course of the year. Entering through "the gate of good life" (analogous to Cancer, Macrobius's "gate of the gods"), they proceed through the seasons with their corresponding humors. Moreover, the ages are compared not only to the course of the year but to the passage of the sun through the day, marked by the four rung canonical hours.[106]

The analogy was still pertinent in Donne's day, although the custom of ringing the hours had suffered considerably by his time. The *Picta poesis* of Barthelemy Aneau (1556), for example, presents an emblem entitled "The Undying Nature of Man" (fig. 11), which consists of a quartered circle, representing eternity, that depicts the life of man from spring, with its rising sun, through summer and autumn, to winter with its setting sun. At the bottom of the circle lies man in the grave, presumably awaiting the final Resurrection; at the top is Jove, enthroned in clouds. Appended to the emblem are the verse:

> Spring, Summer, Autumn, Winter. These are the four
> Seasons in the years turning in the sphere.
> So the entire man has four ages of life.
> He is a boy, then a young man, then a man, and
> finally an old man.
> Such that a conversion of a life similar to the
> eternal world
> Argues so many times that we men are eternal.[107]

---

[105] Ibid., p. 139.

[106] In the *Convivio*, Dante compares the four ages of man to the four seasons and then to the canonical hours. Adolescence corresponds to the period up to the ringing of tierce; manhood, from tierce to nones (sext was commonly unrung); age, from nones to vespers; and decrepitude, from vespers onward. *Dante's "Convivio,"* tr. William W. Jackson (Oxford: Clarendon Press, 1908), p. 274 (Tract. 4, xxiii).

[107] *Picta poesis Ut pictura poesis erit* (London, 1556), sig. B5v:

> Ver, Aestas, Autumnus, Hyems, Hae quattuor annis
> Sunt Tempestates, orbe volubilibus.

Another emblem, on the title page of John Case's *Lapis philosophi-cus*, actually presents the sun moving downward on the arch of the zodiac above the recumbent figure of a man (fig. 12). Dante, in the twenty-third chapter of the *Convivio*, had made the comparison of man's life to an arch, its highest point placed between the years thirty and forty, identifying the perfection of age as thirty-five. Ages forty-five through sixty-nine were given over to age, and, at seventy, man entered decrepitude. Seventy years, it may be remembered, was the biblical limit to man's life, and in its association with the Babylonian captivity the number had come to represent, as Christopher Butler points out, "man's enslavement to the world of sense—a captivity ter-minated only by the redemptive action of Christ, who releases the soul of man from the fetters of the flesh, permitting him to ascend above the sphere of time." Thus, it symbolizes the whole course of time from Adam to the Second Coming, as well as the span of one man's life.[108]

As we have seen, Donne was particularly interested in the number 70. In *Essayes in Divinity* he had held forth at some length on its sym-bolism. The *Devotions* contains six specific references either to the number or to its integer. After explaining that "seuen is infinite,"[109] Donne sets out the pattern of the seven critical days of his fever, drawing attention to the span in its hopeful resolution: "*Seuen dayes, O my God*, haue we looked for this *cloud*."[110] He associates the number with the eternal Sabbath and the ages of the world, wherein the poets "extend the *worke of a day*, to a *thousand yeere*."[111] Twice he alludes to the life-span limit of threescore and ten ("*an eternity* of threescore & ten yeares"; "wee need *sleepe* to liue out our *threescore and ten yeares*"),[112] and in the final Expostulation he alludes to the doubled integer as the infinite number of pardon: "thou who hast com-manded me *to pardon my brother seuenty seuen* times, hast limited thy selfe to no Number."

G. A. Starr has remarked on the tendency of spiritual autobiogra-phies to assume a regular shape, particularly an organization in inter-

---

Quattuor aetates homo sic habet integer aevi,

Qui puer, hinc juvenis, mox vir, & inde senex.

Aeterno ut similis mundo revolutio vitae

Nos itidem aeternos arguat esse homines.

[108] Maren-Sofie Røstvig, *The Hidden Sense*, Norwegian Studies in English, 9 (Oslo, 1963), p. 88.

[109] Prayer 4, sig. E10r.

[110] Expostulation 19, sig. Y11r.

[111] Prayer 19, sig. Z1r.

[112] Meditation 7, sig. I6v; Meditation 15, sig. R5r.

vals of seven, corresponding to the ages of man.[113] The *Devotions* also demonstrates this tendency. One remembers that each of its twenty-three prose sections is divided into three—a Meditation, an Expostulation, and a Prayer—a total of sixty-nine prose units, one short of the number 70. This number had traditionally been put to use in treatises on contemplation; Bonaventura's *Itinerarium mentis in Deum*, for example, was organized in a *scala* of sixty-nine steps. (Indeed, Bonaventura's three-part division of *apprehensio*—the exploration of the corporeal and temporal world for *vestigia* of the Creator, *oblectatio*—the movement of the mind from macrocosmic evidence to the higher truths of form, measure, and operation, *diiudicatio*—the passing of the mind beyond itself to the eternal—bears strong resemblance to Donne's three-part division of Meditation, Expostulation, and Prayer. It seems very possible to me that this model answers most strongly to Donne's meditative progression.)

The number 69 has been associated with incomplete perfection, for it is one short of 70, which signifies the imminent fulfillment of man's life and, in extension, that of the macrocosm. This is the arch of the *Convivio*, an incomplete circle of time. When one begins to consider the *Devotions* in the light of Dante's arch, interesting possibilities come to light, for the work seems structured in a scheme based on the incomplete span of human life. The true center falls at the thirty-fifth prose unit, the high point of the arch—the Expostulation of Devotion 12, which presents a pyrotechnic display of the possibilities for ascent and descent of those vapors that Donne calls a "hieroglyphic" of his life and death. Matching each of the prose units to a corresponding life year, beginning with the first Meditation and the year 1572, the first of Donne's life,[114] brings to light a significant autobiographical pattern.

Donne himself draws attention to such a pattern in the "*three Births*" of the "Epistle Dedicatory" (his natural birth, his entry to the ministry, and his recovery from sickness). He mentions the second birth again in Expostulation 8:

> Then, when he, first of any man conceiu'd a hope, that I might be of
> some vse in thy *Church*, and descended to an intimation, to a perswasion,
> almost to a solicitation, that I would embrace that calling. And thou who

[113] *Defoe and Spiritual Autobiography* (Princeton: Princeton University Press, 1965), pp. 36–37.

[114] Donne's biographer R. C. Bald places his birth between January 24 and June 19, 1572. Thus 1572 is the first "anno aetatis." Note also that Donne's epitaph is so phrased: His entry into Orders on January 23, 1615, is reckoned as occurring in the forty-second year of his age.

hadst put that desire into his heart, didst also put into mine, an obedience to it; and I who was sicke before, of a vertiginous giddiness, and
irresolution, and almost spent all my time in consulting how I should
spend it, was by this *man of God*, and *God of men*, put into the poole, and
recouerd.

This account of his entry into the ministry, which he equates with
recovery from illness, occurs in the twenty-third of the sixty-nine
prose units of the *Devotions*, exactly one-third of the way through its
progression. The corresponding life year is 1595, which lay, according to his biographer R. C. Bald, at the height of the probable period
of his conversion from Roman Catholicism to the Anglican church.[115]
But given the number and its association in Dante, Suso, and Petrarch with illness, recovery, and conversion, the placement of
Donne's account of his entry into the ministry is startling. Moreover,
when one casts an eye back to the very first Meditation, which corresponds to the year of Donne's birth and baptism, one finds the account of his initial succumbing to the fever couched in terms of original sin, conception, and birth:

> O miserable condition of Man, which was not imprinted by *God*; who as
> hee is *immortall* himselfe, had put a *coale*, a *beame* of *Immortalitie* into vs,
> which we might haue blowen into a *flame*, but blew it out, by our first
> sinne . . . and our *dissolution* is conceiued in these *first changes*, *quickned*
> in the *sicknes* it selfe, and *borne* in *death*, which beares date from these
> first changes.

References to birth, childhood, and youth cluster in the first third
of the *Devotions*. The first Prayer draws attention to God who "leadest
vs from our *beginning*, through all our wayes," to his "mercies afforded mee from the beginning," and to "my beginning in this world,
when thou plantedst me in the *Christian Church*." The second Expostulation, with its comparison of God's Providence to "the hand of my
Nurce," gives a rare detail from his childhood: "My parents would
not giue mee ouer to a *Seruants* correction." And in the third Expostulation: "*Suffer little children to come to mee*, saiest thou. Is there a ver-
ier child then I am now? I cannot say with thy seruant *Ieremy, Lord, I
am a Child and cannot speake*; but, *O Lord*, I am a sucking childe, and
cannot eat, a creeping childe, and cannot goe. . . . I haue this weake,
and childish frowardnes too, I cannot sit vp, and yet am loth to go to
bed." In the seventh Meditation (corresponding to the nineteenth
year on Dante's arch) Donne reminds us that "*death* is at a yong mans
backe, and saies nothing; . . . *Youth* is an *ambush*." Finally, in the tenth

---

[115] *John Donne: A Life* (New York: Oxford University Press, 1970), pp. 63–72.

Prayer (which corresponds to 1601, the year of Donne's marriage) we find him confessing "the *sinnes* of my *youth*."

Given these references to sin and birth and to the events of childhood and youth (coupled with the tradition of the taking of holy orders as a kind of birth),[116] it follows that Donne has placed his "natural" birth at Meditation 1, corresponding to the year of his actual birth, 1572, and his "supernatural" birth at the eighth Expostulation, corresponding to the year 1594, exactly one-third of the way through the *Devotions*: the twenty-third prose unit, containing explicit reference to James Stuart's calling Donne to the ministry and pointing to the "twy-light" of the solstitial day (chart 4).

It now behooves the reader to seek out the third of Donne's *natalia*. And the quest leads down convoluted bypaths worthy of Donne at his most complex and witty. The two-thirds mark of the *Devotions* occurs at, or rather immediately after, Meditation 16, that is, the forty-sixth prose unit. This, the first unit of the digression on bells, corresponds to Donne's own forty-sixth life year, 1617, the year of Anne Donne's death. Appearing as it does at the end of the second group of twenty-three prose units and given the possible reference to the ascension of the soul from carnal to divine love—a reference reinforced by Donne's sermon on the winter solstice of 1617 and reinforced further by the association of the number 23 with the solstice and with conversion—it is legitimate to inquire whether Donne may have placed his third *natalia* at this point. He had, after all, paid his wife the highest of compliments: "Here the admyring her my mind did whett / To seek thee God; so streames do show the head."

And indeed the section is preceded by Prayer 15 in which, concerned with sleep—or rather the lack of it—as an emblem of his condition, Donne presents the equation in language strongly reminiscent of the traditional association of sleeping and waking with contemplation:

O Eternall and most gracious *God*, who art able to make, and dost make the *sicke bed* of thy seruants, *Chappels of ease* to them, and the *dreames* of thy seruants, *Prayers*, and *Meditations* vpon thee, let not this continuall watchfulnes of mine, this inabilitie to sleepe, which thou has laid vpon mee, bee any *disquiet*, or *discomfort* to me, but rather an argument, that thou wouldest not haue me sleepe in thy *presence*. What it may indicate or signifie, concerning the state of my *body*, let them consider to whom that consideration belongs; doe thou, who onely art the *Physitian* of my *soule*, tell her, that thou wilt afford her such *defensatiues* as that shee shall

---

[116] This is an ancient tradition derived from commentary on Ephesians 4.23. See Gregory of Nyssa, "On the Baptism of Christ," *Pat. Gr.*, 46, cols. 577–600.

Chart 4. The Natural and Supernatural Births

Devotion	Year	Life Event	Text		
	1572	1	Born Jan. 24–June 19	"our first sin"	NATURAL BIRTH
1	1573	2			
	1574	3		"my beginning in this world"	
	1575	4			
2	1576	5		"the hand of my nurse; parents' correction"	
	1577	6			
	1578	7			
3	1579	8		"Is there a verier child than I am now?"	
	1580	9			
	1581	10			
4	1582	11			
	1583	12			
	1584	13			
5	1585	14			
	1586	15			
	1587	16			
6	1588	17			
	1589	18			
	1590	19			
7	1591	20			
	1592	21			
	1593	22			
8	1594	23	Conversion from Rome	"I was put in the pool and recovered"	SUPERNATURAL BIRTH
	1595	24			
	1596	25			
9	1597	26			
	1598	27			
	1599	28			
10	1600	29			
	1601	30			
	1602	31			
11	1603	32			
	1604	33			
	1605	34			
12	1606	35			
	1607	36			
	1608	37			
13	1609	38			
	1610	39			
	1611	40			
14	1612	41			
	1613	42			
	1614	43			
15	1615	44			
	1616	45			
	1617	46			
16	1618	47			
	1619	48			
	1620	49			

Chart 4. (*cont.*)

Devotion	Year	Life Event	Text
17	1621	50	
	1622	51	
	1623	52	
18	1624	53	
	1625	54	
	1626	55	
19	1627	56	
	1628	57	
	1629	58	
20	1630	59	
	1631	60	
	1632	61	
21	1633	62	
	1634	63	
	1635	64	
22	1636	65	
	1637	66	
	1638	67	
23	1639	68	
	1640	69	

wake euer towards thee, and yet euer *sleepe* in *thee*; & that through all this sicknesse, thou wilt either preserue mine vnderstanding, from all decaies and distractions, which these watchings might occasion, or that thou wilt reckon and account with me, from before those violencies, and not call any peece of my *sicknesse*, a *sinne*.

On the other hand, if one expects references to death and rebirth at this point, one is disappointed. Both the sixteenth Meditation and Expostulation, which flank the two-thirds point, lack any overt reference to death and birth, or rebirth, which so marked the occasions of Donne's first two structural *natalia*. Rather, Meditation 16 directs us away from Donne's death to the deaths of others: "And when these *Bells* tell me, that now one, and now another is buried, must not I acknowledge, that they haue the *correction* due to me, and paid the *debt* that I owe?" It concludes: "so when these hourely *Bells* tell me of so many *funerals* of men like me, it presents, if not a *desire* that it may, yet a *comfort* whensoeuer mine shall come." The following Expostulation, which inaugurates the final third of the *Devotions*, opens with a rather conservative response to the controversy on church bells then brewing in the English church,[117] and proceeds to an analogy

[117] Normally the church bells were rung two to three times daily: at Morning Prayer—public and choir—and at Evening Prayer. But there was also ringing to sermons (generally at midmorning), ringing of the passing bell and funeral bells (as the

between the trumpets and bells of Old Testament ritual and the bells and final trumpet of Christian funerals and the Second Coming.

Explicitly, Donne focuses our vision on the death of his neighbor: "That [bell] which rung yesterday, was to conuay him out of the *world*, in his *vaunt*, in his *soule*: that which rung to day, was to bring him in his *Reare*, in his *body*, to the *Church*; And this continuing of ringing after his *entring*, is to bring him to mee in the *application*." The matter is perplexing until one takes into consideration the subtitle of the Devotion in question: "*Et properare meum clamant, à Turre propinqua, / Obstreperae Companae aliorum in funere, funus.*" Donne's translation: "*From the bels of the church adioyning, I am daily remembred of my buriall in the funeralls of others.*" This begins a three-part digression on bells that seems to deviate from the formal progression of the *Devotions*. The following Devotions, 17 and 18, are entitled "*Nunc lento sonitu dicunt, Morieris*" ("Now, this Bell tolling softly for another, saies to me: Thou must die") and "*At inde / Mortuus es, Sonitu celeri, pulsuque agitato*" ("The bell rings out, and tells me in him, that I am dead").

Now Donne had, in the very first Expostulation, forecast this pattern:

> O heighth, O depth of misery, where the first *Symptome* of the sicknes is *Hell*, & where I neuer see the feuer of lust, of enuy, of ambition, by any other light, then the darknesse and horror of *Hell* it selfe; & where the first Messenger that speaks to me doth not say, *Thou mayst die*, no, nor *Thou must die*, but *Thou art dead*.

These phrases direct us once again to Dante and the genre of spiritual autobiography. In the twenty-third chapter of his *Vita Nuova*, Dante is prostrated with a fever and in a delirium, experiences a dream-vision in which he is confronted first with the death of Beatrice ("Vero e che morta giace la nostra donna") and then his own, imminent ("Tu pur morrai") and actual ("Tu se morte") death. There is a vision of angels and, after his cure, the recounting of his experience, like Hezekiah, in song ("Donna pietosa e di novella etate")—a song that by its title, moreover, indicates that a conversion of some sort has taken place.[118]

As Charles Singleton has pointed out, this chapter 23, with its con-

---

Devotions attests), and traditional all-night ringing at the summer solstice, on All-Hallows Eve, and on All-Souls. This drew fire from the Puritans: Henry Burton's *A Divine Tragedy Lately Enacted* (Amsterdam, 1636), cites four cases of divine retribution for "superfluous bell-ringing" in the English church. I am grateful to William Barr for drawing this controversy to my attention.

[118] *La Vita Nuova of Dante Alighieri*, trans. Mark Musa (New Brunswick, N.J.: Rutgers University Press, 1957), p. 48.

cerns and language so like those of Donne, falls at the midpoint of the *Vita Nuova*.[119] (Moreover, the twenty-third chapter of Suso's *Exemplar*, which presents much the same conventions, forms the numerical center of its whole.) Thus the third segment of Donne's autobiographical arch commences with a similar vision and a virtually identical *sentence*: your neighbor has died, you will die, you are dead. This leads us to question whether the three-part digression on bells may not point directly to the conventions of early spiritual autobiography. Examination of the digression and of the material which surrounds it will, I think, confirm the postulate.

The forward movement of the *Devotions*, with the exception of the digression on bells, is given over to the progress of the disease from the first symptoms to the critical days. Then comes the interruption of the digression, followed by signs of health and finally recovery. The episode of the bells occurs just after the crisis of the fever with its accompanying insomnia. Devotion 14 presents, in its three parts, an extended metaphorical treatment of the critical or climacteric years, those multiples of 7 that were thought to be occasions of great change, danger, or fortune by our predecessors. Most important were, on the basis of the significance of their factors, the years 42 (7 × 6), 49 (7 × 7), and 63 (7 × 9), this last known as the grand climacteric. The prose sections of Devotion 14 correspond to Donne's life years—40, 41, and 42—in the years 1611, 1612, and 1613, when he was "sicke . . . of a vertiginous giddiness, and irresolution," The fourteenth Prayer, prose segment 42, reflects verbally the Hezekiah theme:

> Let thy mercifull prouidence so gouerne all in this *sicknesse*, that I neuer fall into vtter *darknesse, ignorance of thee*, or *inconsideration of my selfe*; and let those *shadowes* which doe fall vpon mee, *faintnesses of Spirit*, and *condemnations of my selfe*, bee ouercome by the power of thine irresistible *light*, the *God* of *consolation*; that when those *shadowes* haue done their office vpon mee, to let me see, that of my selfe I should fall into irrecouerable darknesse, thy *spirit* may doe his *office* vpon those *shadowes*, and disperse them, and establish mee in so bright a *day* here, as may bee a *Criticall day* to me.

In the following Meditation, the fifteenth, Donne takes his reader through an extended and rather conventional meditation on sleep as

[119] *An Essay on the Vita Nuova* (Cambridge: Harvard Univ. Press, 1958). Considering the first and last poems of the series as prologue and epilogue, he maintains that the poetic scheme of the *Vita Nuova* can be stated in terms of 9, 3, and 1, with Canzone II (chapter 23) falling in the central position, that is: 1, 9; I; 4-II-4; III; 9, 1. Thus the number 9, to which Dante attached so much importance, occurs three times.

the figure of fearful death, but closes with the association of wakefulness as encumbrance with worldly concerns: "why is none of the *heauinesse* of my *heart*, dispensed into mine *Eie-lids*, that they might fall as my heart doth?" In the fifteenth Expostulation, he equates sleep with salvation: "but shall not they to whom thou art *Saluation*, sleepe? or wilt thou take from them that *euidence*, and that *testimony*, that they are thy *Israel*, or thou their *saluation*?" The Expostulation concludes with Donne himself presented as an icon of sleeplessness. It is an ancient figure—the iconography generally presents a reclining sleeper, head on hand, eyes wide open[120]—and is often represented in connection with Jacob's ladder as a figure of contemplation. (In this light Donne's phrase "that they are thy *Israel*" takes on new meaning.)

Although the figure could also be taken *in malo* as a sign of moral and intellectual sloth, sleep generally signified the *quies vitae* which only God can give. The concept of sleep as contemplation and of insomnia as the inability to achieve that state persisted throughout the Christian Middle Ages and well into the Renaissance, achieving a late epitome in the works of Juan de la Cruz. It is not remarkable then that immediately after Devotion 15, which so strongly echoes this iconography, there should followed the three-part digression on bells which taken *in toto* constitutes a dream vision. Devotions 16, 17, and 18 depict Donne in a delirium, passing through the fevered crisis of his illness and, as in a dream, witnessing the drama of his own death and burial played out by the funeral bells for his neighbors.

The message is a central one not only to the *Devotions* and the *Vita Nuova* but to such related visions as that in Chaucer's *Book of the Duchess*:

> Myselven can not telle why
> The sothe; but trewly, as I gesse,
> I holde hit be a sicknesse
> That I have suffred this eight yeer,
> And yet my boote is never the ner;
> For there is phisicien but oon
> That may be hele; but that is don.[121]

The poet, bereaved by worldly loss, wanders in a waking delirium seeking a physician. Only by his own death to sin and by entrance

---

[120] The most comprehensive study of the iconography of the dream-vision can be found in Francis X. Newman, "Somnium: Medieval Theories of Dreaming and the Form of Vision Poetry" (Ph.D. diss., Princeton University., 1962).

[121] *Works*, ed. F. N. Robinson (New York: Houghton Mifflin, 1957), p. 267 (ll. 34–40).

into a *vita nuova* with Christ is the dreamer healed and granted Divine Vision. Thus we find the expected congruence of sin, death, and birth not in Devotion 16, where we might at first expect it, but at the end of the digression on bells in Devotion 18. The bells were the means by which Donne was "daily remembered" of death.

I suggest that this three-part digression corresponds to the illness of Hezekiah, who on the third day went up to the temple. The section ends on a jubilant note, for Prayer 18 presents us with Donne's final *natalia*: "*a* preter-naturall Birth, *in returning to* Life, *from this Sicknes*":

> O Eternall and most gracious *God*, I haue a new occasion of *thanks*, and a new occasion of *prayer* to *thee*, from the *ringing* of this *bell*. Thou toldst me in the other *voice*, that I was *mortall*, and approaching to *death*; In this I may heare thee say, that I am *dead*, in an *irremediable*, in an *irrecouerable* state for bodily health. If that bee thy *language* in this *voice*, how infinitely am I bound to thy heauenly *Maiestie*, for speaking so plainly vnto mee? for euen that *voice*, that I *must die now*, is not the voice of a *Iudge*, that speaks by way of *condemnation*, but of a *Physitian*, that presents health in that: Thou presentest mee *death* as the *cure* of my *disease*, not as the *exaltation* of it; if I mistake thy voice herein, if I ouer-runne thy pace, and preuent thy hand, and imagine *death* more instant vpon mee than thou hast bid him bee, yet the voice belongs to me; *I am dead*, I was *borne dead*, and from the first laying of these *mud-walls* in my *conception*, they haue *moldred* away, and the whole course of *life* is but an *actiue death*.

The return to life is immediate: The following Devotion chronicles the signs of cure and the physicians' optimism. Thereafter Donne describes their practice and his own rising from the sickbed.

I do not think that the placement of the moment of recovery immediately after Donne's acceptance of "*death* as the *cure* of my *disease*" in the eighteenth Devotion is arbitrary. For one thing, if one accepts the three-part unit of Devotions 16 through 18 as a formal digression, then the point of recovery occurs immediately after the forty-sixth prose unit (Prayer 15)—the numeric two-thirds point in the *Devotions'* progress. More than this, however, is the presence of a long-standing tradition dating to Augustine's *De Trinitate* that reinforces Donne's choice of this textual division and his subtle insinuation of a change from the significance of 23 as a number of justice to its emphasis as a truly hexaemeral number, embodied in his statement that God now speaks to him with "not the voice of a *Iudge* . . . but of a *Physitian*."

There was first, of course, the connection of the number 18 with the woman of Luke 13 who was cured of crippling arthritis. (The King James version describes her as "a woman which had a spirit of infirmity eighteen years, and was bowed together, and could in no wise lift up herself.") The consensus of the commentators, Lapide points out, was that the woman was possessed of a demonic spirit, her malady incurable by human agency. Anagogically this was held to signify the world held in bondage to sin before the Law, a period reflecting the six days of Creation, then six days under the Law, and finally, six days under the New Law—hence, an eschatological 18. This sense is echoed by Ambrose, again cited by Lapide, who divides the number into 10 for the Decalogue and 8 for the Resurrection.[122] (He in turn is echoed by the *Glossa Ordinaria*, which sees the crippled woman as a figure of corrupted human nature cured only by the combination of the Law and the Resurrection.)[123] It is Augustine, however, who makes the crucial jointure, for he connects the woman of Luke's gospel to the nature of mankind by means of a long disquisition on the ratio of the single to the double, which, among other things, signifies the relationship between the single death of Christ to mankind's double death in soul and in body. Understanding the implications of that ratio will go a long way, I think, toward our understanding Donne's division of the *Devotions* by the three births mentioned in his "Epistle Dedicatory."

To Augustine, the death of Christ meant that men, while they are subject both to the death of the flesh through the curse on Adam and the death of the soul through sin, are promised a twofold resurrection:

> Therefore the soul, which was before ungodly and is now godly, is said to have come alive again from the dead and to live, on account of the righteousness of faith. But the body is not only said to be about to die, on account of that departure of the soul which will be; but on account of the great infirmity of flesh and blood it is even said to be now dead, in a certain place in the Scriptures, namely, where the apostle says, that "the body is dead because of sin, but the spirit is life because of righteousness" [Rom. 8.10]. Now this life is wrought by faith, "since the just shall live by faith" [1.17]. But what follows? "But if the Spirit of Him that raised up Jesus from the dead dwell in you, He that raised up Christ from the dead shall also quicken your mortal bodies by His Spirit which dwelleth in you" [8.10,11].[124]

[122] *Commentaria in Scripturam Sacram* (Paris, 1874) 2:188–89.
[123] *Pat. Lat.* 114, col. 303.
[124] *Pat. Lat.* 42, cols. 890–91. Anima igitur jam pia, quae fuit impia, propter justitiam fidei dicitur ex morte revixisse atque vivere. Corpus autem non tantum moriturum propter animae abscessum qui futurus est, sed propter tantam infirmitatem carnis et sanguinis, quodam in loco in Scripturis etiam mortuum dicitur, loquente Apostolo: *Corpus quidem*, inquit *mortuum est propter peccatum, spiritus autem vita est propter justitiam.*

Augustine then defines the ratio: "Therefore on this double death of ours our Saviour bestowed His own single death; and to cause both our resurrections, He appointed beforehand and set forth in mystery and type His own one resurrection."[125]

In order to understand the application of this ratio to Donne's three births, it is necessary to quote Augustine at still greater length on number theory, for his comments on the divine ratio underlie this final division of the *Devotions*:

> Now this ratio of the single to the double arises, no doubt, from the ternary number, since one added to two makes three; but the whole which these make reaches to the senary, for one and two and three make six. And this number is on that account called perfect, because it is completed in its own parts: for it has these three, sixth, third, and half; nor is there any other part found in it, which we can call an aliquot part. . . . And Holy Scripture commends to us the perfection of this number, especially in this, that God finished His works in six days, and on the sixth day man was made in the image of God. And the Son of God came and was made the Son of man, that He might recreate us after the image of God, in the sixth age of the human race. For that is now the present age.[126]

Hence the woman of Luke 13 becomes a type of the Church, for, imprisoned and bowed down by the powers of Satan, she is released by the healing power of the Son of God. In her eighteen years of infirmity, Augustine finds the third multiple of six, for this is the sum of the months of her captivity.

Augustine goes on to relate the number 6 to the year's calendar and from there to the calendar of the Year of Grace, for he reckons the days of the pregnancy of the Virgin—from March 25 to Decem-

---

Haec vita ex fide facta est; quoniam justus ex fide vivit (Rom. 1.17). Sed quid sequitur? *Si autem Spiritus ejus qui suscitavit Jesum a mortuis, habitat in vobis; qui suscitavit Christum Jesum a mortuis, vivificabit et mortalia corpora vestra per inhabitantem Spiritum ejus in vobis* (Rom. 8.10–11).

[125] *Pat. Lat.* 42, col. 891. Huic ergo duplae morti nostrae Salvator noster impendit simplam suam: et ad faciendam utramque resuscitationem nostram, in sacramento et exemplo praeposuit et proposuit unam suam.

[126] *Pat. Lat.* 42, col. 892. Haec autem ratio simpli ad duplum oritur quidem a ternario numero; unum quippe ad duo, tria sunt: sed hoc totum quod dixi, ad senarium pervenit; unum enim et duo et tria sex fiunt. Qui numerus propterea perfectus dicitur quia partibus suis completur: habet enim illas tres, sextam, tertiam, dimidiam; nec nulla pars alia, quae dici possit quota sit, invenitur in eo. . . . Cujus perfectionem nobis sancta Scriptura commendat, in eo maxime quod Deus sex diebus perfecit opera sua, et sexto die factus est homo ad imaginem Dei (Gen. 1.27). Et sexta aetate generis humani, Filius Dei venit et factus est filius hominis, ut nos reformaret ad imaginem Dei. Ea quippe nunc aetas agitur. . . .

ber 25—as 276 days, "which is forty-six times six."[127] Forty-six is the number of years spent in building the temple that Christ promised to raise up in three days. "And in this number of years the temple was built, because in that number of sixes the body of the Lord was perfected; which being destroyed by the suffering of death, He raised again on the third day."[128]

When one moves to the *Devotions*, one finds the three-part digression on the bells following immediately after the forty-sixth prose division, a built-in pattern of death and resurrection. Donne has moved from an emphasis on the number 23 as a number of Justice (2 + 3) to a ratification of its hexaemeral meaning as a number of mercy. As 2 × 3, the number points toward his double Resurrection from sin and from death. Thus, the final structural segment that follows the eighteenth Devotion, the third segment of Donne's life arch, opens with a structural finesse of particular delight, one of the "curious and daintie conceits, not for common capacities," to which John Chamberlain referred so many years ago. But what is even more evocative of "holy delight," when the reader casts an eye at the end of the eighteenth Devotion and Donne's third *natalia* (which incidentally, follows on the heels of the year of his illness, 1623, and which corresponds to Donne's coming fifty-fourth year, the age at which on many astrological calendars one actually passes through the Gates of Capricorn), one finds that there remain fifteen prose units—Devotions 19 through 23—a number which corresponds to the fifteen extended years granted to King Hezekiah (chart 5).

Immediately after the digression on bells, the *Devotions* moves quickly to its narrative conclusion. In the remaining five Devotions, signs of digestion are perceived in the urine; the patient is purged, rises from bed (at the sixty-third prose segment, reflective perhaps of the grand climacteric), embarks on convalescence, and fortifies himself against relapse. In its upward movement from desolation, in the very fact that its hero recovers his life and his health, the *Devotions* takes its place in the tradition of spiritual autobiography, where victim ultimately takes on the role of victor, and the costume is Christ. But unlike Shakespearean comedy, Donne's *Devotions* ends with no fine marital balance. Chapter 24 is yet to be written, and the circle is imperfect until God completes its drawing.

[127] *Pat Lat.* 42, col. 894.

[128] *Ibid.*, "In that number of years the temple was built: because in rationale of sixes the body of the Lord was completed—destroyed by the passion, it rose in three days." (Quo numero annorum templum aedificatum est, quia eo numero senariorum corpus Domini perfectum est, quod mortis passione destructum, triduo resuscitavit.)

Chart 5. The Preternatural Birth

Devotion	Year	Life Year	Life Event	Text	
	1572	1	Birth		NATURAL BIRTH
1	1573	2			
	1574	3			
	1575	4			
2	1576	5			
	1577	6			
	1578	7			
3	1579	8			
	1580	9			
	1581	10			
4	1582	11			
	1583	12			
	1584	13			
5	1585	14			
	1586	15			
	1587	16			
6	1588	17			
	1589	18			
	1590	19			
7	1591	20			
	1592	21			
	1593	22			
8	1594	23	–– Conversion–––––––––––	Calling to ministry by James I–– 1/3 –––	SUPERNATURAL BIRTH
	1595	24			
	1596	25			

9	1597	26			
	1598	27			
	1599	28			
10	1600	29			
	1601	30			
	1602	31			
11	1603	32			
	1604	33			
	1605	34			
12	1606	35	– – – – – – – – – – – – – – – – – – –	Discourse on ascent/descent – – – – – –1/2 – – – – – – – – – – – –	
	1607	36			
	1608	37			
13	1609	38			
	1610	39			
	1611	40		Critical days	
14	1612	41		Climacterics	
	1613	42	Major climacteric year	His own critical day	
	1614	43		Waking dreams	
15	1615	44	Holy Orders	Insomnia	
	1616	45			
	1617	46	– – Anne Donne dies August 15 – –	"Dreams of thy servant [are] prayers" – – – 2/3 – – – – – – – – – –	
16	1618	47		BELLS FOR OTHERS	
	1619	48			
	1620	49			
17	1621	50		BELLS FOR DONE	DREAM VISION
	1622	51			
	1623	52	} Illness, recovery, *Devotions*	DEATH KNELL	
18	1624	53			PRETERNATURAL BIRTH
	1625	54		"I am dead"	
	1626	55			

Chart 5. (*cont.*)

Devotion	Year	Life Year	Life Event	Text
19	1627	56		
	1628	57		
	1629	58		
20	1630	59		
	1631	60		
	1632	61		
21	1633	62		
	1634	63	Grand climacteric	Rising from bed
	1635	64		
22	1636	65		
	1637	66		
	1638	67		
23	1639	68		
	1640	69		

Chapter VI

AN AFTERWORD

To Discharge Myself of Myself

IN THE YEARS since its publication, the *Devotions Upon Emergent Occasions* has suffered more than its share of neglect due to changing religious sensibility and literary taste, the inseparable coils of which have served during the last three and a half centuries either to bind its author's temples with laurel or, until recently, to tether the work to the ecclesiastical bookshelf. How is one to come to terms with this (to the modern eye) very difficult book? Are we to respond merely to those vibrations moving each way free that have so enamored our century of Donne's poetry, despite its scholastic underpinnings? Or should we anatomize Donne's book, as he anatomized himself in it, with a fine critical scalpel, tracing out this generic sinew, that vein of form? Both of these questions are unnecessary, since Donne defies both our *altitudos* and our postmortems. And because he does so, I have found the preparation of this study, with all its "lightenings, sudden flashes; . . . thunders, sudden noises; . . . eclipses, sudden offuscations and darkenings of [the] senses" an enjoyable task, even a "holy delight."

But such delight does not come easily. The world and humanity's attitude toward it have undergone great change since the publication of *De revolutionibus orbium coelestium* in 1543. No longer do we perceive a rationally ordered universe, created in six days and restlessly awaiting the seventh. Ours is more often a world where, in the words of one recent autobiographer, all is "chance, accident, absurdity," so that the notion of a "continuous personality which is identical with itself through all the changes it suffers in time" is an illusion, and autobiography hence a "trick," experience a "flux of impressions."[1]

It is not the intention of this study to mourn a lost ontological paradise where knowledge and experience once fused in a cohesive vision of the self, but rather to maintain that a sense of self—unfragmented, undisjointed, safe in the individual because lost in the common Christian identity—made the daring introspective adven-

[1] Goronwy Rees, *A Bundle of Sensations* (New York: Macmillan, 1961), p. 15.

tures of a poet like Donne not a terminal risk nor their autobiographical expression a "trick." Rather, what seems a distortion of truth imposed by the act of contemplation (according to some modern
theorists, so overriding a qualification of autobiography that it is a
necessary qualification of it)[2] proves for pre-Romantic autobiographers not so much a distortion as a stretching of the self, assimilating
the individual into all of humanity through the *imitatio Christi*. This
distortion, this stretching, was one which sought to fit subject to form,
even sometimes imposing a fictive framework, in which events are
recounted and placed to fit a pattern that reflects the individual's
deepest perception of God's universe and his own place in it—so that
personal data are denied importance save in their extension outside
the individual into the general pattern of creation and redemption.

James Olney has recently addressed this issue in terms readily applicable to Donne. His study, *Metaphors of the Self*, merits quotation at
length:

> These order-produced and order-producing, motion-producing, mo-
> tion-satisfying theories and equations—all the world view and world pic-
> tures, models and hypotheses, myths and cosmologies—it may be that
> another, for our purposes better and more comprehensive, name for
> these would be "metaphors": they are something known and of our mak-
> ing, or at least of our choosing, that we put to stand for, and so to help
> us understand, something unknown and not of our making; they are
> that by which the lonely subjective consciousness gives order not only to
> itself but to as much of objective reality as it is capable of formalizing
> and of controlling. The focus through which an intensity of self-aware-
> ness becomes a coherent vision of reality, the point through which the
> individual succeeds in making the universe take on his own order, is met-
> aphor: the formal conjunction of single subject and various objects.[3]

But Olney speaks from a century whose single subject is all too single, where external "reality" can bring little to the completion of a
coherent whole, whether it be of self or art. Thus, his "metaphors"
are a reflection of an internal rather than of any external reality, so
that he concludes:

> In the given, whether it be external reality or internal consciousness,
> there is nothing to be called meaning: the world means nothing; neither
> does consciousness per se. Our sense that there is a meaning in some-

---

[2] Roy Pascal, *Design and Truth in Autobiography* (London: Routledge and Kegan Paul,
1960), p. 72.

[3] *Metaphors of the Self: The Meaning of Autobiography* (Princeton: Princeton University
Press, 1972), p. 30.

thing—in a poem, in experience—comes only when the elements that go to make up that thing take on a relation to one another; in other words, the meaning emerges with our perception of a pattern in chronologically or geographically discrete items and elements. We must connect one thing with another and finally assume the whole design of which the element is only a part.[4]

For the writer of early spiritual autobiography, meaning emerged not with perception of pattern, for pattern was a given. Donne, in his many catalogings of the Book of the Creatures rarely asks, "What does this mean?" Rather, he inquires, "Where does this fit?" Of man's condition, for example, he wonders:

> Is he a *world* to himselfe onely therefore, that he hath inough in himself, not only to destroy, and execute himselfe, but to presage that execution upon himselfe; to assit the sicknes, to antidate the sicknes, to make the sicknes the more irremediable, by sad apprehensions, and as if hee would make a fire the more vehement, by sprinkling water upon the coales, so to wrap a hote fever in cold Melancholy, least the fever alone shold not destroy fast enough, without this contribution, nor perfit the work (which is *destruction*) except we ioynd an artificiall sicknes, of our owne *melancholy*, to our natural, our unnaturall fever.[5]

The emphasis is not on finding an overall pattern and hence inducing meaning, but rather on deducing meaning from the process whereby the individual self, as perceived in its lived experience, articulates with the wholeness of Creation. My conjecture is that the movement away from such articulation instigated the rift between early spiritual autobiography and later forms of the genre. Certainly our reading of the early spiritual autobiography demands a focus on points of articulation in the design—as I have just done with the *Devotions*—as much as on the integrity of the whole or on "where the work comes out." Moreover, such points of articulation, determined as they are by the individual life and the poet's individual perception of it, open to the reader a means of approaching the delicate question of the poet's "originality."

In the *Devotions* Donne works with material well known to his audience—even in some aspects well worn. The reader who is aware of his participation in this long history of poetic design can move between the discursive text and its underlying structure, perceiving a set of tensions and articulations belonging wholly to Donne the individual, the innovator. If the *Devotions* partakes of the tradition of ex-

[4] Ibid., pp. 30–31.
[5] Meditation 1, sigs. B3v–B4r.

emplary spiritual autobiography—as its explicit structural references
to the *Vita Nuova* suggest—it is on Donne's own terms, and as always,
they are unique.

But such one-of-a-kind-ness as the *Devotions* displays was not his
overriding purpose. For Donne, the reality behind the pattern, not
his and our flawed perception of it through the artifact, was the goal.
The poet does not supply meaning, nor does the reader; meaning
need not be supplied, only accepted. The poet-autobiographer's responsibility is to conform his account of his life to the truth of his
experience, but the better the poet, the better the individual, the
more his experience reflected in its narrated form the form of God's
Creation itself—in its immanence, its beauty, its permanence, no matter that they were limited by his human condition and short time.

Whether an awareness of self-existence and an awareness of God
are coextensive—as Cardinal Newman would have them, virtually
identical—there can be no doubt that an understanding of God and
his universe (or the laws of the natural world, or the structure of human society) must come out of, and will be deeply colored by, the
nature of the self and the knowledge that one has of that self.

What one finds in the *Devotions* can be called a "liturgical" self: a
sense of being that is at once private and public, in service of personal
salvation and at the same time committed to the spiritual fate of king
and nation; a sense of being in harmony with the movement of the
seasons and the temporal progress of the Incarnation and Redemption. Hence we find Donne, falling ill at the beginning of Advent,
following the liturgy from his sickbed, hearing the music of Morning
and Evening Prayer from the church of St. Gregory, living with the
church through the dying of the natural year. He stood literally at
the gates of death, "the yeares dark midnight," when he might well
have expected to enter through the door of Capricorn to the house
of the Water-Bearer. But the symbol unfolds, for liturgically, the
movement through the Gate of Death in December leads to the feast
of the Incarnation, and the promise of new life through the death of
Baptism, the new Water-Bearer, and the Year of Grace ends, significantly, in the sign of Pisces.

The framework of the *Devotions* is rich with the acknowledgement
of ultimate regeneration. At the moment of darkness, beginning the
long night of the solstice, Donne turns his eyes to the morning: "Who
casts not vp his *Eie* to the *Sunne* when it rises?"[6] The rising *sol iustitiae*
lighted a darkness both personal and universal, for in allying the
movement of his life with that of the church and of all mankind,

---

[6] Meditation 17, sig. T4r.

Donne could ask for whom the bell tolled with the greatest pertinence.

The view of time in the *Devotions*, is, as in the Sermons, sacramental. For Donne, Advent and Christmastide of 1623 must have been
poignantly personal in meaning, and his mind turned to the application of the Advent matter—of Hezekiah, of the merciful extension of
the king's life by fifteen years, of the ages of the world and of man,
and of the coming of the Son of Justice, the death in darkness of the
old year and the coming of the light which would bring the new—to
his own life. More than one critic has remarked on the apparent lack
of a time progression in the *Devotions*, a progression necessary to the
genre of spiritual autobiography. Yet by submitting the years of his
life, in actual progression, to the framework of macrocosmic time,
Donne has produced a highly literary spiritual autobiography, bely-
ing what has been called the tendency of English autobiography "to
minimize the importance of literary form as an end in itself."[7] Rather,
Donne has found a form truly answerable to his own experience, and
it is answerable because form and subject correspond to the same cosmic and historical reality.

We no longer possess that world and that perspective. But we cannot deny its validity for those who lived and wrote within its hierarchical confines.

An autobiography, it has been maintained, is invalid without outward narrative shape, so that the self unfolds "not solely according to
its own laws, but also in response to the world it lives in."[8] Moreover,
it must encompass the entire perceived span of life. To repeat the
definition of Professor Zimmerman:

> Ideally practiced, autobiography involves the formulation of a coherent
> interpretation of the self from a particular viewpoint in time. What dis-
> tinguishes it from memoirs, diaries, writing is the author's viewing of his
> past life in an effort to construe it as a whole. Through the process of
> reflection, there emerges an interpretation of past experience which at-
> tempts to clarify the development of the self.[9]

The autobiographer, whatever the century in which he writes, must
confront his full historical self.

---

[7] Donald Stauffer, *English Biography before 1700* (Cambridge: Harvard University
Press, 1930), p. 216.

[8] John N. Morris, *Versions of the Self* (New York: Basic Books, 1966), p. 216.

[9] T. C. Price Zimmerman, "Confession and Autobiography in the Early Renaissance," in *Renaissance Studies in Honor of Hans Baron*, ed. Anthony Molho and John A.
Tedeschi (Dekalb, Ill.: Dekalb University Press, 1971), p. 33.

But the spiritual autobiographer must go a step further, for he must document interior history as well. Indeed, this documentation of inward shape is his chief aim. Read discursively, its interior narrative framework ignored, Donne's *Devotions* does not qualify as spiritual autobiography. But then, perhaps it is not too late to learn to read such a text. What will happen when we abandon our preconceptions and approach the *Vita Nuova*, the *Historia Calamitatum*, Suso's *Exemplar* in the manner of the audiences for whom they were written? The autobiographies of Thomas Whythorne, of William Chappell, Matthew Robinson, even of Lodowick Muggleton, the horse doctor's son, may seem less eccentric and far more true to autobiographical norm if we do so. It would be interesting as well to turn a formal eye on the autobiographical sonnet sequences such as Fulke Greville's *Caelica* or on the obvious autobiographical structures in Spenser, Shakespeare, and Milton. For Donne himself, we would be wise to reexamine the autobiographical content of the *Anniversaries*, the "Holy Sonnets," even the Sermons, for their formal intent.

Donne's mode of composition was once characterized as "explicit complexity at the literal surface, not something working away complexly in its interior."[10] Yet in 1624, in a bedside chair, forbidden the use of his books, he composed in one month's time the *Devotions Upon Emergent Occasions*, a spiritual autobiography of intricate thematic and structural complexity. In a time of physical pain and great personal anguish, he took the necessary distancing step, with all its ensuing complexities of invention, that distinguished him as a true "maker." His literary descendant, W. B. Yeats, said: "If it be true that God is a circle whose centre is everywhere, the saint goes to the centre, the poet and artist to the ring where everything comes round again."[11] Witty to the end, John Donne did both.

[10] A. Kent Hieatt, *Short Time's Endless Monument: The Symbolism of the Numbers in Edmund Spenser's "Epithalamion,"* (New York: Columbia University Press, 1960), p. 6.

[11] "Discoveries," *Essays and Introductions* (London: MacMillan, 1961), p. 287.

OCULAR PROOF: THE SPIRITUAL AUTOBIOGRAPHY OF OPICINUS DE CANISTRIS

SPATIAL and numerological structuring in premodern literature has been only slowly accepted by the scholarly community, to some extent because of the sheer difficulty involved in recognizing such structures and also because the subject is classed with the "occult," an areas presently divorced from the intellectual mainstream but one deeply embedded in premodern thinking. Hence to propose a deliberate schematic structure in any work, one must adhere to certain rules of evidence. Otherwise, it is very easy to go astray, supposing every bush a numerological bear.

Alastair Fowler has mandated five categories of evidence for the numerological critic: (1) deliberate authorial statements concerning the work's structure, (2) internal consistency of the perceived pattern, (3) commentary on the structure by contemporary critics, (4) recognition by contemporary poetic theory, and (5) imitation of the pattern in later literature.[1] Thus far, no one structure has been clearly supported by all five kinds of evidence, although examples of all five kinds do occur, as in the instances of Henry Constable's authorial statement prefacing an arrangement of his sonnets and the spatial schema set forth by Henry Ferrers for his projected "Enneads."[2] One recalls as well the correspondence of Sir John Chamberlain concerning the "holy delights" of Donne's *Devotions* and the discussions revolving around the Castle of Alma. Moreover, the attention paid to pattern by contemporary theorists like Puttenham, combined with the multiplicity of medieval commentaries, indicates that the art of spatial construction was an accepted one. But a work as complex as Donne's *Devotions* must have drawn on more than just a generally accepted tradition. Surely it must have been preceded by some schema—what Sidney called the "fore-conceit"—which governed its internal complexities. Is it not logical that Donne worked from a diagram or a life calendar?

[1] *Triumphal Forms: Structural Patterns in Elizabethan Poetry* (Cambridge: Cambridge University Press, 1970), pp. 1–2.

[2] *The Poems of Henry Constable*, ed. J. Grundy (Liverpool: Liverpool University Press, 1960); Elizabeth K. Berry, "Henry Ferrers, an Early Warwickshire Antiquary, 1550–1633," *Dugdale Society Occasional Papers* (Oxford) 16 (1965): 30.

Such a schema would constitute ocular proof and would add a sixth catgory of evidence to Fowler's list. Given the ravages of time, fire, and worm, the remainder of premodern rough copy is understandably sparse, but it is not impossible that some such evidence of interior pattern planning exists. Recently, one such has come to light: a spiritual autobiography, conforming in content and structure to the tradition I have elucidated in this study, and accompanied by a diagrammatic life calendar in the hand of its author, Opicinus de Canistris.

A scriptor in the papal office of the Poenitentiaria Apostolica at Avignon, Opicinus (1296–ca. 1350), once known as the Anonymous Ticinensis, was identified in the early twentieth century as the author of a defense of John XXII, *De preeminentia spiritualis imperii*, and of a description of his native Pavia, entitled *De laudibus Papiae*. He appears to have been no more than a bureaucratic functionary and a producer of minor literature. But in 1334 he fell seriously ill, an event that proved significant to the tradition of spiritual autobiography. Prostrated and paralysed, fearing to lose his scribal hand, he was consoled by a vision of the Virgin and, cured, he rose from his bed, proclaiming his thanks by means of his autobiography. The resulting manuscripts—a twenty-three-part autobiography and an accompanying set of illustrations—are described below:

Cod. Vat. lat. 6435 consists of a total of twenty-three parts: twenty-two paper quires of four double pages each plus a custodian. It is a collection of adversaria written down day-by-day—short notes and long essays seemingly disparate in character, concerning the inner life and experiences of the author, interspersed with meditations, dissertations, and exercises. The manuscript is illustrated with drawings that seem to be derived from the companion manuscript. It was moved to the Vatican from the archives at Avignon in 1594.

Cod. Pal.lat. 1993 consists of twenty-seven whole parchment skins used on both sides. The skins are full of designs in black and colored inks of extremely varied nature: maps, calendars, rose windows and other architectural designs, zodiacs, Christological medallions, angelic figures, and other mysterious figures which are obviously alchemical, sexual, cabbalistic, and political in nature. The manuscript was moved from the Palatine library in Heidelberg to the Vatican in 1623.

Interest in Opicinus was first sparked in 1927 when Faustino Gianani identified him as "l'Anonimo Ticinese," the previously unknown author of the description of Pavia and the papal defense already mentioned.[3] Then Roberto Almagia described the strange maplike

---

[3] *Opicino de Canistris, l'Anonimo Ticinese* (Pavia: Tipografia Successori Fusi, 1927).

illustrations of *Cod. Pal. lat.* 1993, which had been filed in the Vatican map collection, presumably because of the geographical illustrations that (among others) it contains. The manuscript was initially of interest to historians seeking the medieval sources of Columbus's navigational charts, but further study was abandoned when what had at first appeared to be maps turned out to be graphic autobiographical charts. Luckily Opicinus' principal student, Richard Salomon, did not abandon his work before publishing an edition of the drawings[4] and identifying the companion autobiographical manuscript they served as illustrations and, I think, plans.[5] Salomon's edition of the illustrations makes them available to the scholarly community, although his commentary amounts to little more than perplexed head scratching. But the autobiography itself has yet to be edited for publication. I regret that it has come to my attention after the completion of the present study; hence I am able only to offer it to the scholarly community for study.

The deciphering of Opicinus and the investigation of the complex relationship between the written autobiography and its underlying diagrams will be some fortunate scholar's work, but for present purposes, I would like to direct the reader to the year-by-year astrologically structured chart of the forty years of Opicinus's life that provides our ocular proof (fig. 13). It is a year-by-year, day-by-day autobiographical calendar bounded by the four points of the compass, its exterior circle drawing attention to the four stages of the author's life (emphasized by four self-portraits), its interior circles chronologically cataloging life events, and its center featuring the geography of the Mediterranean and the icon of the Madonna and Child. It is clearly a spatially ordered calendar of one man's life. I maintain that it provides the fore-conceit of the twenty-three-part autobiography.

In addition, an interesting if perhaps still tenuous connection with Donne has turned up. The collection of illustrations, *Cod. Pal. lat.* 1993, was among the manuscripts which composed the famous "occult" collection of the Palatine library at Heidelberg, seized by the Vatican in 1623. In the course of his travels, Donne had occasion to visit the city at least four times, and given his scholarly bent—and his intimate connection with an even more frequent and enduring visitor to Heidelberg, the scholarly Sir Henry Wotton—the possibility of his examining the collections and Opicinus's autobiographical chart is a

[4] *Opicinus de Canistris. Weltbild un Bekentnisse eines Avignonesischen Klerikers des 14. Jahrhunderts. Studies of the Warburg Institute.* IA and IB: text and plates (London, 1936).

[5] "A Newly Discovered Manuscript of Opicinus de Canistris," *Journal of the Warburg and Courtauld Institute* 16 (1952): 45–57.

real one. However, although the illustrations were housed at Heidelberg, the autobiography lay at Avignon until 1594 when it was moved
to Rome. Given the data of Bald's biography, we know that Donne
could not have visited Italy after 1591 and never visited Avignon.[6]
Thus, the chances of his acquaintance with Opicinus's autobiography
are slim. The question of how the tradition made its way from the
fourteenth to the seventeenth century is open. But that such a tradition does exist seems to me now established. The Opicinus chart
opens a rich opportunity to study it in finely drawn detail.

[6] *John Donne: A Life* (Oxford: Oxford University Press, 1970), pp. 50–52.

INDEX